CW01096260

The
STAINMORE
&
EDEN VALLEY RAILWAYS

Deepdale Viaduct with an eastbound freight crossing on 21st August 1952. The train locomotive is an Ivatt 2-6-0, No. 46478 with J21 Class 0-6-0 No. 65047 banking.

W. A. Camwell

The picture used to commemorate the 100th anniversary of Belah Viaduct amidst speculation by the *Herald* – "How much longer will it stand?" Their suspicions were remarkably accurate. Two years after this picture was taken Belah was no more. An act of legalised vandalism reduced Belah's graceful girders to scrap iron.

Courtesy The Cumberland & Westmorland Herald

Contents

Kirkby Thore c 1895.

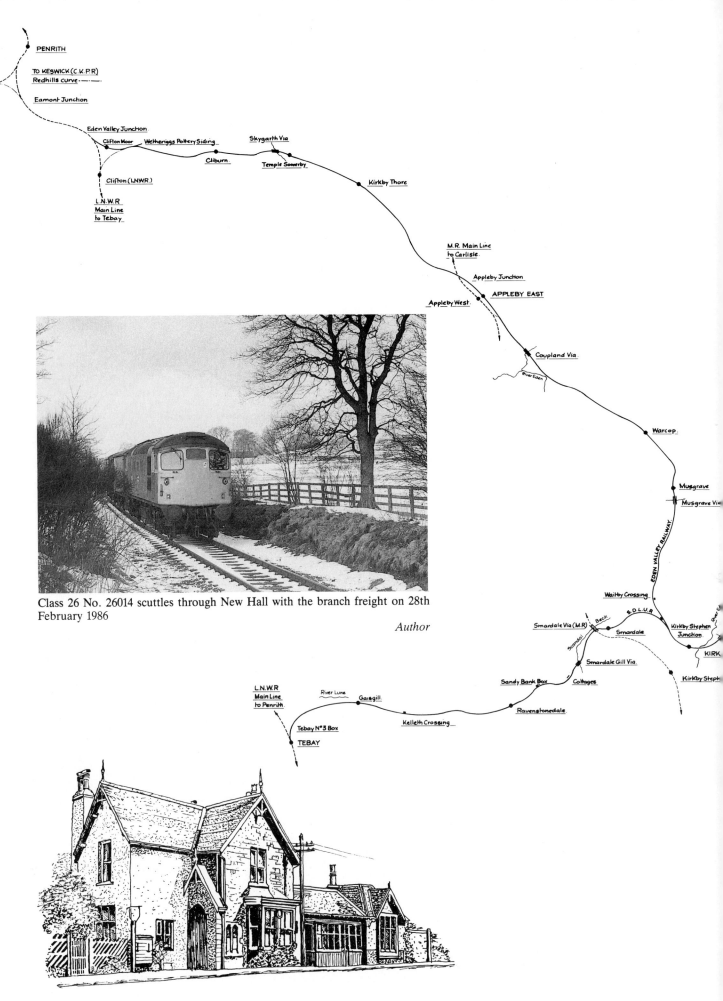

PENRITH

TO KESWICK (C.K.P.R)
Redhills curve

Eamont Junction

Eden Valley Junction.

Clifton Moor   Wetheriggs Pottery Siding

Skygarth Via

Cliburn.

Temple Sowerby

Clifton (LNWR.)

L.N.W.R
Main Line
to Tebay

Kirkby Thore

M.R. Main Line
to Carlisle.

Appleby Junction

APPLEBY EAST

Appleby West.

Coupland Via

River Eden

Warcop.

Musgrave

Musgrave Via

EDEN VALLEY RAILWAY.

Waitby Crossing

S.D.L.U.R

Smardale Via (M.R)

Beck

Smardale

KIRKBY STEPHEN
Junction

KIRK

Scandal

Smardale Gill Via.

Sandy Bank Box   Cottages

KIRKBY STEPH

L.N.W.R
Main Line
to Penrith.

River Lune   Gaisgill.

Ravenstonedale

Kelleth Crossing

Tebay Nº3 Box

TEBAY

Class 26 No. 26014 scuttles through New Hall with the branch freight on 28th February 1986

Author

Ravenstonedale

6

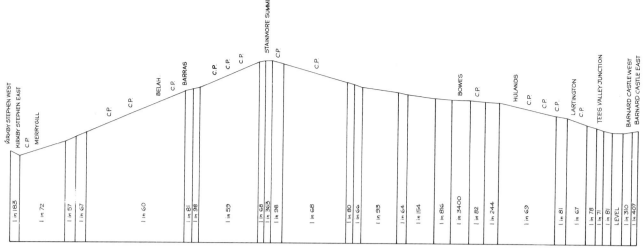

Kirkby Stephen West to Barnard Castle East 21 miles approx

Not to Scale

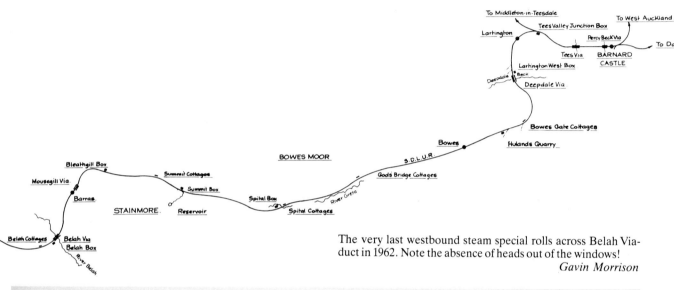

The very last westbound steam special rolls across Belah Viaduct in 1962. Note the absence of heads out of the windows!

Gavin Morrison

7

Introduction

Even now, with weed covered, collapsed trackbeds, the former North Eastern Railway complex in Cumberland, Co. Durham and Westmorland holds a unique, almost possessive attraction. I often find myself inexorably drawn to some part of its long past rural wanderings - pondering and wishing, remembering glimpses of faded glory from the late 1950s when the country junction of Kirkby Stephen could still be seen alive with the sights and sounds of a railway linking the North East with the North West.

Just over thirty years ago this splendid route was still in operation. A line of remarkable contrasts, running westward away from the attractive, historical market town of Barnard Castle (the focal point for the feeder routes from Darlington and Teesside and West Auckland, North Durham and Northumberland) over wild moorland and down into the valleys of the Lune and Eden in Westmorland.

Even today, the impact of the route's closure is still felt in the communities it once served so comprehensively. The railway became an integral part of everyday life in these communities and remained so until the axe fell in 1962.

A visit to any site along the route invariably transmits a sense of loss and regret. The enormity of this feeling of loss extends well beyond the withdrawal of the last few remaining services from the national timetable in 1962, to a sense of intense frustration that future generations will never be able to enjoy a "trip over Stainmore", as countless thousands of railway travellers, including myself, once did. The railway may well have closed, but the memory of this marvellous route will remain for many years to come.

Let us then imagine that the year is 1957, just before the dreadful, ominous rumblings regarding closure were first felt. The Stainmore Line was still in full swing. First a few background notes, then a trip over the route from the eastern end during that period is perhaps the most appropriate way of setting the scene for the history, photographs, plans, etc., to follow.

BR Class 4MT 2-6-0s Nos 76045 and 76050 guide the 11.05 Blackpool – Newcastle train down the bank near Waitby on 3rd August 1957.

R. H. Leslie

1

Background

In common with so many other railway histories, the seeds of the Stainmore Line were sown in the year of the great 'Railway Mania' of 1845.

The 1840s heralded the start of a new era for the railways of Great Britain. After years of experimentation and consolidation, railways became accepted as part of the industrial fabric of the country. They were used not only for the transport of freight but by this time had added the Post Office, the Army and Royalty to their list of regular customers. Investment in 'the railways' was one of the most attractive commercial activities of the time.

A considerable number of proposals for railways in the North Yorkshire, Durham, Cumberland and Westmorland areas emerged at this time. New speculators and existing companies were all unwilling to miss out on any potentially lucrative railway development. The commercial attractions of reaching Scotland via the Yorkshire Dales and the Pennines attracted a number of concerns during the 'Railway Mania' period.

On 8th June 1850 the discovery of the main iron ore seam at Eston in Cleveland altered the fortunes of the whole North East of England's economy. The vast iron and steel making complexes which eventually emerged in the North East created the need for a direct line of communication between the Cleveland area and the industrial coast of West Cumberland. However, the low quality ore available from Cleveland was not suitable for the production of high quality iron and steel. This could only be achieved by the use of high quality haematite ore available in West Cumberland, itself a producer of iron and steel requiring vast quantities of coke. Thus an ideal opportunity arose to transport coke westward, and haematite iron ore eastwards.

In 1839 a commission appointed by the Lords of the Treasury gave its blessing to a direct line between Lancaster and Carlisle. The Act of Parliament was granted in June 1844. Whilst the Lancaster & Carlisle line was under construction, its directors, hearing of possible proposals to link Durham with Westmorland by railway, proposed to further construct a branch southwards from Penrith to Appleby with a view to possibly joining any lines which might be constructed either from the south from the Richmond area or from Durham or Darlington.

There were a variety of schemes proposed to build a link over the Pennines at this time. The three major proposals can be summarised as follows:

The York & Carlisle
In April 1845 a prospectus was published to announce the formation of a very ambitious scheme - The York & Carlisle Railway which estimated a requirement of £1,500,000 to build its line.

The proposal was to construct a railway leaving the East Coast Main Line at Northallerton, travelling via Catterick Bridge, Richmond, the Greta Valley to Barnard Castle, there amalgamating with a branch from Bishop Auckland and then proceeding through the Tees Valley and crossing Stainmore to Brough and Appleby. It would then continue down the Eden Valley to Clifton where it would join the Lancaster & Carlisle Railway.

There was to be a branch through Ravenstonedale to Tebay. The promoters persuaded the Lancaster & Carlisle Railway to abandon their idea of a branch south from Penrith and join with them in the much more comprehensive York scheme. The Lancaster & Carlisle agreed and accepted a third share in the direction of the new company.

The Yorkshire & Glasgow Union
However, two months later another concern set out to make a rival line known as the Yorkshire & Glasgow Union Railway. This was to leave the East Coast Main Line at Thirsk, cross the Pennines through Wensleydale to Hawes and so to reach Kirkby Stephen, Appleby and the Lancaster & Carlisle at Clifton.

The Leeds & Carlisle
In October of the same year, a third group of promoters announced the formation of the Leeds & Carlisle Railway. This proposed route was to leave the Leeds and Thirsk line near Headingley and reach Clifton via Wharfedale, Hawes and the Eden Valley. Amongst other heavy engineering works it would have required a tunnel over three miles in length in the Mallerstang area, and a viaduct over quarter of a mile long south of Appleby.

Each of these three undertakings held attractive prospects of carrying vast quantities of traffic from Yorkshire and the East Coast into Scotland, and each promised to develop the resources of the barren country through which they passed.

However, of the three proposals, only one, the original York & Carlisle scheme, recognised the additional value of connecting the industrial district of Durham with the Furness District.

The Leeds & Carlisle and Yorkshire & Glasgow Union schemes joined forces almost immediately, agreeing to concentrate on making the Thirsk to Clifton line with a branch from the Leeds and Thisk route near Ripon to enable West Riding traffic to reach the Wensleydale route near Bedale.

In April 1846, the York & Carlisle scheme was examined by a parliamentary committee. The Yorkshire & Glasgow Union strongly opposed the York & Carlisle Scheme. Lord Palmerston, chairman of the committee, suggested that the two concerns should come to terms with each other. This resulted in the amalgamation of the two schemes which formed the Northern Counties Union Railway. The new project encompassed the best and optimum parts of the previous proposals, consisting of the Thirsk to Clifton line through Wensleydale, the branch near Bedale and the cross-country line from Bishop Auckland to Tebay. The company obtained its act of Incorporation on 27th July 1846.

The York & Carlisle scheme had involved crossing the Pennines at Stainmore only, but the Northern Counties plan required the Wensleydale route to be made also, and this additional expense appears to have been the company's first serious mistake. To make matters worse, another railway - the Liverpool, Manchester & Newcastle-upon-Tyne Junction, a combination of two other schemes: The Liverpool, Manchester & Newcastle Junction and The Lancashire & North Yorkshire, had also been empowered to make its line through Wensleydale. This concern obtained their act on 26th June 1846. Although the Liverpool, Manchester & Newcastle scheme never came to fruition, the pressure placed upon the Northern Counties Union Railway by this rival proposal must have been a cause for serious concern.

According to W.W. Tomlinson's fine history of the North Eastern Railway, "The lines which the Liverpool, Manchester & Newcastle-upon-Tyne were authorised to make were the main line of the Lancashire & North Yorkshire company from Elslack to Scorton (47½ miles) and the Hawes Branch of the original Liverpool, Manchester & Newcastle Junction company (9 miles). Those which the Northern Counties Union Company were empowered to make were the main line of the Yorkshire & Glasgow Union company from Thirsk to Clifton (69 miles) and a portion of the York & Carlisle Railway between Bishop Auckland and Tebay (50¼ miles), with the Wath Branch (7 miles) and the Auckland Branch (¾ mile). Total 127 miles."

The NCU Act presented a further problem. Because the company was a combination of three projects, it had been thought necessary to guard against any one part of the whole being sacrificed to provide for another, and it was enacted that the construction of the Thirsk-Clifton and Bishop Auckland-Tebay lines must proceed simultaneously.

When the shareholders met after the passing of their Act, their chairman, Major Beresford MP (formerly of the Leeds & Carlisle) addressed them frankly. The number of railways contemplated at that time would make it impossible to raise their capital quickly and it was explained, in an able and straightforward manner, that they would be wise not to undertake the heavy outlay, but to re-survey the most expensive part of the work; apply for an amended Act and come to some arrangement with the Newcastle Junction in making the line through Wensleydale.

The Bishop Auckland-Tebay route was therefore re-examined with the object of getting rid of a proposed tunnel two miles long, through limestone, but the engineer considered the alternative route over Stainmore impracticable. So the company sought to repeal the 'simultaneous' clause in its Act.

The remedy was strongly resisted by Mr Henry Howard of Greystoke (a director of the LCR and of the former York & Carlisle) who contended that the proposed Bishop Auckland to Tebay line had induced many people to support the company and it must not be set aside to provide money for the Thirsk-Clifton line. He was supported by Mr William Crackenthorpe of Newbiggin (Temple Sowerby) who stressed Westmorland's need for Durham coal. Nevertheless the majority voted for the amendment of the Act and so alienated the York & Carlisle party.

The NCU 'Deviation' Bill was presented to Parliament in 1847 and the committee was sympathetic to the Westmorland opposition, refusing leave to repeal the 'simultaneous' clause. A Bill for Amalgamation with the Newcastle Junction was withdrawn owing to the uncertain position of that company.

It became quite impossible for the Northern Counties Union Company to raise the necessary finance for this ambitious combination of schemes to be constructed simultaneously, especially in the period which followed the 'Railway Mania'. Nevertheless an attempt was made and a short section of line was started at the Yorkshire end while (some rumours suggest), a start was also made on the Durham section at Tebay.

In 1848 the company again sought to repeal the clause which would paralyse its efforts. Once again the parliamentary committee declined to remove the restriction and the NCU found itself bound to carry out the simultaneous construction programme during the slump which followed the 'Railway Mania'. It had no alternative but to suspend work, cut expenses to the bone and wait for better times.

Spirits rose again in 1851 when the Great Northern and the Glasgow & South Western railway companies proposed to take over the NCU and form a main line from King's Cross to Glasgow, but the LCR and LNWR successfully defeated the plan.

The NCU company lived on for a while and even continued to hold annual meetings. However, its powers eventually lapsed and such money that remained was returned to the shareholders. It was no mere 'bubble' company and its failure was unfortunate, for though its plans were grandiose in their conception, they were not impracticable. Had their railway been completed, there would have been no cause for the piecemeal construction of various lines which replaced it, less efficiently, and at greater expense, some years later.

In an age when railways were bringing prosperity wherever they went, the little towns 'off the line' were declining. In this respect, the unfortunate inability of the Northern Counties Union Railway to complete its lines in Westmorland was a bitter blow to the communities waiting for 'The Railway'. The people of Appleby, and of the communities along the Eden Valley, seemed to be in real danger of being miles away from any railway.

Meanwhile in 1852 there were plans to construct a railway from Darlington to Barnard Castle. After numerous difficulties the necessary Act of Parliament received the Royal assent on 3rd July 1854, the line being opened to Barnard Castle on 8th July 1856.

By this time, further attempts to bring a railway to Appleby and the Eden Valley had been made (in 1852) when Sir Richard Tufton of Appleby Castle commissioned a survey of a line from Clifton, on the

Lancaster & Carlisle line to Appleby via Morland. The Westmerian contingent no doubt followed with interest the advances by the Stockton & Darlington Railway towards Barnard Castle and possibly the West.

The directors of the Stockton & Darlington Railway were also showing interest in the possibility of a railway to Westmorland. The increasing need to carry Durham coke to the Barrow-in-Furness area and bring back Furness ore to Cleveland was the main consideration. This traffic was travelling via the circuitous route between Newcastle and Carlisle at that time.

On 1st November 1854, a very important meeting was held in Appleby over which Mr William Wilkinson of Warcop presided. The subject under discussion was the possibility of an extension of the Darlington and Barnard Castle route over Stainmore, through Appleby to join the Lancaster & Carlisle line at Hackthorpe. No real conclusion was achieved at this time and proceedings were then further interrupted by the outbreak of the Crimean War, 1854-56.

The resumption of meetings and negotiations resulted in the proposal, at a meeting in Brough in September 1856, that a line be constructed between Barnard Castle and Tebay with a branch from Kirkby Stephen through Appleby to Penrith (or Clifton).

It would seem that the proposal to make the main line between Barnard Castle and Tebay, and not Penrith, was greatly influenced by Mr Joseph Pearce, a director of the Stockton & Darlington Railway. With his fellow directors he had now fully assessed the potential of sending Durham coke east and bringing haematite ore to Durham to smelt with the poorer grades of Yorkshire ore currently being used. The path to Furness and southern Lakeland via Tebay, the Lancaster & Carlisle line, Hincaster Junction and Arnside was the most economically attractive route.

The abandonment of the Hackthorpe route and the choice of Tebay as the western end of the main line was not met with any great favour in the Eden Valley.

On 20th September 1856 William Wilkinson again took the chair at a meeting in Appleby where strong feelings were expressed, which viewed this proposed choice of Tebay as a break of faith. The initial outcome of this controversy was the formation of two companies: The South Durham & Lancashire Union Railway and The Eden Valley Railway.

In the November of 1856 a bill was promoted for an extension to the Haggerleases branch of the Stockton & Darlington Railway near Lands Colliery to join the Darlington and Barnard Castle line at Barnard Castle and then cross the Pennines to Kirkby Stephen and Tebay. The junction of the line at Lands Colliery became known as Spring Gardens Junction, effectively and historically marking the eastern end of the Stainmore Line. A promotional meeting for the Barnard Castle-Tebay line was held in Kirkby Stephen on 18th November 1856.

The economically and superbly surveyed route of the South Durham & Lancashire Union Railway by the engineer - Thomas Bouch - received the Royal assent on 13th July 1857. The Stainmore Line was born. The capital originally authorised to build the route was £553,000.

Unfortunately the Appleby party could not agree on a route down the Eden Valley for their 'Eden Valley Line' and the engineer, again Thomas Bouch, surveyed two lines. One was to pass through Warcop and

along the east side of the River Eden to Temple Sowerby, while the other followed the west side of the river through Morland. The former was longer by a mile or so but cheaper by some £50,000 and on 24th October 1857 another meeting at Appleby, with William Crackenthorpe in the chair, resolved to build the Eden Valley Railway from Kirkby Stephen to Clifton by way of Warcop, Appleby and Kirkby Thore.

So strong was local enthusiasm that 146 landowners and farmers immediately took up shares; the Bill was presented to the House of Commons on 4th February 1858 and received the Royal assent on 21st May, the Company being empowered to raise £135,000 by shares and borrow an amount not exceeding £45,000.

Instead of making for Penrith, the new railway turned southwards at Wetheriggs to join the Lancaster & Carlisle Railway at Clifton station. The L&CR had not forgotten earlier attempts to use a similar line as a means of reaching Scotland and, being allied to the London & North Western Railway, it was on guard against some future concern taking over the Eden Valley line as part of a larger scheme.

So while its directors were kindly and courteous to the project the LNWR declined to assist with a subscription, saying that so long as the line turned south at Clifton, they were "inclined to look favourably upon the scheme".

On the other hand, the Stockton & Darlington Railway (which had much to gain and nothing to lose by the line) guaranteed £25,000 worth of shares and undertook to work the railway, as they had already agreed to do with the South Durham & Lancashire Union Railway.

The directors included a number of local gentlemen - Sir Richard Tufton and Admiral Russel Elliot of Appleby, James Atkinson of Winderwath, William Brougham of Brougham Hall, William Crackanthorpe of Newbiggin and John Crosby of Kirkby Thore among others. The secretary, George Brown, was also secretary of the Barnard Castle and South Durham Railways and Thomas Bouch the engineer as mentioned before was also engineer for those lines. Bouch was a Cumberland man who had been employed, under Locke, on the construction of the Lancaster &

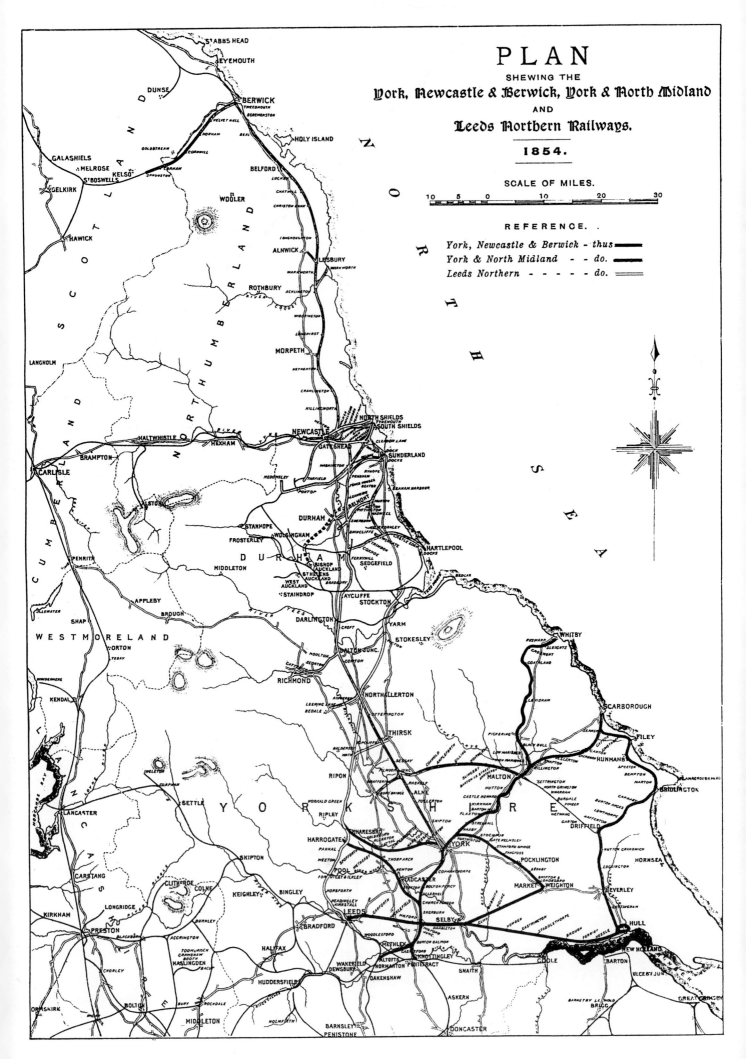

PLAN
SHEWING THE
York, Newcastle & Berwick, York & North Midland
AND
Leeds Northern Railways.
1854.

SCALE OF MILES.

10   5   0   10   20   30

REFERENCE.

York, Newcastle & Berwick - thus ━━━━
York & North Midland   - - do. ━━━━
Leeds Northern - - - - - do. ═══

Carlisle Railway but unfortunately he is best remembered for his ill-fated Tay Bridge.

And so it began. The passing of the Acts for the construction of the Stainmore and Eden Valley Railways in 1857 and 1858 paved the way for a hundred years of railway involvement and connection between the industrial North East of England and the counties of Cumberland and Westmorland. From the unsure beginnings of the 1840s emerged the first tentative foray by a railway company over the mighty, unpredictable Pennines through the pass at Stainmore.

The use of this route had for centuries been the link between North East and North West England. Bronze age traders, then hundreds of years later the Romans used the pass, building a notable fort at Bowes to protect this line of communication. In much later times the Normans built a keep on the same site, utilising masonry left by the Romans.

Marauding Scots, cattle drovers and coaches between England and Scotland used the Stainmore Route (including the Glasgow Mail Coach upon which Charles Dickens travelled to Bowes in 1838 – Dickens subsequently writing his novel "Nicholas Nickleby" based upon the contemporary, educational injustices evident at the nearby Dotheboys Hall).

Interestingly, the Richmond to Brough coach was extended to Tebay on three days a week to connect with trains there as from 4th June 1849. The coach returned on alternate days. Additional users were horse dealers who travelled to the famous fairs at Brough and Appleby, some via Gilsland and the 'Great North Road' towards Scotch Corner, and others via the green road over Cotherstone Moor.

The coming of the railway radically changed the transport pattern over the Pennines and in fact had far-reaching effects on the economy and life of the communities through which it passed. So much so that only a few years after the passage of the first train, the road over Stainmore had reverted to an ill-defined grass track.

A report from the *Westmorland Gazette* as soon after the opening as 7th October 1865 remarked, in relation to the decline of Brough Fair, "that local people could now shift their cattle by rail and that the fair itself had greatly degenerated. Regular attenders thought it "the smallest they had seen"."

2

A Brief Description of the Routes

The double-track main line leaves the 1865 station at Barnard Castle, passes the West signal box to the south of the line and runs over Percy Beck Viaduct, crossing the River Tees for the first time at Flatts Wood. It then sweeps south west over the Tees for the second time by means of the massive stone-piered, steel-topped Tees Viaduct - 132 ft high and 732 ft long.

Tees Valley Junction signal box is passed to the south of the line which is already at 550 ft above sea level, and now climbing steadily at 1 in 70 as the Middleton-in-Teesdale branch diverges towards the North West. The slopes of Teesdale diminish as the route passes through the picturesque, secluded station at Lartington on a curve climbing at 1 in 67, preceding a stretch of open embankment at the end of which can be seen the long-disused entrances to the quarries at Cat Castle.

The start of the epic journey over Stainmore. This classic photograph shows the junction at Barnard Castle East. Note the excellent signal gantries. The line diverging to the left, rear of the train, ran to West Auckland, the line descending behind the train to Darlington and the line to the right of the tended area ran to the original Barnard Castle, 1856 station, latterly this was a goods depot.

J. W. Armstrong

Class G5 No. 67305 waits at the head of the 5.30 pm train to Middleton-in-Teesdale on 14th September 1957.

J. F. Mallon

An eastbound train passes the West box on 8th November 1952, hauled by No. 46480, an Ivatt 2-6-0. Note the beautifully tended gardens.

J. W. Armstrong

A lovely picture of J21 class 0-6-0 No. 65110 piloting a sister engine on a westbound train, preparing to leave Barnard Castle in 1949.

J. W. Armstrong

Percy Beck Viaduct before the trees made this view impossible to photograph.

J. L. Birkbeck

Signalman Chapman offers the single line token to the fireman of Ivatt 4MT No. 43102 as it takes the pick-up freight onto the Middleton-in-Teesdale branch in 1963.

J. L. Birkbeck

Signalman Chapman relinquishes the single line token for the Middleton-in-Teesdale branch dmu at Tees Valley Junction.

J. L. Birkbeck

A Darlington to Middleton-in-Teesdale dmu crosses Tees Viaduct near Barnard Castle in October 1964.

Maurice Burns

Fireman Arthur Watson of Brough and his Driver, the late Bill Dickson of Kirkby Stephen, prepare to leave Lartington station for the West. The Darlington – Penrith local train is hauled by Ivatt Class 2MT 2-6-0 No. 46474.

J. W. Armstrong

Lartington West box, on the eastern side of the line, warns of the impending, magnificent, curving viaduct carrying the line over Deepdale Beck at the base of a heavily wooden ravine. The viaduct here is 161 ft high and 740 ft long and identical in basic design, although slightly smaller than Belah Viaduct, still to come.

Looking east from the decking of Deepdale Viaduct towards the box at Lartington West. Note the similarity between this box and that at Tees Valley.

J. F. Mallon

The disused main line to the east of Lartington West signal box looking east. The former quarry entrance can just be detected to the left hand side of the picture.

J. L. Birkbeck

A Q6 Class 0-8-0 on track lifting operations at the A67 road overbridge on 19th April 1963.

J. L. Birkbeck

A dramatic sweeping reverse curve guides the route westward under an unusual aqueduct of 1872 (still extant), prior to passing under the A67 main road at Bowes Gate where two single-storey cottages mark the defunct junction with the quarry tramway to the south of the line at Boldron Kip.

A view of the rail deck of Deepdale Viaduct in July 1962. Just over a year later it was gone.

J. L. Birkbeck

An interesting picture, again in July 1962, of the catwalk arrangement under the decking, of Deepvale Viaduct, allowing access for maintenance, etc.

J. L. Birkbeck

British Railways Standard locomotives cross in front of the signal box at Bowes. Class 3MT tank No. 82027 on a Darlington train, left, and Class 3MT 2-6-0 No. 77011 on a westbound freight, right.

J. W. Armstrong

Climbing continuously the main line parallels the A67 road past the quarry sidings, workmen's platforms and the signal cabin at Hulands before running into the station at Bowes, some 23 miles from Darlington. Bowes station, similar to Lartington, is built in a style more or less unique to the South Durham & Lancashire Union Railway and Eden Valley Railway companies.

A platform signal box, island platform and goods shed accompany the main station building at Bowes which is sited to the east of the road overbridge. Adjacent to this bridge, on the north side, is a flight of steps affording access to the 'up' platform from the nearby village. The line leaves Bowes on a relatively level section known as Bowes level, before beginning the hard, bleak, forbidding trek toward Stainmore Summit as it passes the railway cottages at God's Bridge, at which point the infant River Greta passes under a huge stone slab over which the 'Pennine Way' crosses.

Class Q6 0-8-0 No. 63373 stands on a track lifting train in Bowes station on 28th December 1962. Even the snow did not significantly impede the pace at which the Stainmore line was destroyed.

J. L. Birkbeck

The timeless scene at Bowes. Class J25 0-6-0 No. 5663 ambles through with an eastbound freight in LNER days. Note the beautifully cared for gardens.

J. W. Armstrong

Ivatt Class 4MT No. 43099 shunts the pick-up freight at Bowes.

Ian Robinson

Ivatt Class 4MT No. 43102 penetrates the overgrown goods yard at Bowes.

Ian Robinson

A gradient of 1 in 68 heralds the approach to the isolated cottages at Spital. The site of the signal box on the north side of the line can be detected by a platelayer's cabin, a flat piece of ground and the surviving concrete water butt.

Crossing substantial stone bridges the line passes over a small bridge near a platelayer's cabin where a brook, known as Welcome Stream, diverges away from the line. Whether the stream was so named because this is the boundary between Durham and Westmorland, or whether it marked the point of welcome relief for crews of westbound trains, I'm not sure.

Former North Eastern Railway Class C, later to become LNER/BR Class J21 No. 65092 eases a westbound freight past Spital cottages. The infant River Greta meanders eastward in the background. No. 65092, former NER No. 1565, was one of the first two 0-6-0 Class C locomotives to receive superheated boilers in August 1914.

J. W. Armstrong

A front end study of Class J21 No. 65100 standing at Stainmore Summit. Note the wire device attached to the front coupling. This system theoretically enabled assisting engines to be uncoupled without stopping.

J. W. Armstrong

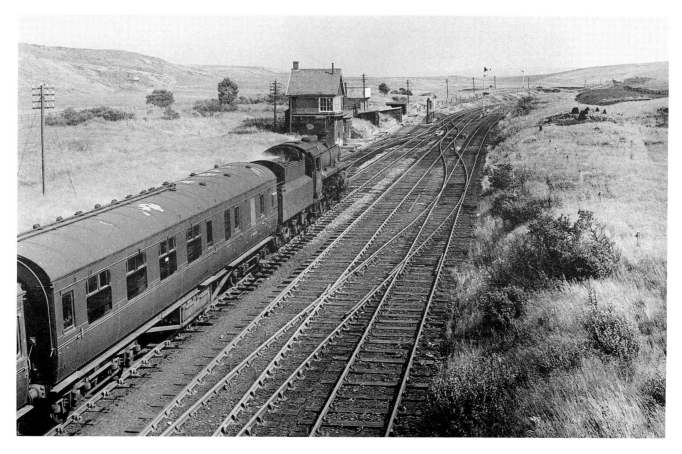

The bleak, exposed layout at Stainmore Summit boasts commodious siding facilities. The problems with bad weather necessitated the longer runs of signal wire from the signal box to the signals being elevated on posts. Comprehensive watering facilities are available at Stainmore, fed from the former North Eastern Railway's own reservoir, high in the fells to the south of the Summit.

A touch of sunshine as BR Standard Class 4MT No. 76050 hurries eastward over the Summit.

Gavin Morrison

Kirkby Stephen shed's smartly turned out British Railways standard Class 4MT No. 76047 storms over the Summit with the 11.05 on Blackpool – Darlington train on 26th July 1958.

R. H. Leslie

British Railways Standard Class 3MT No. 77002 pilots a Class 4MT 2-6-0 over the Summit and past the summit sign on a westbound North East – Blackpool excursion.

Derek Cross

The substantial signal box is of a different style to the others on the route. A former signalman at Stainmore, Mr N. Pearson, described his years in the box as follows: "I spent the happiest days of my life in this isolated cabin; as an aspiring young signalman I became acquainted with the beauty of a sunrise on a summer morning, the call of the grouse in the heather, the far-off sounds of the shooting parties on the Glorious Twelfth, or the simple breathtaking majesty of a sunset over the valley. I treasure most of all the memory of the brilliance of the Northern lights seen during the night shift when it *did* seem as if the stars could be picked out of their velvet background, so near did they appear. When one of the coloured searchlights of the aurora shot across the sky, things began to happen in the cabin. Bells used to jingle, block indicators danced and the phonophone telephone circuit would crackle like a demented Geiger counter".

The interior of Stainmore box with signalman Whealams in charge.

J. F. Mallon

The Summit and signal box, from the east.

Courtesy North of England Newspapers

A huge pair of summit marker boards erected by the LNER proudly proclaim that Stainmore Summit is 1,370 feet above sea level. These boards were probably introduced about 1930, replacing earlier timber units.

The line begins its west side descent under a stone overbridge which, in 1947, was actually filled with snow to the parapet allowing observers of the time to walk over the telephone wires! The cottages built to house Stainmore signalmen nestle to the north west side of the overbridge.

One of the Summit signs erected by the LNER. These replaced an earlier timber sign which erroneously informed passengers that Stainmore Summit was 1,378ft above sea level. One of the current signs can now be seen in the National Railway Museum, York.
Maurice Burns

Power on for BR Standard Class 3MT No. 77003 piloting sister engine No. 77002 as they attack the last half mile to the Summit with the 11.20 am Blackpool – Newcastle train on the 2nd August 1958.

R. H. Leslie

Two former NER 0-6-0s battle up the curve between Bleathgill and the Summit. Notice the new, concrete permanent way hut, left. A great deal of expenditure on non-essential work took place immediately prior to the issue of the closure proposals. This involved signalling, trackwork 'rationalisation', etc. Figures for this work were then introduced into the case for closure.

J. W. Armstrong

The start of a sequence mentioned and illustrated later, as Standard Class 2MT No. 78013 blasts its way through Barras, assisted in the rear by No. 78017 on an eastbound freight on 16th August 1958.

Gavin Morrison

The descent towards Bleathgill begins at 1 in 59 as the vista of the Eden Valley appears to the north. A mile or so to the west of the Summit is the boarded-up signal box at Bleathgill, preceded by a rock cutting - here too there were remarkable snow scenes during the severe winter of 1947.

The line swings southward from Bleathgill, high above the rooftops of nearby farmhouses on this bleak, near treeless edge of Westmorland, eventually crossing Mousegill by means of a very tall stone viaduct before running through the famous, substantial stone station at Barras - the highest main line station in England.

Class J21 0-6-0 No. 65047 leaves Barras with an eastbound passenger train.

J. W. Armstrong

An eastbound train leaves Barras. The locomotive is a North Eastern Railway G1 Class 4-4-0 rebuilt from an earlier 2-4-0 locomotive. These locomotives replaced the "Tennants" and earlier Fletcher locomotives on the Stainmore route.

Eddie Foster

One of the earliest snow pictures taken at Barras in 1905. Barras station was the highest main line station in England. The section of line between the Summit and Belah in particular always suffered problems with snow. Although conditions needed to be particularly severe to cause complete blockages notable such occasions being in 1942, 1947 and 1955. In the 1980s the main road over Stainmore was frequently closed due to inclement weather.

K. L. Taylor Collection

Another early (1907) snow scene between Kirkby Stephen and Barras.

K. L. Taylor Collection

A selection of shots taken in 1942 and 1947 in the Bleathgill – Barras – Belah area.

F. Dargue Collection

British Railways Standard Class 3MT No. 77002 and a 4MT blast towards Barras with a Newcastle bound train.

R. H. Leslie

The incomparable Belah Viaduct, from the north-west. An eastbound train of empties hauled by a J21 and banked by a 2MT leaves Belah box wreathed in smoke.

J. W. Armstrong

A remarkable picture of an eastbound freight crossing Belah. Notice the freshly painted girders and also the fact that there is no banking engine.

J. W. Armstrong

Continuing the descent we pass over Belah Viaduct. If Deepdale can be described as 'magnificent' then Belah is 'incredible' - 1,040 ft long and 196 ft high, like a huge, exiled Big Dipper from Blackpool's Pleasure Beach, bridging a rift in the valley side thus crossing the virgin River Belah. The SD&LUR altered the course of the river here to fit in with the pitching of the massive piers.

Once over the viaduct the line passes what must surely be the loneliest of signal boxes – Belah, perched high upon the embankment at the eastern side of the line at the Kirkby Stephen end of the viaduct. Both box and viaduct are visible for many miles down the Eden Valley.

A former Belah signalman, Mr G. A. Bishop, worked the boxes at Belah and Stainmore Summit from 1901 to 1905. Mr. Bishop, as 'fifth man', worked four hours in each box, walking over Belah Viaduct twice a day in all weathers to reach Belah signal box. Mr Bishop was a keen cricketing enthusiast and had an arrangement with a guard to deliver his evening paper so that he could follow the Australian Test Match scores. One night the wind blew the paper out of the guard's hand and over the viaduct. But such was

Mr Bishop's interest in cricket that he searched below the viaduct (no mean feat!) and found his paper to read that R.E. Forster was 287 not out, winning for England! Mr Bishop's outdoor activities included an occasional swim in the reservoir at Stainmore.

The line, still descending rapidly, passes the single-storey signalmen's cottages at Belah, beyond which Redgate or Aitygill Viaduct of five stone arches, carries the line over a small stream. It thus effectively leaves Stainmore and drops towards Kirkby Stephen and the more friendly terrain of Upper Eden, through Big Hill cutting high above Winton at Rookby Scarth. Still clinging to the fell side Merrygill Viaduct is crossed, passing the throat of the large quarry to the east and the box controlling entry and exit of quarry rail traffic to the west, prior to crossing the wooded ravine bridged by Podgill Viaduct. Then, round a flange-screeching corner, still at the now relatively gentle rate of 1 in 72, past the engineer's sidings, over the River Eden at Stenkrith (Coopkarnal Hole) and into Kirkby Stephen itself, always quietly active with signal boxes, sheds, the station, cattle docks, etc. spread either side of the five-arched road overbridge to the south of the pleasant country town.

A complete contrast in weather conditions to those shown earlier as a westbound summer Blackpool train steams down through Barras before sweeping round the curve high above New Hall towards Belah Viaduct.

Derek Cross

Ivatt Class 4MT 2-6-0 No. 43129 guides the 11.15 am Blackpool – Darlington train over Belah's 196ft high girders on 18th July 1959. This view is taken from the north-eastern side of the viaduct. Note the recently (1956) painted structure.

R. H. Leslie

Repairs to Aitygill Viaduct in the 1950s necessitated the temporary re-alignment of trackwork and the introduction of single-line working, even though double-track still existed normally for the rest of the section between Belah and Merrygill signal boxes.

J. W. Armstrong

An eastbound freight beyond Merrygill heads towards Big Hill Cutting high above Winton. The train locomotion is an Ivatt Class 4MT 2-6-0 banked by sister locomotive No. 43056.

Neville Bousfield

A Class J21 0-6-0 on the 'down' line near Merrygill.

Eddie Foster

A snowbound Big Hill Cutting looking down towards Kirkby Stephen. The long closed and disappeared Rookby Scarth signal box was situated on the north-eastern side of the line between the cutting and the road underbridge.

Neville Bousfield

Some of the workforce celebrating the opening of the new kiln at Hartley Quarry.

G. W. Simpson collection

Class J21 0-6-0 No. 65103, at the head of an eastbound passenger train, attacks the stiff climb away from Merrygill.

Neville Bousfield

Either *Helen* or *Billy* a Hawthorn, Leslie built 0-4-0ST, handles a train of internal wagons loaded with stone.

G. W. Simpson

Merrygill Viaduct and Hartley Quarry.

Author

39

A J21 drifts down towards Merrygill in LNER days. Hartley Castle Farms' horses graze in the foreground. The town of Kirkby Stephen can be seen in the middle distance, with the Eden Valley beyond.

Eddie Foster

One of the new kilns – 'Jubilee', with quarry engine *Helen* 0-4-0 Hawthorn, Leslie 3890 of 1936 on top.

G. W. Simpson collection

The quarry viewed from the top of the now-demolished gas kilns. The blacksmith's shop and engine shed are shown in the foreground.

G. W. Simpson collection

An early scene at Kirkby Stephen (East) goods yard showing staff preparing cattle wagons ready to accept stock from the local auction mart.

Harold Robinson collection

Class J21 No. 1516 shunts the quarry. This locomotive did not quite make it into British Railways' ownership, being withdrawn in July 1947. Built as a compound engine in 1889 and rebuilt in 1907.

Neville Bousfield

Hartley Quarry was owned by Sir Hedworth Williamson. Sir Hedworth and colleagues are seen here at the quarry on the day of the opening of the new kiln, 'Elizabeth'.

G. W. Simpson collection

One of the quarry locomotives, *Charles Hedworth*, a Sentinel, Chester rebuild (CH6218 of 1915) of 0-4-0ST Hunslet 683 of 1903, with crew Randall Loadman and Tommy Miller.

G. W. Simpson

The end of the line before the mid-70s cutback at Merrygill, looking east.

J. L. Birkbeck

Merrygill Viaduct and the layout of the quarry entrance. The power house and water cooling system can be seen to the left handside of the picture.

G. W. Simpson collection

The view towards Merrygill and the East from Podgill. Merrygill's splendid 'down' bracket signal is worthy of comment, to the right hand-side of the picture.

J. F. Mallon

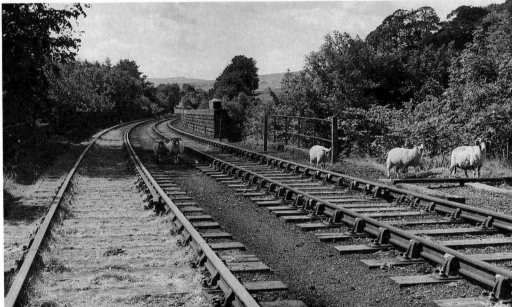

Merrygill Viaduct looking towards Kirkby Stephen in 1974 when the line was still open for freight to and from Hartley Quarry. The bridge in the foreground has since been demolished.

Author

British Railways Class 3MT 2-6-2 tank No. 82028 at Merrygill.

Neville Bousfield

Ivatt Class 4MT 2-6-0 No. 43120 in the snow with the "Merrygill trip" preparing to leave the quarry on 4th January 1966. Guard Finlay of Carlisle Kingmoor converses with the locomotive crew. Due to deteriorating trackwork the practice of main line locomotives penetrating quarry lines ceased in 1967.

Author

45

Sister engine No. 43028 shunts in front of the box on the same working.

Author

Another "Ivatt", No. 43106, trundles away down towards Kirkby Stephen running on the 'up' line with the thrice weekly train from Merrygill to Carlisle. All the railway has since disappeared from Merrygill, but No. 43106 is, happily, preserved on the Severn Valley Railway.

Author

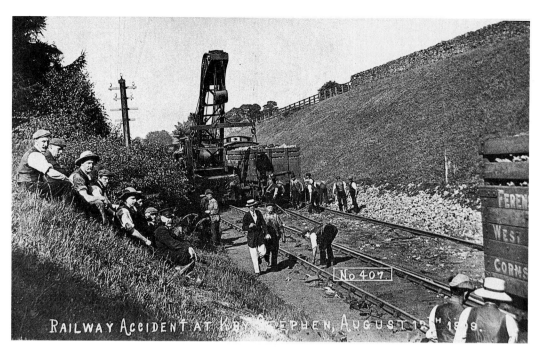

Derailment of 12th August 1909, between Merrygill and Podgill Viaducts.

Iain Smith collection

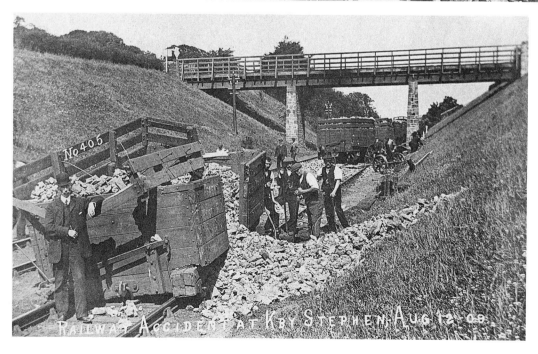

Podgill Viaduct from the east.

Author

An Ivatt Class 4MT 2-6-0 works from Kirkby Stephen East over Podgill Viaduct. The engine-in-the-middle formation enabled easier working arrangements when Warcop, the goods yard and Merrygill Quarry traffic was all being handled by one locomotive, especially when run-round facilities had been removed, as was the case when this picture was taken.

Author

Ivatt Class 4MT 2-6-0s Nos 43073 and 43028 ease the 11.5 am Blackpool – South Shields/Darlington train away from Kirkby Stephen East over the River Eden at Stenkrith. The fine East signal box can be seen behind the trees to the left of the picture dated 16th August 1958.

R. H. Leslie

No. 43028 still in action eight years later shunts the depleted remains of Kirkby Stephen goods yard. By this time the fine North Eastern signalling, the East box, the station lift, engine shed, etc., had all been demolished.

Author

From Kirkby Stephen Junction signal box to the west of the station, the route climbs hard again at 1 in 77, now single track, through deep cuttings and over high embankments up through the small halt at Smardale and into the valley of the River Scandal, passing underneath the southernmost arch of the Midland Railway's impressive Settle and Carlisle Smardale Viaduct.

KIRKBY STEPHEN EAST

British Railways standard Class 2MT No. 78016 approaches the platform at Kirkby Stephen East with an eastbound train.
Neville Bousfield

The classic scene at Kirby Stephen. The late Owen Jackson looks down upon the station and engine shed which houses a variety of NER 0-6-0s and one of the ill-fated former Great Northern Railway Class D3 locomotives. The picture was taken between 1930 and 1936.

Eddie Foster

The eastern approach to Kirkby Stephen East. A couple of former NER 0-6-0s shunt in the foreground, whilst a former Great Eastern Railway Class E4 2-4-0 approaches with a westbound train.

Eddie Foster

Class J21 No. 981 of 1889 vintage at the rear of a westbound freight in the busy yards at Kirkby Stephen.

Eddie Foster

A Class Q5 0-8-0, No. 443, stands at the head of a westbound freight close to the shed. Class Q5s were banned from working between Kirkby Stephen and Barnard Castle from 1929.

Eddie Foster

A splendid study of Class Q5 No. 2125 standing to the east of the five-arch stone over-bridge. Notice the electric shunting signal in the foreground. No. 2125 became British Railways No. 63259 and was withdrawn in 1951. *Harold Wright/John Mallon collection*

Kirkby Stephen, looking west, as BR Standard Class 4MT 2-6-0 No. 76024 pilots Ivatt Class 4MT 2-6-0 No. 43129 under the cattle overbridge, just prior to taking the Tebay line. Signal No. 5, Kirkby Stephen Junction box's Down Main signal for Tebay is lowered on the splendid vintage gantry beyond the bridge.

Derek Cross

By 1961 freight had been deliberately diverted away from the Stainmore line and the shed closed on 20th November 1961. Long before then the fine station and facilities at Kirkby Stephen had taken on an almost ghostly air. The deserted shed and near empty sidings tell their own story.

The calm was broken on Saturdays during that last summer by a succession of North East – Blackpool excursions which called at Kirkby Stephen for water. One cannot help but speculate how much, if any, revenue from these trains was ever credited to the Stainmore route when the case for closure was prepared. The Blackpool excursions travelled via Newcastle once the Stainmore line was closed. There are now no regular Newcastle – Blackpool trains – yet another traditional travelling pattern having been destroyed.

Derek Cross

A number of years earlier in busier times, Class J21 No. 1564 leaves Kirkby Stephen for the West.

Eddie Foster

Semi-retired signalman Dick Alderson, along with his memories of much busier days in the large box at Kirkby Stephen Junction.

Sid Steadman

The only train of the day, hauled by Ivatt Class 4MT 2-6-0 No. 43120, relinquishes the single-line tablet to signal man Dick Alderson standing on the specially-constructed tablet catching platform.

Author

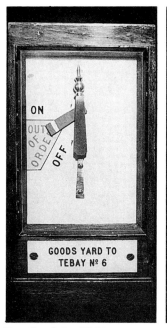
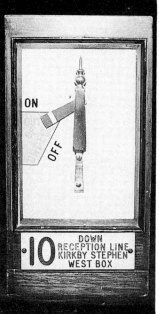

Details of the Kirkby Stephen Junction signal indicators.

Author

The 1905 derailment at the entrance to the West sidings. The track layout here seems to differ from that shown on various track plans in existance. A third west siding appears to begin and there is some evidence of further pointwork on the Eden Valley branch running below signals controlling 'up' line entry to the station and goods lines on the right of the picture.

Iain Smith collection

A last look at the Junction, looking east shortly after closure. Notice the earlier signal box on the right-hand side of the picture. This was used latterly by the Permanent Way Department. By the late 1980s only the metal overbridge remained.

J. T. Hall

Tablet taking at the southern side of the box, many years earlier. A Class J21 on a 'special' swings on to the main line to Tebay. The Signal box was then named 'Kirkby Stephen West'.

Eddie Foster

Two excellent views of British Railways Standard Class 4MT 2-6-0s No. 76020 banked by No. 76023, easing approximately 300 tons of coke and mixed freight up the gradient near Waitby on 17th August 1957.

R. H. Leslie

A rather poor picture but an interesting one showing the Eden Valley branch, complete with northbound train, diverging away from the climbing Tebay line in the foreground.

Eddie Foster

Not too many years previously, two former NER 0-6-0s handle a Blackpool excursion. The previous photographs of Nos 76020 and 76023 were taken from the bridge in the distance.

Eddie Foster

Smardale Halt gained a second class prize in the best kept station garden competition in the 1930s. Amy Wearmouth was in charge at the time. This picture shows that station in its prime with Amy standing on the platform.

Amy Wearmouth collection

Smardale station building viewed from the north east, shortly after the line's closure. Smardale halt did not issue passenger tickets. Instead a splendid system prevailed whereby the staff at Smardale assessed the passenger situation and then telephoned either Ravenstonedale or Kirkby Stephen stations so that tickets and cash could be exchanged via the carriage window when Smardale passengers passed through (or alighted at) the respective station.

J. T. Hall

Below: The view towards the west from underneath bridge No. 161 at Smardale station. Note the Class 45 diesel on a southbound express crossing the Midland, Smardale Viaduct in the distance.

J. T. Hall

Above: An NER Class G1 of the late 1880s, rebuilt as a 4-4-0 early this century, whisks its train through the lovely gill between Smardale Halt and Smardale Gill Viaduct.

Iain Smith collection

Below: Smardale Gill in 1957 as Ivatt Class 4MT 2-6-0 No. 43072 disturbs the peace of the gill with the 7.32 am South Shields – Blackpool service on 3rd August 1957.

R. H. Leslie

The North Eastern main line between Smardale and Ravenstonedale passed underneath the Midland Railway's Settle – Carlisle line at Smardale, through the southern most arch of the Midland Viaduct. The close proximity of the two routes can be judged from this picture looking eastward along the NER line.

J. T. Hall

The first in a series of pictures showing the beautiful Smardale Gill Viaduct. Here, Ivatt Class 4MT 2-6-0 No. 43129 trundles over the high arches with the 11.5am Blackpool – Darlington train on 17th August 1957.

R. H. Leslie

A westbound train handled by an Ivatt Class 4MT 2-6-0 with steam to spare, climbs over the viaduct.

R. H. Leslie

A great study of a Class J25 0-6-0 and a banker struggling up towards Sandy Bank Summit (889 feet above sea level). The train of approximately 500 tons of coke would be bound eventually for the blast furnaces of West Cumberland via Tebay, the London North Western Railway main line to Hincaster Junction and the Furness line around the Cumbrian coast.

Iain Smith collection

The view looking west, from high above the viaduct.

Eddie Foster

The single line clings almost perilously to the wooden slopes of the valley before swinging dramatically across the valley on the South Durham & Lancashire Union Railway's own Smardale Gill Viaduct; 14 arches, 553 ft long, still climbing past lime kilns and two railway cottages, eventually achieving the summit at Sandy Bank, via a fine stone-lined cutting.

Local farmers pose for a picture on the boarded crossing at Sandy Bank Summit. The horse was called 'Morphet'.

Eddie Foster

Ivatt Class 4MT 2-6-0 No. 43073 leaves the double-track section to the east of Ravenstonedale station. The train is bound for South Shields on 19th July 1958.

R. H. Leslie

Ivatt Class 4MT 2-6-0 No. 43129 hauls its Blackpool – Darlington train off the eastbound main line, onto the single-track section, just beyond Ravenstonedale station.

R. H. Leslie

Standard Class 4MT 2-6-0 No. 76051, hauling a Tebay to West Auckland mineral empties train, prepares to receive the single-line tablet for Kirkby Stephen.

R. H. Leslie

Many enthusiasts of the line consider the stretch between Smardale and Sandy Bank to be one of the finest in the country. I can do no more than agree. The line at Sandy Bank doubles (latterly at Ravenstonedale) before descending to the lovely staggered platformed station at Ravenstonedale which is actually sited at Newbiggin-on-Lune. The name was altered from Newbiggin to Ravenstonedale in 1877 to avoid confusion with Newbiggin on the Settle-Carlisle line which opened in 1876.

The long, easy run along the Lune Valley through Gaisgill eventually brings the line past Tebay No. 3 box and into the junction station with the West Coast Main Line at Tebay.

Ivatt taper-boiler Class 2MT 2-6-0 No. 46471 coasts over an occupation crossing near Gaisgill with a 'down' Kirkby Stephen – Tebay class K stopping freight train on Friday, 30th May 1952.

E. D. Bruton

The eastbound Millom – Derwenthaugh empty coke wagon block train (from Millom Ironworks) seen from the east of Tebay en route for the Darlington area. Motive power is Kirkby Stephen shed's Worsdell Class J25 0-6-0 No. 65695 (one of the 1898 design of saturated steam locomotives with slide valves) which made a quick turn round in less than half an hour at Tebay, NE yard following arrival with the morning down goods and coke from Darlington, on Friday, 30th May 1952.

E. D. Bruton

Standard Class 3MT 2-6-2 tank No. 82026 pilots Class 4MT 2-6-0 No. 76048 at the head of the 11.5 am Blackpool – Newcastle train through Gaisgill on 8th September 1956.

R. H. Leslie

A view from the west side of the LNWR West Coast Main Line showing BR Standard Class 9F 2-10-0 No. 92017 with a 2-6-4 tank banking, about to attack the climb to Shap. The NER approach to Tebay is defined by the line of wagons in the background.

Author

Perhaps the sun always shone at Tebay in the glorious days of steam! BR Standard Class 4MT 2-6-0 No. 76049 pilots Ivatt 4MT No. 43056 on a westbound summer Saturday train, just 'inside' Tebay's 'down' distant signal.

Derek Cross

The famous picture of Ivatt Class 2MT 2-6-0 No. 46471 leaving the NE Yard at Tebay at the head of the Fridays only 8.42 am Ulverston – Durham 'Miners' special on 6th June 1952. Notice the splendid train of mixed origin stock.

E. D. Bruton

A Penrith train conveying six horse boxes and two lovely clerestory-roofed coaches speeds northwards past milepost No. 1 and Waitby 'down' distant signal.

Eddie Foster

Class J21 0-6-0 No. 65047 of 1889 vintage trundles away from Kirkby Stephen with a Penrith bound train.

Eddie Foster

Above: Looking towards the south at milepost No. 1 near to Waitby.

Author

Left: The now long-demolished crossing cabin at Waitby, complete with outside lever frame to control the two distant signals.

Author

Below: Class J21 0-6-0 No. 1613 heads a Penrith train, entering Musgrave station.

Eddie Foster

The substantial bridge over the River Eden at Musgrave, seen from the north-east. This bridge was unfortunately (and unneccessarily) demolished in 1985.

Author

Looking north over the bridge. Musgrave station can be seen in the distance.

Author

Class G5 0-4-4 Tank No. 1916 pauses at Warcop with a northbound train in LNER days.

Eddie Foster

The branch from Kirkby Stephen going northwards departs from Kirkby Stephen Junction in single line form, dropping gently into the Eden Valley through picturesque cuttings and over embankments. Skirted by typical NER wooden fencing it passes Waitby Crossing, crossing over Musgrave Viaduct, 221 ft in length, then through the tiny station at Musgrave (change for Brough) and eventually into Warcop.

Warcop, due to its proximity to the Army camp and local quarries at Brough, is well equipped with sidings, loading ramps and other goods facilities, although it is a single platform station with a platform signal cabin. The branch crosses Coupland Beck Viaduct and begins the climb of 1 in 100 up to the beautiful Appleby East station area, tucked behind the County

The view north of the Valley branch at milepost 12. Appleby's fixed distant signal can be seen in the distance.

J. F. Mallon

School and easily missed by enthusiasts travelling over the S&C route which passes 200 yards away. The NER junction with the S&C occurs some 500 yards beyond Appleby East station (Appleby Junction), before dropping underneath the Midland line and wandering in close proximity to the A66 main road for four miles to Kirkby Thore station which nestles below the road overbridge. A metal-topped river crossing bridge is passed prior to the quick run down through Temple Sowerby, over the 439 ft long Skygarth Viaduct to Cliburn, into the woods past Wetheriggs Pottery siding and to Clifton Moor. All the way that lovely sleepy feeling that the Eden Valley exudes with its secret lanes and pathways criss-crossing the railway is enjoyed as the line rolls gently through the Vale of Eden, spread like a patchwork quilt from the feet of the mighty Pennines to the edge of the Cumbrian Lakeland. Clifton Moor is the last station before the meeting with the WCML at Eden Valley Junction. The stretch of track between Clifton Moor and the Junction is double, while a short stretch of 'sharing' with the WCML affords the final access to the bay platform at Penrith.

The Midland Railway's extension to the North – The Settle – Carlisle line, crossed the Eden Valley branch to the north of Appleby. This photograph shows the overbridge in question, with the decaying remains of the branch underneath. Unfortunately this scene has been completely swept away by the Appleby Bypass. The S&C line crosses the new road by means of a large concrete bridge.

Author

Two views of a derailment at Powis, between Appleby and Kirkby Thore.

Mrs N. Hudson collection

Permanent way workers between Appleby and Cracken-thorpe.

Gordon Shaw collection

British Railways Class 3MT 2-6-2 tank No. 82028 accelerates the 10.2 am Sundays only Darlington – Penrith train away from the crossing at Cliburn.

R. H. Leslie

A derailment to the north of Kirkby Thore.

Iain Smith collection

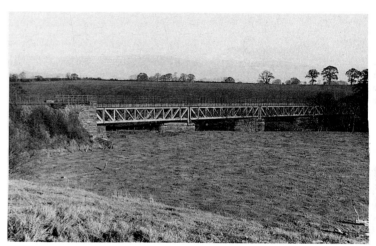

The rarely photographed Skygarth Viaduct to the north of Temple Sowerby.

J. F. Mallon

The view north along the branch, between Appleby and Kirkby Thore.

J. F. Mallon

The last revenue earning service had long since trundled away to the west leaving Cliburn station to await its fate. In the event, Cliburn fared much better than many of the other Eden Valley/ Stainmore line structures. The present owner has retained much of the character of the main building, renovating this as a private dwelling, and much to his credit has also preserved the signal box.
Alex Fraser

Class 3MT 2-6-2T No. 82029 coasts towards Clifton Moor.
R. H. Leslie

A BR Standard Class 3MT 2-6-2 tank eases the 2.57 pm Penrith – Darlington train away from Clifton Moor towards Wetheriggs on 21st May 1956. I wonder what other railway delights the picnic party sampled on that spring day more than thirty years ago.

R. H. Leslie

The pottery siding at Wetheriggs, looking south

J. F. Mallon

Class G5 0-4-4T No. 439 leaves Clifton Moor with a Penrith-bound train in 1929.

Locomotive & General Railway Photographs

Ivatt Class 2MT 2-6-0 No. 46488 faces south as Class J21 0-6-0 No. 65103 draws an Eden Valley train gently past Penrith No. 2 signal box and into the Valley platform at Penrith.

J. W. Armstrong

Standard Class 3MT 2-6-2T No. 82027 coasts between Eden Valley Junction and Clifton Moor on 28th April 1956. The track between the junction and Clifton Moor was double, becoming single to the south of the Clifton Moor platforms.

R. H. Leslie

Standard Class 3MT 2-6-2T No. 82027 hurries a Penrith – Darlington train off the West Coast Main Line and onto the Eden Valley branch. To the left of the picture is a LNWR lower quadrant signal. This remained operational until electrification of the West Coast Main Line and closure of the box at the junction.

R. H. Leslie

Standard 2-6-2T No. 82029 waits at the head of an Eden Valley branch and Stainmore line train at Penrith. The door of the first carriage beckons would-be passengers to join the train – if only we could do so now and enjoy a trip over this marvellous railway as the passengers on this summers day in the 1950s must have done.

R. H. Leslie

Class J21 No. 65100 (NER No. 1122) eases a train from the Eden Valley towards Penrith, past the junction of the West Coast Main Line and the Keswick branch. Passed fireman Monty Dickinson can be seen on the footplate.

Derek Cross

Standard 2-6-2T No. 82029 enjoys the section of flat bottomed West Coast Main Line as the 8.55 am Saltburn – Penrith train travels the last mile into Penrith on 5th August 1956.

R. H. Leslie

The Clifton Moor coal working passing Penrith No. 1 (LNWR) box. The locomotive is Ivatt Class 2MT 2-6-0 No. 46458. Part of the locomotive shed can be seen over the guard's van, while Penrith No. 2 signal box is beyond the tender of the rebuilt 'Royal Scot' in the distance.

Derek Cross

3

The Construction of the Lines

The engineer appointed to survey and construct both routes was Thomas Bouch, as mentioned previously, who accepted this position on 5th January 1857 by a letter which read:

Chambers 78 George Street,
Edinburgh Jan 5th, 1857

To the Provisional Committee,
of the South Durham & Lancashire Union Railway,

Gentlemen,

The terms upon which I am willing to undertake the engineering of the proposed South Durham and Lancashire Union Railway are as follows:

For preparing the Parliamentary Plans and Sections including the engraving of them, for preparing the Parliamentary Estimates giving evidence and fighting the Bill through Parliament and for undertaking all the expenses incident to the Engineering department up to the passing of the act excepting the Engineering witnesses that may be brought in support of the Bill at the rate of (£50) fifty pounds per mile,

For preparing the Working Plans and Sections, Specifications and Working Drawings of all bridges and works and all Land Plans and for finding all resident Engineers, Inspectors and Superintending the works and for undertaking all the expenses incident to the engineering department from the passing of the Act up to the opening and completion of the Railway to be paid at the rate of one hundred and fifty pounds per mile (£150).

I am gentlemen
your most obedient servant
Thomas Bouch

Meanwhile the South Durham & Lancashire Union Railway were experiencing difficulty with the Lancaster & Carlisle Railway regarding junction arrangements at Tebay and Clifton.

The Lancaster & Carlisle (still independent of the London & North Western Railway) was particularly anxious about the Eden Valley Line. The 'Little' North Western Railway had been trying to extend its Skipton to Morecambe line by making a branch to Tebay and it was also understood that the Great Northern Railway was endeavouring to extend its line to Scotland (as the Midland Railway did later via Settle and Carlisle).

An alternative route from Tebay to Penrith might thus have taken the Great Northern, or any other railway, well on the way to Carlisle and the Scottish Border. For this reason the Lancaster & Carlisle Railway took the view that, if the Eden Valley line was intended to serve only local places and not form part of the more comprehensive through route, then the junction at the northern end of the valley branch should be at Clifton - facing south.

The Lancaster & Carlisle Railway was similarly cagey regarding siding and station facilities at Tebay and made no move, despite earlier encouraging offers, to accept the new railway at Tebay.

Following a long period of fruitless negotiation, the South Durham & Lancashire Union Railway decided to show that they did not want to be delayed further. In late 1858/early 1859 they instructed their solicitors to prepare a formal notice to inform the Lancaster & Carlisle Railway that the SD&LUR were going to proceed with their junction at Tebay as provided for in their Act of Parliament. They also informed the Lancaster & Carlisle of expenses and inconvenience the new railway had incurred due to the delay.

In the event a large and comprehensive interchange and southward facing junction was built at Tebay. The southward facing and inadequate junction at Clifton, on the Eden Valley line, was also built.

Work on the South Durham & Lancashire Union main line began on 25th August 1857 when the Duke of Cleveland cut the first sod at Kirkby Stephen.

Ironically the Duke of Cleveland had originally opposed the construction of the Darlington & Barnard Castle Railway. The Duke also wished to preserve part of his estate and game reserves by having a portion of the line between Barnard Castle and Evenwood laid in a tunnel. Construction of this part of the route east of Barnard Castle was deferred until arrangements were made for some deviation of the line at this point. During the same period an agreement was made to improve the original course of the line at Gaisgill.

The Duke of Cleveland arrived at the King's Arms Hotel at 11.30 am and a procession led by a navvy with a wheelbarrow and spade was formed. The barrow was of 'polished mahogany with handsome mouldings, polished brass nobs and felloe'."

It was doubted whether the 'navvy' was really a workman as the newspaper says, "whether the navvy who bore the barrow on his shoulders was a real son of the soil or embankment and the cutting we are not prepared to say, but he looked stalwart and sturdy and sunburnt enough". Behind him came the band, followed by the railway's silk banner, then came the chairman, vice chairman, noblemen, MPs and directors.

More banners followed and then the directors of the Stockton & Darlington Company and of the Darlington & Barnard Castle Co. Mayors, clubs and societies brought up the rear of the procession.

LORD BROUGHAM CUTTING THE FIRST SOD OF THE EDEN VALLEY RAILWAY, AT APPLEBY.

A fine engraving from the *Illustrated Times* of 21st August 1858 showing Lord Brougham cutting the first sod of the Eden Valley Railway. An extract from the accompanying text read:
"All being ready, Rear-Admiral Elliott, in a neat little speach, called upon Lord Brougham, in the name of the directors, to turn the first sod. "With the greatest pleasure", replied his lordship. Then (says the *Carlisle Journal*) "Lord Brougham received from the brawny navvie who stood beside him, a neat spade with which he cut the first sod, and threw it into a handsome mahogany barrow which had been provided for the occasion".

A contemporary account of the occasion in the *Westmorland Gazette* stated:
"On the day of the sod cutting ceremony all the shops in Kirkby Stephen were closed and the town enjoyed a general holiday. Triumphal arches and flags were everywhere and the bells of the parish church rang forth a peal.

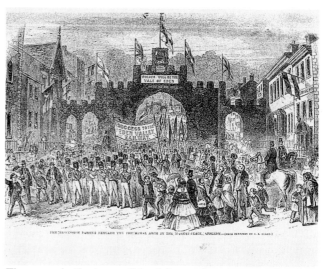

THE PROCESSION PASSING BENEATH THE TRIUMPHAL ARCH IN THE MARKET-PLACE, APPLEBY.—(FROM SKETCHES BY A. A. CLARK.)

The scene in the town of Appleby on the same occasion.

The ceremony took place about half a mile from the town on the right hand side of the road leading to Tebay and Kendal, on ground belonging to Mr Matthew Thompson, approximately where the booking office was built later. The Duke lifted a sod or two with the spade and placed it in the barrow which he wheeled away. Spade and barrow, which bore commemorative plates, were given to the Duke.

The first sod of the Eden Valley line was cut at Appleby on 28th July 1858 by Lord Brougham in a ceremony amply illustrated by the engravings. The construction of the Valley branch actually began on 11th February 1859 on Julian Bower Farm, Whinfell. The relatively new Eden Valley Railway Company held its first half-year meeting in 1859 at the King's Head Hotel Appleby. The chairman was Admiral Elliot.

At a speech following the sod cutting ceremony, Mr William Crackanthorpe of Newbiggin mentioned that Appleby had once been a great posting town but its post houses had not been used since the opening of the Lancaster & Carlisle Railway. Appleby's markets had been thinly attended and the town was to a certain extent falling into decay. He saw in the coming of the Eden Valley line hopes of a revived prosperity. A procession comprising 16 banners (three of which were "May Westmorland Flourish", "Peaceful & Plenty" and "Civil & Religious Liberty") took place and at 2.30 pm a large company sat down to a dinner in a tent which had been erected behind the King's Head Hotel. A ball was held in the hotel later in the day.

Table of Viaducts on the South Durham and Lancashire Union Railway					
		Length	Greatest and least height		Width and
Name of Viaduct	Construction	ft	ft	ft	No. of spans
Tees	Iron	732	132	65	2 of 21ft 5 of 120ft
Deepdale	Iron	740	161	50	11 of 60ft
Belah	Iron	1,040	196	60	16 of 60ft
Gaunless	Iron	640	93	70	4 of 120ft
Percy Beck	Stone	260	66	20	6 of 30ft 2 of 13ft
Mouth-Gill	Stone	244	106	40	6 of 30ft
Haty-Gill	Stone	324	94	30	7 of 30ft 2 of 12ft
Merry-Gill	Stone	366	78	40	9 of 30ft
Pod Gill	Stone	466	84	60	11 of 30ft
Smardale	Stone	553	90	40	14 of 30ft
Langleydale	Stone	411	76	27	11 of 30ft
Forthburn	Stone	248	43	16	4 of 35ft 2 of 15ft
Eden Valley Railway					
Sky-Garth	Iron	439	35	21	4 of 98.3 ft
Copeland	Stone	200	31	27	5 of 30ft
Musgrave	Iron	221	20	12	3 of 63ft

Sufficient land was purchased by the respective railways to allow both the main line over Stainmore and the Valley branch to be built as single lines but doubled if required at a later stage. Overbridges in particular were built with eventual doubling in mind as were the famous viaducts at Tees Valley, Deepdale, Belah and Smardale Gill. Other viaducts and overbridges were built for single track and doubled later.

The Darlington & Barnard Castle Railway had reached Barnard Castle on 8th July 1856 where a rather pleasant terminal station was built pointing towards the town. This was obviously an unsuitable location if further extensions to the West were to be considered and later a junction, about half a mile away from the town, was built and a new station erected there, the 1856 station and the line to it being retained for goods purposes.

Construction of the line over the Pennines proceeded rapidly without incident and was actually opened for mineral traffic on 4th July 1861. A locomotive reputedly crossed Belah Viaduct for the first time on 19th November 1860 - celebrated by the ringing of church bells at Brough and Kirkby Stephen.

It is incredible to note that in less than four years the whole complex (excluding the section between Bishop Auckland and Barnard Castle which was opened for passenger traffic on 1st August 1863) was operational, the formal opening taking place on 7th August 1861 with the passenger service following a day later.

Developments in the Bishop Auckland area in 1863, namely the construction of the connection between Bishop Auckland and Fieldon Bridge Junction at West Auckland, effectively completed the full North East to Tebay line.

The Bishop Auckland to Barnard Castle section ran from Bishop Auckland to Fieldon Bridge, then through West Auckland to Spring Gardens, using a section of the Stockton & Darlington Railway's Haggerleases branch. The 'new' line then proceeded through Evenwood, Cockfield, Forthburn and Coal Road to merge with the Darlington and Barnard Castle line at Barnard Castle East Junction.

The completion of the route between Bishop Auckland and Barnard Castle eliminated the need for complicated reversals and latterly diversions between Charity Junction on the Bishop Auckland-Darlington line and Stooperdale Junction on the Barnard Castle-Darlington line for Bishop Auckland area to Tebay services.

In common with many others of the time, the routes were built by a series of contractors who had tendered for various sections of the proposed line.

The section between West Auckland (a point to the west of the River Tees), including Percy Beck Viaduct and the foundations and masonry for the Tees and Deepdale viaducts was built by D.P. Appleby of Barnard Castle. The next section to Bowes was built by J. Anderson of Middlesbrough.

The section from Bowes to the Barras side of Mousegill Viaduct, including the building of the viaduct and the foundations and masonry for Belah Viaduct was built by Boulton of Wakefield.

The next section, from the Barras side of Mousegill Viaduct and Rookby Scarth, including the building of Aitygill Viaduct, was constructed by Chambers & Hilton, who also built the section between Rookby Scarth and Smardale, including Merrygill and Podgill viaducts.

The final section, between Smardale and Tebay, including the building of Smardale Gill Viaduct, was constructed by Wrigg of Preston. The metal viaducts crossing the River Tees were constructed by Kennaird, while those across Deepdale and the River Belah were built by Gilkes Wilson.

The Eden Valley branch was constructed by Lawton Bros of Newcastle. The actual construction proceeded relatively smoothly with few problems although the road overbridge at Kirkby Stephen collapsed on 3rd March 1860. A "great fall of congealed earth near Kirkby Thore" resulted in a workman breaking a leg. Other minor landslips also occurred on occasions.

The ubiquitous railway navvies were compelled to work on the bleak, unsympathetic wastes of

Stainmore, and relieved their frustration by becoming something of a nuisance in the surrounding towns and villages. The South Durham & Lancashire Union Railway covered the cost of a special constable in an attempt to control the navvy-associated problems. Approximately two hundred navvies and fifty stone masons were involved with the building of the route.

On Monday 20th February 1860, the next half yearly meeting of the Eden Valley Railway Company was held at the King's Head Hotel, Appleby. The minutes of this meeting indicate that Admiral R. Elliot (agent for the Hothfield Estates) presided at the meeting, accompanied by the company secretary George Brown.

It was recorded that land purchases had proceeded very satisfactorily and that the directors had been engaged in arrangements with the Stockton & Darlington Railway Company, "with a view to giving a more fixed and permanent character to your shares". (The Eden Valley line was absorbed by the Stockton & Darlington Company in 1862).

Thomas Bouch in his report regretted that progress "has not been so satisfactory as I could wish" but continued by noting "an improvement during the last two weeks"; he gave details of the work done - 23 miles of fencing erected, 185,000 cubic yards of excavation carried out (nearly a third of the total required), one under-bridge completed and thirteen other bridges in course of construction, over 1,900 tons of rails and 311 tons of rail chairs delivered and about 5½ miles of permanent way laid. He concluded, "I am of the opinion that not withstanding past delays, the contractors may, with proper exertions, complete the line so as to have it opened simultaneously with the South Durham & Lancashire Union Railway".

One of the few legal problems encountered by the project occurred when, in May 1861, the Eden Valley Railway Company was summoned by Mr John Ker of Langton Field, surveyor of roads for Bongate, for damage to the 2½ mile road between Langton and Gallows Hill, Appleby.

The road was being used by the railway contractor, Mr Joseph Lawton, to transport stone from Hilton at the feet of the Pennines, to the Appleby area. Due to the passage of Mr Lawton's 16 horses and carts per day on average, the road was almost destroyed. The magistrates ruled that the Eden Valley Railway Company should repair the road within a month under a penalty of £5 per day.

Of interest at this time was one of the earliest instances of the railway's effect upon the community through which it passed. The Eden Valley contractor, Joseph Lawton of Newcastle, married a local girl - Miss Arabella Fairer, daughter of Mr William Fairer of Warcop. The marriage was in Warcop church on 30th January 1861. Before the honeymoon Mr Lawton "entertained" the men working on the railway, when toasts were given and songs were sung.

Various problems did occur within the respective companies, not least of which was the death in February 1860 of the Kirkby Thore banker Mr John Crosby.

The eventual cost of the Eden Valley line can be gleaned from a contemporary balance sheet which reported that, "the amount received on shares was £45,980 and disbursements included £6,673 for land, £16,034 for labour and £11,971 for materials. The balance in hand is £17,806".

The ultimate cost of the main line over Stainmore exceeded the original estimate of £9,000 a mile by £3,683, a total of £12,683 per mile. The average cost of a mile of British railway at the time was £54,152. Although these figures are not strictly comparable, they do indicate the economy with which Bouch managed to create his railway.

At about the same time Bouch also reported that 17 miles of the 34½ miles of the main line had also been laid and that the major viaducts were nearing completion. Both Stainmore and Eden Valley lines opened in 1861, further details of which are given later.

The link between the North East and the North West had been made.

The remoteness of parts of the line is illustrated here, where it passed the cottages adjacent to the kilns at Smardale.

4

The Development of the Routes

As mentioned earlier, the route between Barnard Castle and Tebay as well as the Valley branch, was built as a single line with future doubling in mind.

Initial operation on the single line basis involved signal boxes at Barnard Castle, Bowes, Stainmore Summit, Kirkby Stephen and Tebay with no boxes on the Valley branch.

The earliest method of working the route over the Summit was by 'staff and ticket', later replaced by tablet, token and absolute block systems as appropriate.

The rapid increase in traffic and the concurrent interest and improvement of signalling systems led to the construction of further signal boxes and facilities, and very quickly to the doubling of all but 4.66 miles of the Barnard Castle to Tebay main line. The Valley branch remained essentially single track apart from a short stretch between Appleby station and Appleby Junction, and eventually the last short section into Penrith between Clifton Moor and Eden Valley Junction.

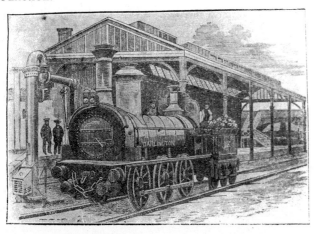

A copy of an early (1864) engraving of the scene at Kirkby Stephen. The locomotive illustrated was a standard Stockton & Darlington short-coupled 0-6-0, No. 103 *Darlington* built by Gilkes, Wilson & Co., Middlesbrough in October 1855. Builder's No. 68. Cylinders 17in x 18in, wheels 4ft 2½in dia. It became NER No. 1103 and was later rebuilt with 17in x 24in cylinders. After various renumberings (No. 1951 in January 1892, 1724 in January 1894 and 2263 in July 1899) it was finally withdrawn and scrapped circa 1905.

Stainmore enginemen were rightly acclaimed to have a tough reputation. Imagine driving and firing No. 103 over the Summit in the teeth of a February blizzard with only a plate provided for protection! It was possible to fire from Shildon all the way to Cockermouth, which could take 16-18 hours. There was a shed at Cockermouth reputed to be of Stockton & Darlington origin. In fact until the 1950s one of the sidings at Cockermouth was known as the 'Stockton Siding'.
Courtesy Cumberland & Westmorland Herald

The doubling of the first section of main line between Bowes and Stainmore Summit was begun in 1866, five years after the opening of the route. This was followed rapidly by the section between Barnard Castle and Tees Valley Junction.

A further pause occurred before the next section was approved for doubling - Tees Valley Junction to Bowes in 1870. Approvals for the doubling of all the remaining sections of the main line, with the exception of the sections between Belah and Kirkby Stephen and Kirkby Stephen to Sandy Bank, had been received by 1875.

The last approval for the Belah to Kirkby Stephen section occurred in 1889 followed shortly by the agreement to double the section of the Valley branch between Appleby station and Appleby Junction. The delay in the doubling of the Belah to Kirkby Stephen section was undoubtedly influenced by the original and rather odd decision to build Aitygill, Merrygill and Podgill viaducts, all relatively large structures - especially Podgill - for single track only.

Obviously, with the ever-increasing pressure to handle more traffic the 'doubling' of these viaducts became inevitable. All three viaducts were still standing in the late 1980s and the skilful method of joining the old to new viaducts could be investigated as shown in the illustrations of Aitygill Viaduct.

Ironically the superb stone viaduct at Smardale Gill, which also still stood in the late 1980s, was built to carry double track but never did so. Instead a single track was economically slewed over the viaduct to ease the curve.

The deceptively high viaduct at Mousegill (106 ft), the highest all stone viaduct on the route, and the smaller Percybeck Viaduct to the west of Barnard Castle, were built to accommodate double track from the outset. To further confuse the issue certain underbridges, No. 107 to the east of Barras and occupation underbridges in the Winton area, were built as single track structures and doubled later.

Mousegill Viaduct, along with bridge No. 108, was blown up by the Army in an act of legalised vandalism in June 1966. An application to demolish Aitygill Viaduct was made at about the same time as the Mousegill episode. Fortunately, the farmer upon whose land the viaduct stands prevented the proposed destruction.

In the late 1860s the signalling arrangements were fairly elementary and obviously as doubling and consolidation occurred improvements in this direction were essential.

By 1875 signalling arrangements were provided at Barnard Castle East and West, Tees Valley Junction, Lartington, Bowes, Stainmore, Barras and Kirkby

Aitygill Viaduct surrounded by trees, is difficult to photograph in its entirety today. These two photographs show details of the viaduct. Note paticularly, in the first view the joint between the original single-track viaduct (nearest) and the subsequent addition.

Author

Stephen East and West. The West box at Kirkby Stephen replaced an earlier box which stood immediately to the west of bridge No. 148 on the exit from Kirkby Stephen. Ironically the original box stood as a linesman's cabin until the late 1960s and its foundations can still be seen, whereas the modern West 'Junction' box has disappeared without trace.

By the mid-1890s additional boxes had been provided at Spital, Belah, Rookby Scarth, Smardale, Sandy Bank and Kelleth (between Ravenstonedale and Gaisgill), followed shortly by a box at Bleathgill and at Gaisgill (to replace Kelleth).

The consolidation before the First World War saw further new boxes at Ravenstonedale and Hulands Quarry (between Lartington and Bowes) with Rookby Scarth closing completely, probably before 1908 although it is shown as intact on the 1915 Ordnance Survey map. Also shown is the ground frame arrangement which was required at Bowes Gate cottages to serve the quarry there, between Lartington and Hulands. The presence of the cottages here suggests there may have been some requirement for railwaymen/signalmen here.

After the First World War Smardale box appears to have been the first casualty, followed variously by Bleathgill and Spital and in 1931 Sandy Bank, when the line between the Summit at Sandy Bank and Ravenstonedale (almost a mile) was singled.

The major quarry facility at Hartley (Merrygill) was served by the railway from the late 1920s. Extensive siding facilities were constructed in the quarry at this time and a signal box was erected on the north side of the line.

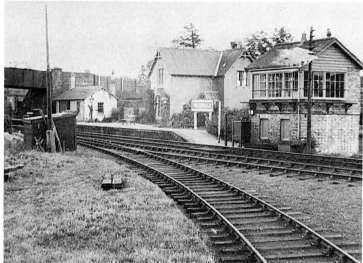

A rare picture of Smardale Halt prior to 1922 showing the signal box which disappeared without trace in that year. Notice the tablet catching platform. The box appears to have been almost identical to the crossing cabin at Cliburn.

Iain Smith collection

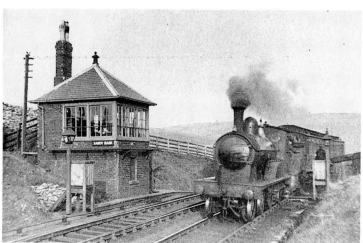

Class G 4-4-0 No. 274 at the head of a Tebay train, passes the single-line token to the Sandy Bank signalman – probably Dick Alderson. This is one of the very few pictures of Sandy Bank signal box to have been discovered.

Eddie Foster

79

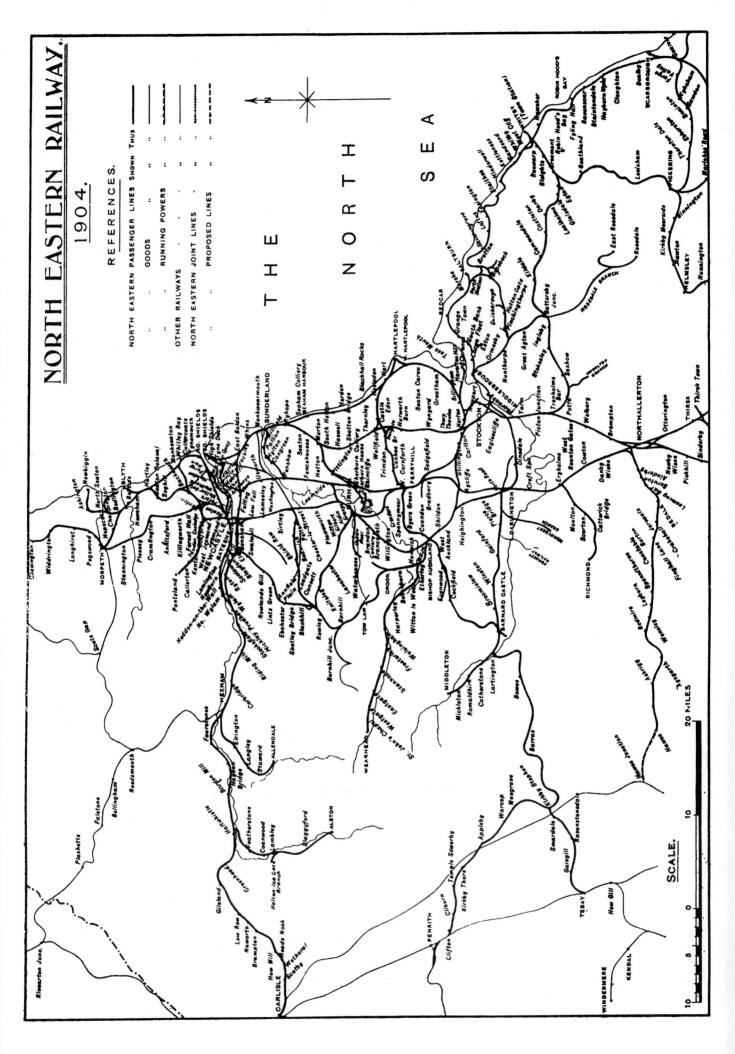

NORTH EASTERN RAILWAY.

1904.

REFERENCES.

NORTH EASTERN PASSENGER LINES SHOWN THUS

GOODS " : "

RUNNING POWERS " : "

OTHER RAILWAYS " : "

NORTH EASTERN JOINT LINES " "

PROPOSED LINES " "

N

THE NORTH SEA

SCALE.

20 MILES

Some time between 1930 and 1936, one of the former Great Northern Railway Class D3 4-4-0s leaves Ravenstonedale with an eastbound train.

Iain Smith collection

By the mid-1930s the station, siding and signal box arrangements had consolidated to constitute the following:

1. Barnard Castle East box controlled the level crossing to the east of the station as well as access to the goods branch and the junction between the West Auckland and Darlington lines. This box also controlled access to and from the small engine shed at Barnard Castle which was situated to the east of the level crossing. The shed opened in 1865 and closed in 1937.

2. Barnard Castle station.

3. Barnard Castle West box.

4. Tees Valley (Junction box).

5. Lartington station, complete with ground frame controlled access to and from the goods yard.

6. Lartington West box, which by now no longer controlled the two quarries at the western side of the line that had closed about the time of the First World War. The box conveniently split the section between Tees Valley and Bowes and provided a crossover facility, affording a view of the viaduct at Deepdale. The signalmen here and at Belah were paid extra to keep watch for fire on the timber decking of the viaducts.

7. Hulands box controlled access to and from the Quarry sidings.

8. Bowes box controlled access to and from the goods yard, etc.

9. Bowes station.

10. Spital box. Rumoured to have been closed in 1930 after intermittent use through the 1920s. It is further speculated that Spital was opened for the last time in 1939 to deal with the passage of wartime evacuation specials. The box was destroyed by fire two years later.

11. Stainmore box controlled the siding and crossover arrangements at the Summit.

12. Bleathgill box (closed).

13. Barras station, complete with ground frame controlled access to and from the goods yard.

14. Belah box provided crossover facilities and afforded a view of Belah Viaduct.

15. Merrygill box controlled access to and from the quarry, etc.

16. Kirkby Stephen East box controlled access to and from the goods yard, engineers sidings, etc.

17. Kirkby Stephen station.

18. Kirkby Stephen West box controlled access to and from the West sidings, the junction with the Valley branch and access to and from the locomotive shed, also marking the eastern end of the single line section from Ravenstonedale. An earlier box, to the West of and adjacent to the cattle overbridge No. 148 was replaced by the Junction (West) box during earlier expansion. The original box remained in use as a linesman's cabin.

19. Ravenstonedale station.

20. Ravenstonedale box controlled access to and from the goods yard and marked the western end of the single station section from Kirkby Stephen. Ravenstonedale box incorporated the previous junctions of Sandy Bank Summit box.

21. Gaisgill station.

22. Gaisgill box controlled the level crossing and access to and from the goods yard.

23. Tebay (No. 3) box controlled the eastern end of the yards at Tebay and access to and from the locomotive servicing/turntable area.

24. Tebay station.

25. Waitby Crossing ground frame controlled the small level crossing.

26. Musgrave station, complete with ground frame, controlled access to and from the goods yard.

Barnard Castle East signal box and level crossing taken in 1964. By this time the lovely lower quandrant signals had been replaced. The signal box was of typical large North Eastern Railway "central division" construction with crossed timbers under the eaves.

R. B. Coulthard

27. Warcop box (which by now had been 're-sited' and had become a single-storey platform box replacing a larger box which formerly stood on the western side of the line about 400 yards south of the station) controlled all facilities at Warcop.

28. Warcop station.

29. Appleby station.

30. Appleby station box controlled the level crossing and access to and from the goods yard. Also marked the southern end of the double-line section to Appleby West (NER Midland Junction) box.

Appleby station box, formerly Appleby West until 1909, duplicated to some degree and eventually replaced Appleby East box which was situated on the west side of the line, a few hundred yards to the south of the station. The original East box was demoted initially to a ground frame to control access to and from the southern end of the loop and yard. It eventually closed altogether and was demolished many years ago.

31. Appleby West (NER Midland Junction) box controlled the junction with the Settle-Carlisle line and also marked the northern end of the double-line section from Appleby station.

32. Kirkby Thore station.

33. Kirkby Thore box controlled access to and from the goods yard.

34. Temple Sowerby station, complete with ground frame, controlled access to and from the goods yard, the ground frame being unlocked by Annetts key from Kirkby Thore box.

35. Cliburn station.

36. Cliburn box controlled the level crossing and access to and from the goods yard.

37. Wetheriggs Pottery ground frame controlled access to and from the siding.

38. Clifton Moor station, complete with platform box, controlled access to and from the goods yard. The platform box replaced an earlier separate structure which stood to the south of the platform to the west of the line. Clifton Moor box also marked the southern

end of the double-line section to Eden Valley Junction.

39. Eden Valley Junction (LNWR) box controlled the junction with the West Coast Main Line.

The use of the curve from the LNWR line at Redhills had gradually declined as far as through traffic was concerned. It seems that 1928 was the last time that mineral trains used the 'curve' after intermittent use during the years from 1918.

When the former Great Northern Railway 4-4-0s appeared in 1932 they were turned at Penrith by using the Eamont Junction-Redhills Junction and Penrith No. 1 Triangle. The points to the curve at Eamont Junction were removed in June 1937 and the signal box there and the box at Redhills closed about a year later.

The original names of stations and boxes were subject to revision as the years went by and alterations, additions, etc., took place. Notable amongst these were the renaming of Newbiggin station to Ravenstonedale to avoid confusion with Newbiggin station on the Settle-Carlisle line which opened in 1876.

Kirkby Stephen West box became Kirkby Stephen Junction and Appleby West (NER/Midland Junction) box became Appleby Junction, shortly after Nationalisation in 1948. The North Eastern Region stations at Appleby and Kirkby Stephen were suffixed 'East' at the same time to differentiate between these stations and the neighbouring stations on the Settle-Carlisle main line. Appleby station box became Appleby East.

An intriguing point worthy of mention in relation to the Valley branch, is the construction of earthworks to the south of Appleby East station which would have afforded a connection with the Midland main line. These earthworks were completed along with a substantial overbridge but no record appears to exist of any use of this connection being made or of track ever being laid. However, an inspection many years ago by Mr G.O. Holt revealed that the sleepers had been laid and he speculated that the cutting may have been used whilst the Settle-Carlisle line was being constructed.

Many years later, during the closure controversy, it was proposed that all trains, Midland and North Eastern, could have used the Midland station at Appleby by the laying of this connection with subsequent economies being achieved by closing Appleby East station and Junction boxes. This scheme never materialised.

Frederick Williams' fine history of the Midland Railway refers to "a siding at some little distance from this point, running into the South Durham". The point referred to being Smardale (Midland) Viaduct. It seems probable that a link between the South Durham line just to the east of Smardale station to one or other end of Waitby (Midland) Rock Cutting may have been constructed and used for about eight months to transfer some of the 60,000 tons of stone required for the construction of Smardale (Midland) Viaduct. Certainly there is evidence of earthworks in the area in question.

It would appear that the SDLUR had already constructed a tramway between the quarry and Smardale Gill (SDLUR) Viaduct at an earlier stage to supply stone for this fine structure. The trackbed of this tramway is still clearly defined.

Barnard Castle station from the east. A G5 class 0-4-4 tank waits in the east bay. The track to this platform was lifted in 1954.

W. A. Camwell

The 1861 station offices at Barnard Castle from the approach road. This stone building was sited on the south side of the passenger train shed. The building was constructed from an attractive yellow sandstone in a cottage like style.

Author

The interior of Barnard Castle East signal box.
Courtesy North of England Newspapers

The west end of Barnard Castle station, showing the 1949 canopy which replaced an earlier cast iron structure.

Author

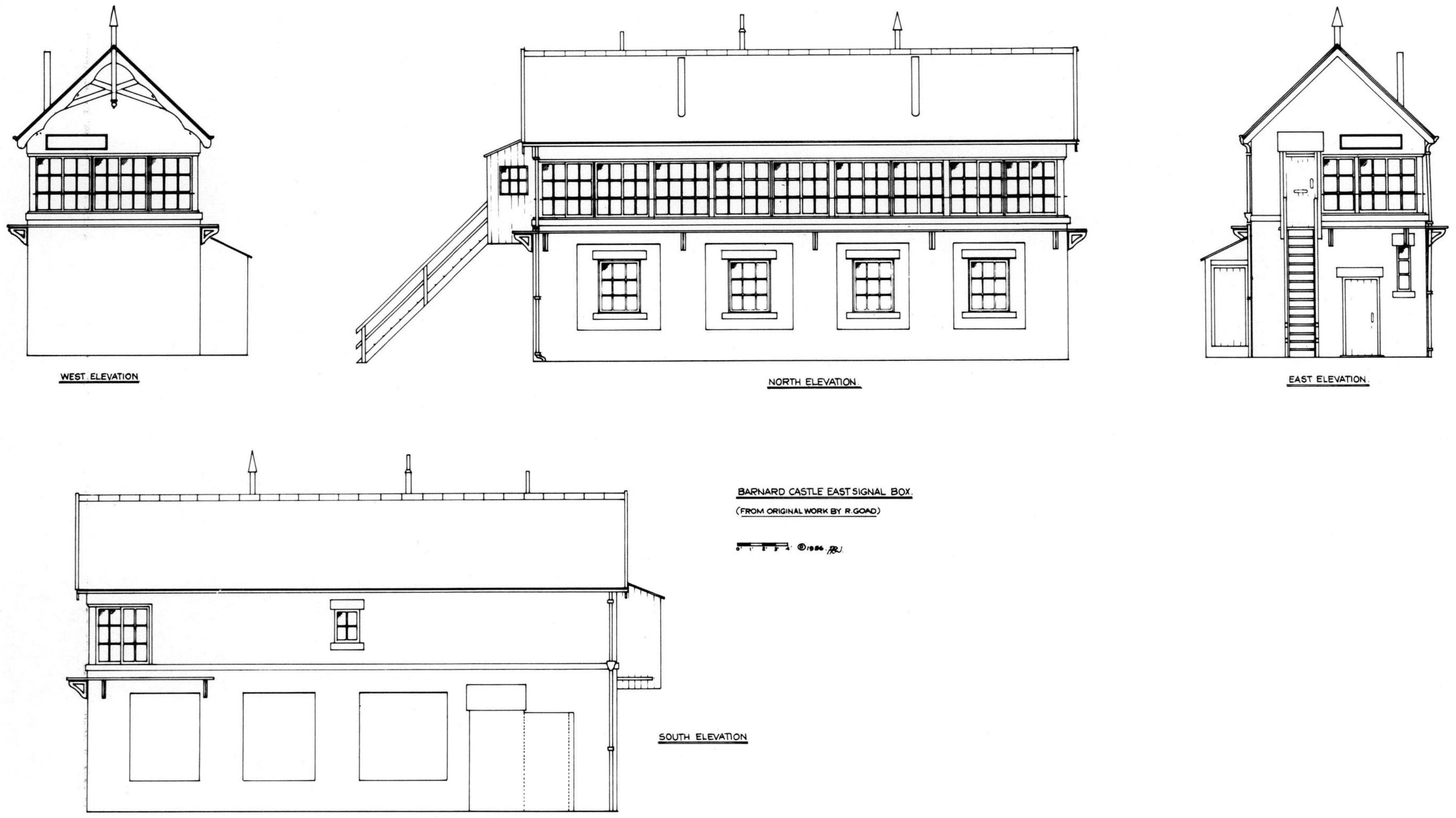

EAST ELEVATION.

NORTH ELEVATION

BARNARD CASTLE EAST SIGNAL BOX
(FROM ORIGINAL WORK BY R GOAD)

© 1984 RGL

SOUTH ELEVATION

WEST ELEVATION

Barnard Castle East Signal Box. East, South, West and North Elevations

Scale: 2mm = 1ft

Author

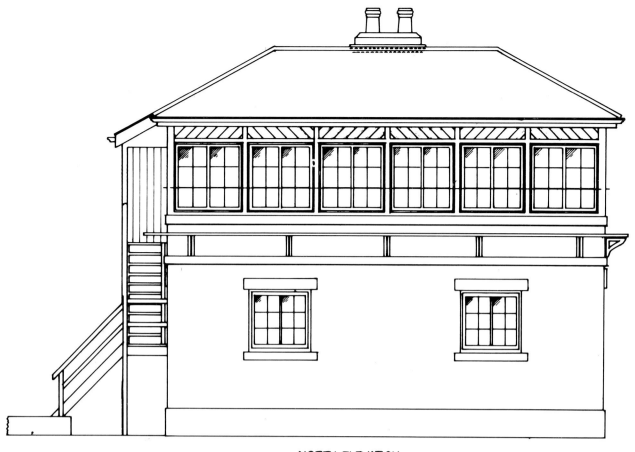

NORTH ELEVATION.

BARNARD CASTLE WEST SIGNAL BOX

(FROM ORIGINAL WORK BY R.GOAD)

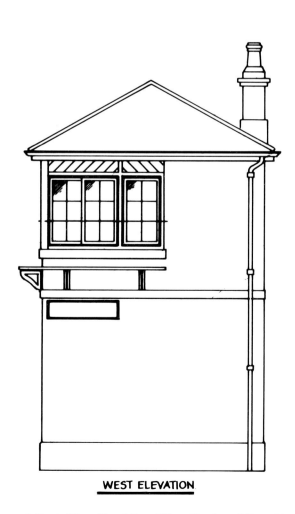

WEST ELEVATION

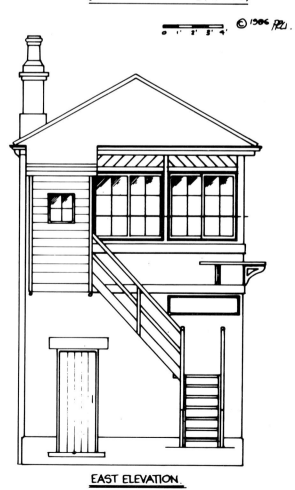

EAST ELEVATION.

Barnard Castle West Signal Box. West, North and East Elevations.
Scale: 4mm = 1ft

Ray Goad/Author

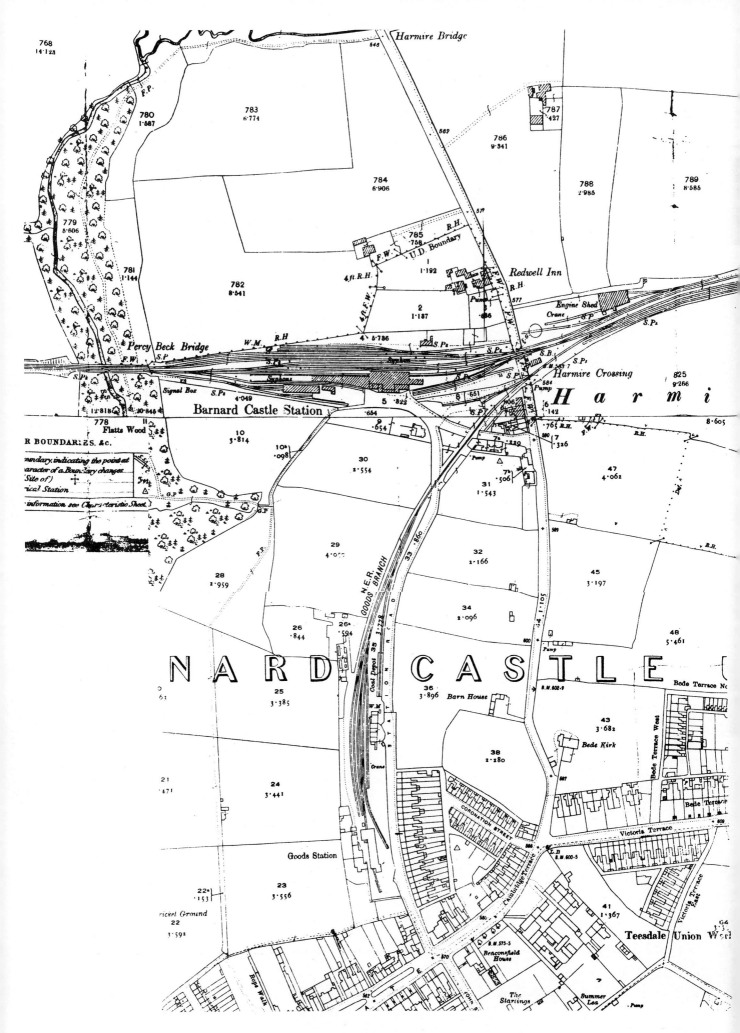

Barnard Castle Station and Goods Station including Percy Beck Viaduct (surveyed 1897).

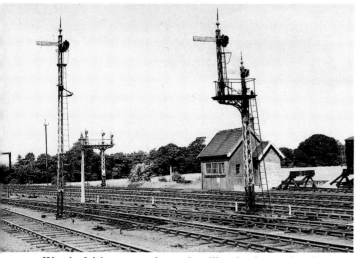

Wonderful lower quadrant signalling in the yard at Barnard Castle on 28th June 1952.

J. F. Aylard

Looking east from Percy Beck Viaduct towards the West box and station.

J. F. Mallon

The weed-grown track as surveyed from his box by signalman Chapman at Tees Valley Junction which was still open in 1963 to handle the Middleton-in-Teesdale branch trains and the demolition trains, working from Merrygill Quarry inexorably to the East.

J. L. Birkbeck

Barnard Castle; the approach from the West.

J. F. Mallon

Tees Valley Junction looking west with the Middleton-in-Teesdale branch diverging to the right of the picture. The double-track main line to Kirkby Stephen passes in front of the box.

J. F. Mallon

The attractive station at Lartington on 12th April 1955. Note the dainty platform cabin. The main buildings still survive as a private dwelling.

F. W. Shuttleworth

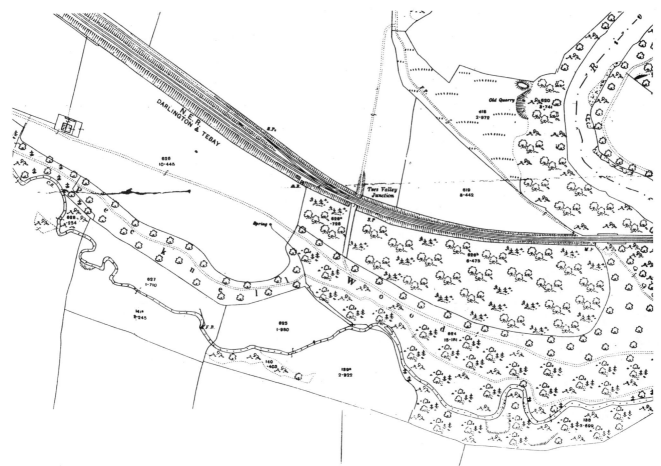

Tees Valley Junction.

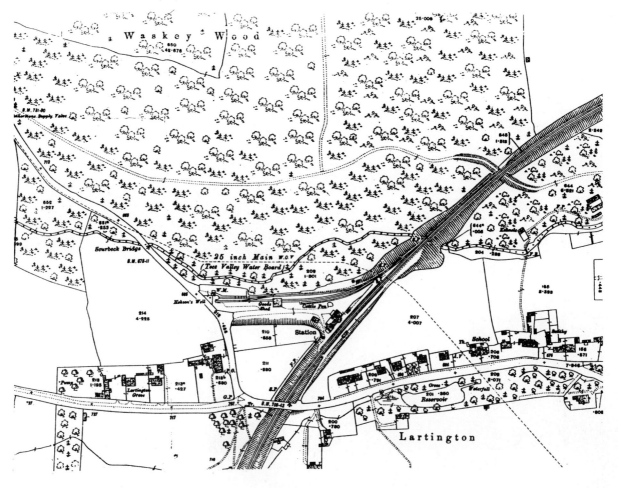

Lartington Station.

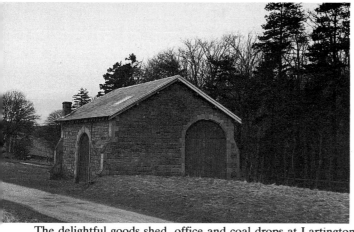

The delightful goods shed, office and coal drops at Lartington, still extant on 12th April 1955.

F. W. Shuttleworth

Above left: A view of the platforms at Lartington taken looking west on 10th June 1959.

J. F. Mallon

Above: The box at Hulands Quarry, looking east.

J. F. Mallon

The quarry platforms at Hulands, looking west. These platforms were erected specially by the North Eastern Railway for workmen at Hulands Quarry.

J. F. Mallon

The rear of the station showing the extensive and ornamental living accommodation.

F. W. Shuttleworth

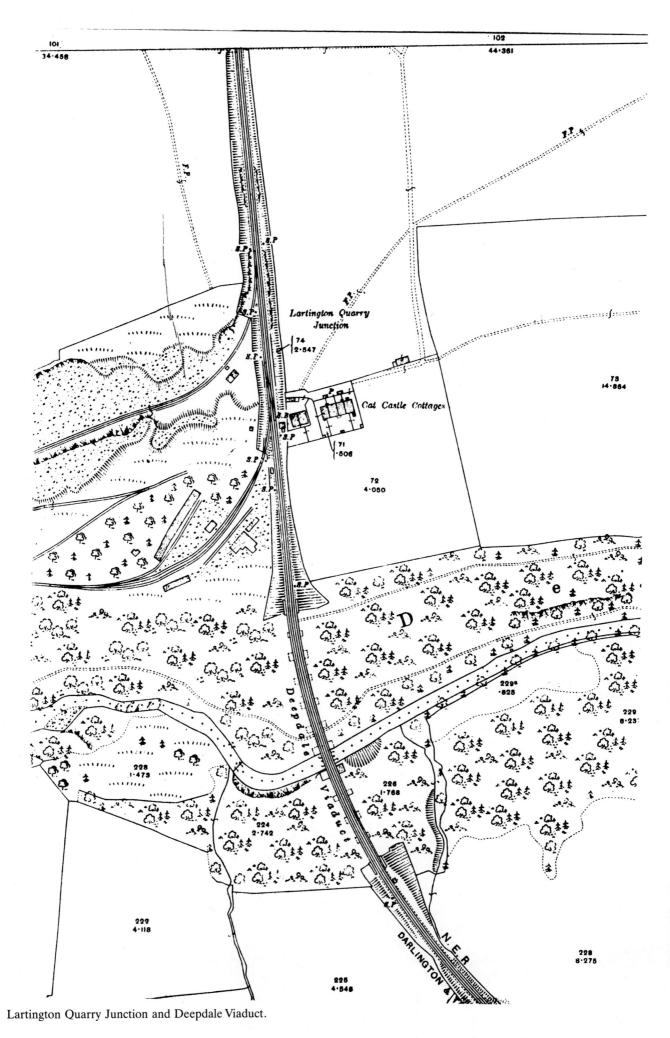

Lartington Quarry Junction and Deepdale Viaduct.

The eastern approach to Bowes.

J. F. Mallon

A 1959 view of Bowes station looking west showing the entrance to the goods yard and the island platform. Note the signal box has lost its brick chimney.

J. F. Mallon

The classic main station building at Bowes. This 1858 structure displays characteristics to be seen in many stations on the route. Stations at Ravenstonedale, Warcop, Kirkby Thore and Temple Sowerby were essentially identical in principle, however, considerable detail differences occurred, the most significant being that Ravenstonedale and Kirkby Thore were 'left handed'. Many of the waiting room screens were different.

J. F. Mallon

Bowes goods yard on 12th May 1959, showing the typical coal office and coal drops.

J. F. Mallon

A lovely view of Bowes station in pristine condition, complete with an array of enamelled advertisements.

Lens of Sutton

Bowes Gate Cottages.

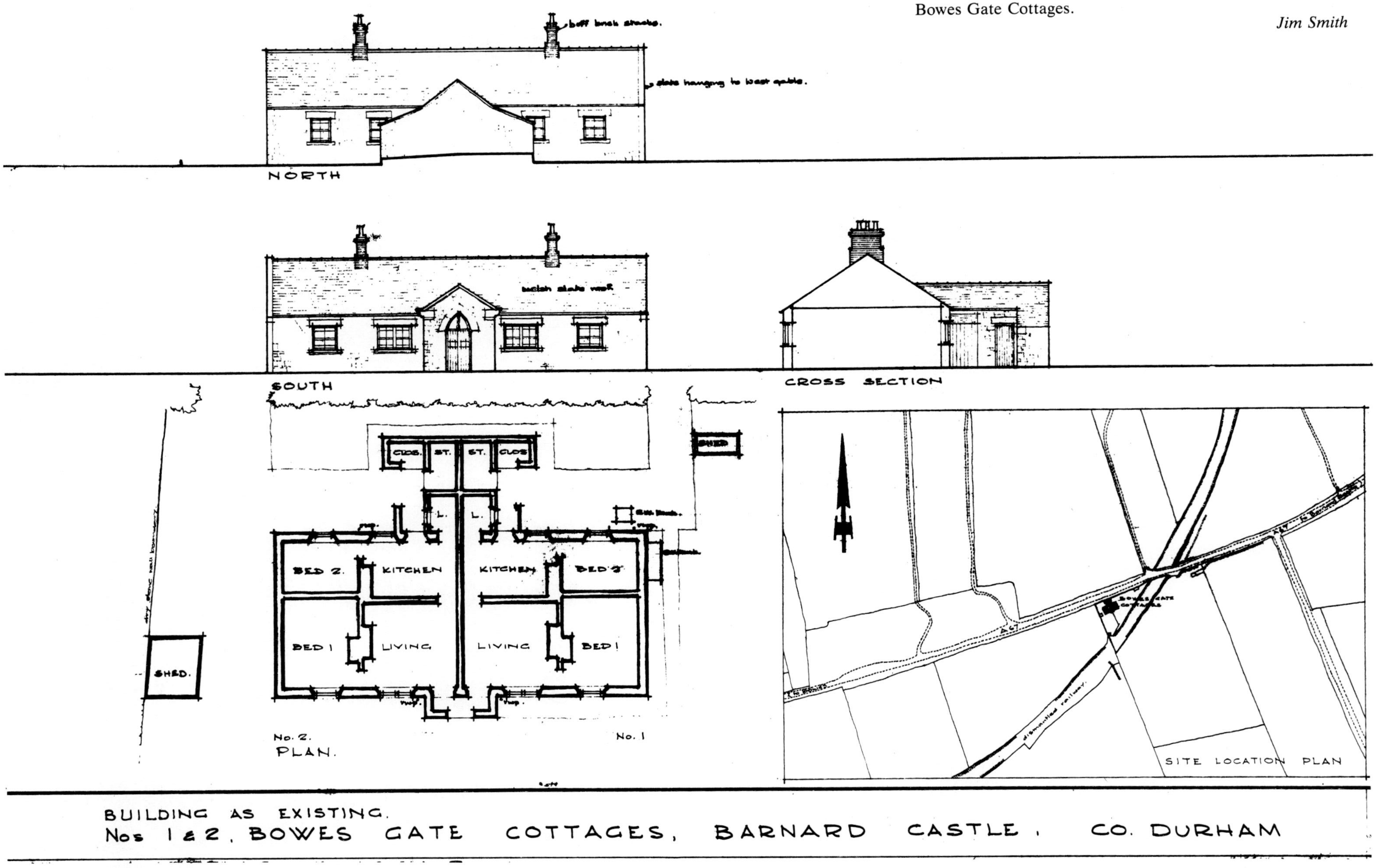

Jim Smith

SITE LOCATION PLAN

CROSS SECTION

NORTH

SOUTH

PLAN.

No. 1

No. 2

BUILDING AS EXISTING.
Nos 1 & 2. BOWES GATE COTTAGES, BARNARD CASTLE, CO. DURHAM

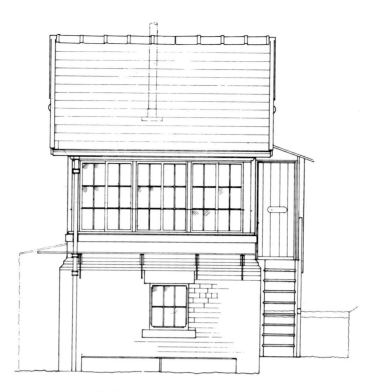

BOWES SIGNAL BOX - SOUTH ELEVATION.

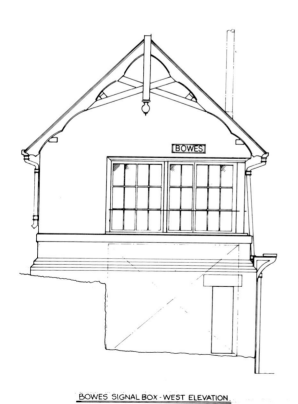

BOWES SIGNAL BOX - WEST ELEVATION.

BOWES SIGNAL BOX - EAST ELEVATION.

Bowes Signal Box. West, South and East Elevation.
Scale: 4mm = 1ft

Author

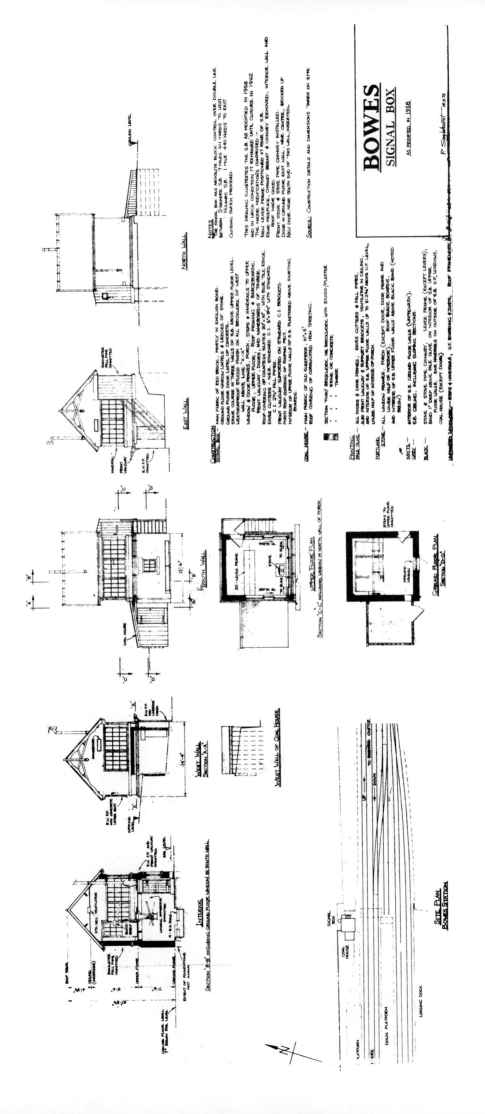

Bowes Signal Box with detailed notes.

Peter Singlehurst

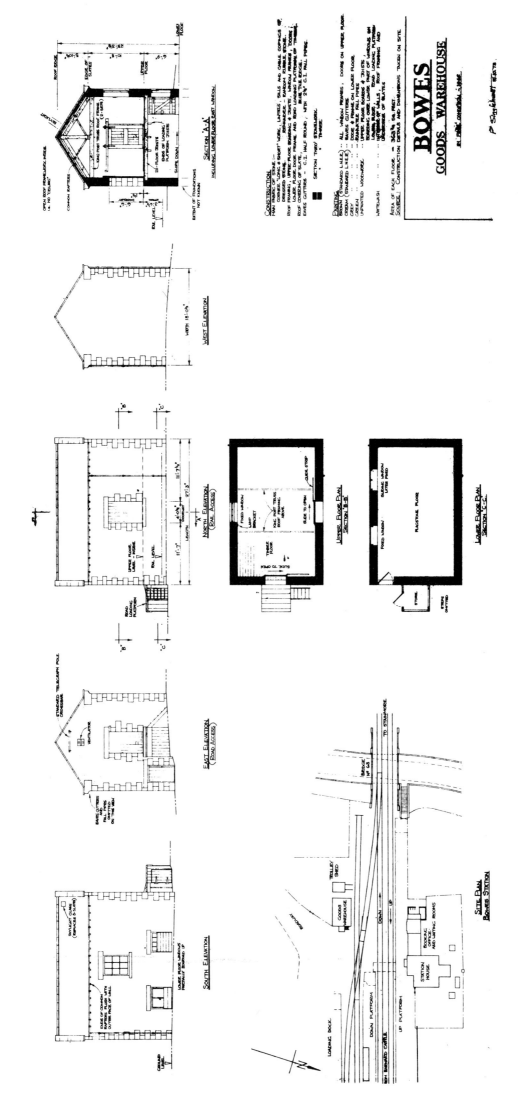

Bowes Good Shed with detailed notes.

Peter Singlehurst

95

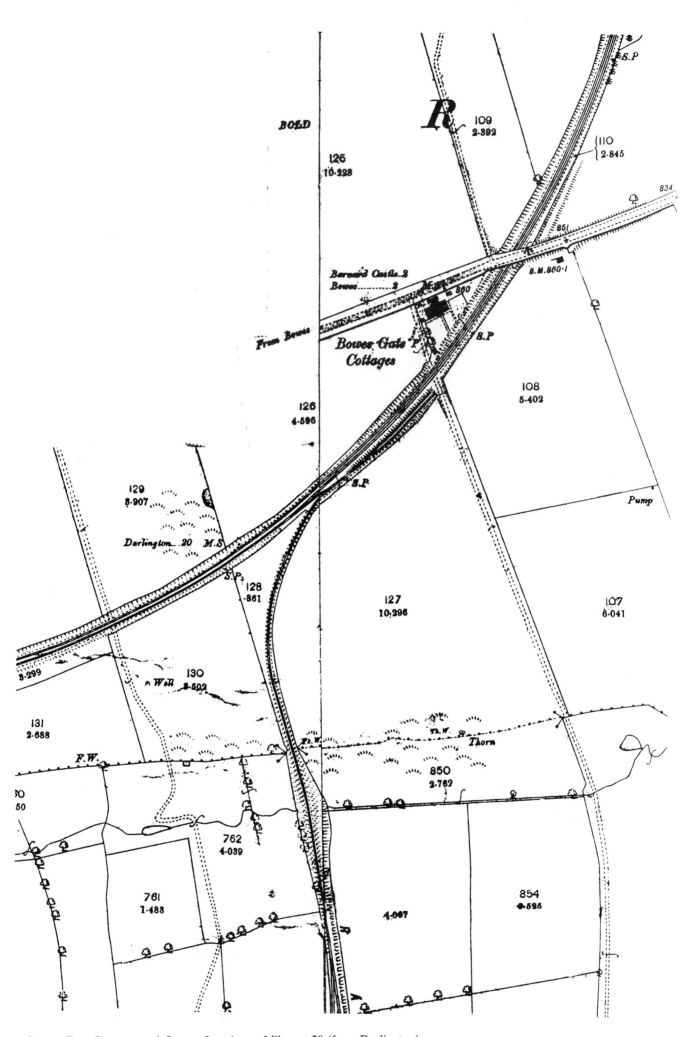

Bowes Gate Cottages and Quarry Junction at Milepost 20 (from Darlington).

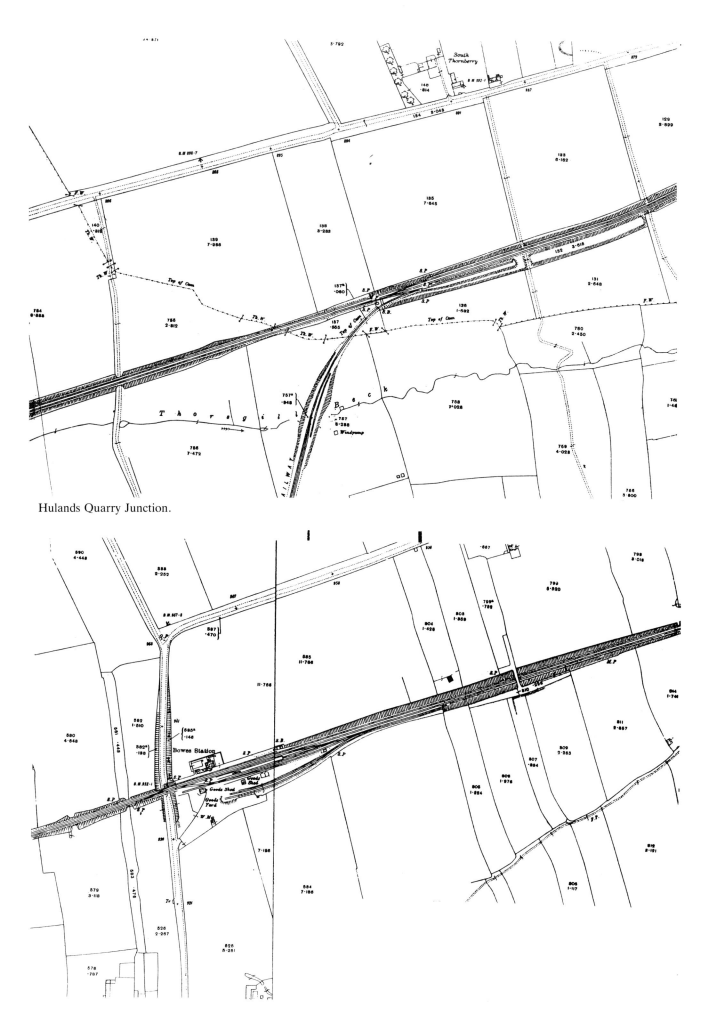

Hulands Quarry Junction.

Bowes Station.

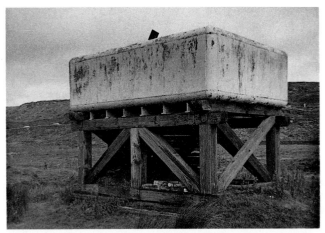

The substantial water tank at Stainmore Summit.

J. L. Birkbeck

The extremely isolated box at Bleathgill situated on the northern side of the line at the western end of a cutting notorious for blockage by snow. The BTF film *Snowdrift at Bleath Gill* must be viewed by all Stainmore enthusiasts to appreciate the dramatic conditions which have prevailed here over the years.

J. F. Mallon

An interesting survivor from the days of the Stainmore Line is the reservoir high on the fells and its accompanying man-made water course to the long-demolished watering facilities at the Summit. The reservoir survives as do parts of the specially constructed channel.

Author

The Summit complex still intact shortly after closure. This view taken from the west.

Maurice Burns

Bleathgill box and cutting viewed from the east.
J. L. Birkbeck

The 'down' waiting room at Barras shortly after closure.
Ron Herbert

The 'up' side station building at Barras, minus clock but otherwise still intact. Note, the closure proposal notice still in position.
Ron Herbert

Barras Station Main Building. East and South Elevations.
Scale: 3mm = 1ft

Author

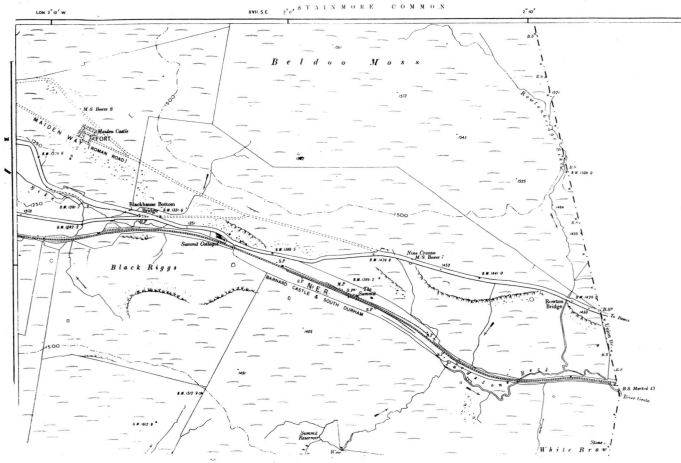

Stainmore Summit 1899.

Bleathgill Signal Box.

The delightful signal box and permanent way cabin at Belah.

J. W. Armstrong

The lonely signal box at Belah, photographed on 28th January 1962, one week after closure.

Ron Herbert

Belah again in January 1962 showing the approach trackwork.

J. L. Birkbeck

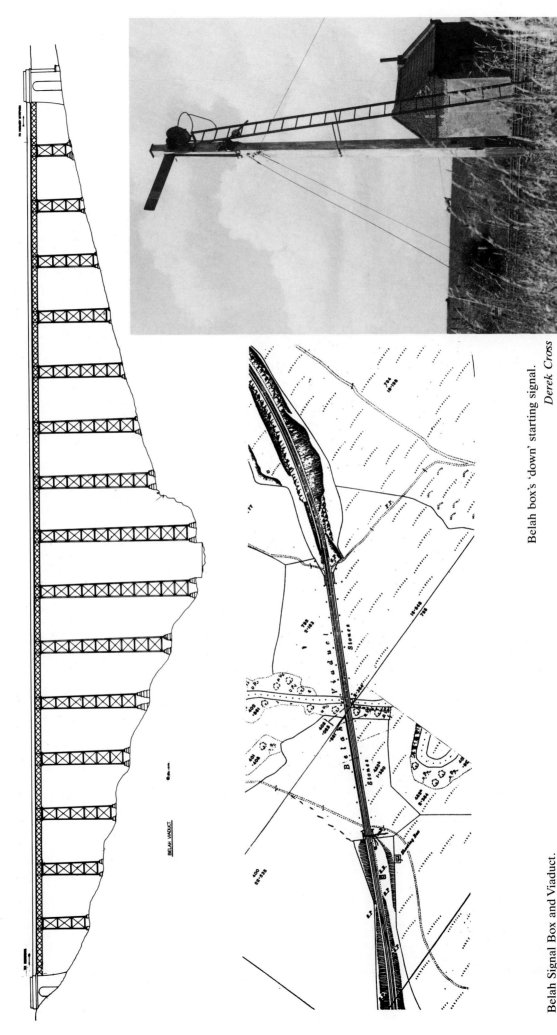

Belah Viaduct. Sketch Elevation.

Author

BELAH VIADUCT

Belah box's 'down' starting signal.
Derek Cross

Belah Signal Box and Viaduct.

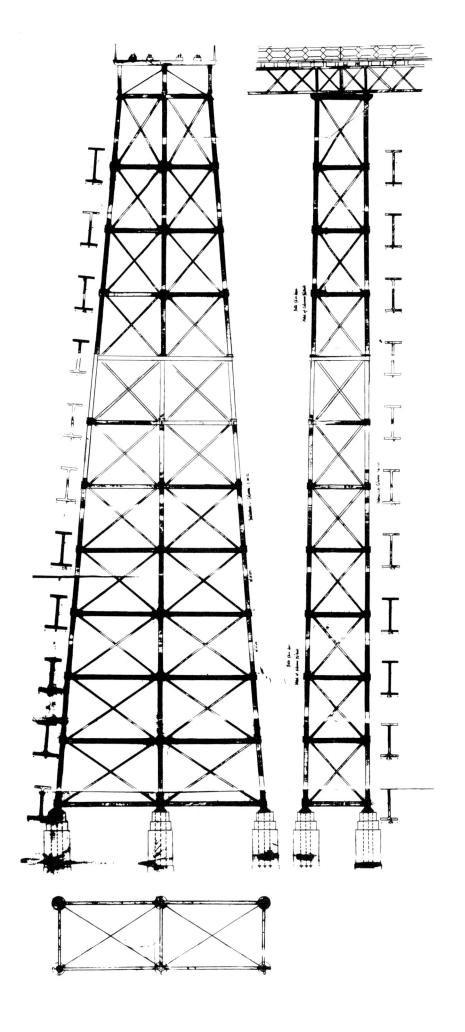

Belah Viaduct. Detail of one of the highest piers. Reproduced by kind permission of the Public Record Office.

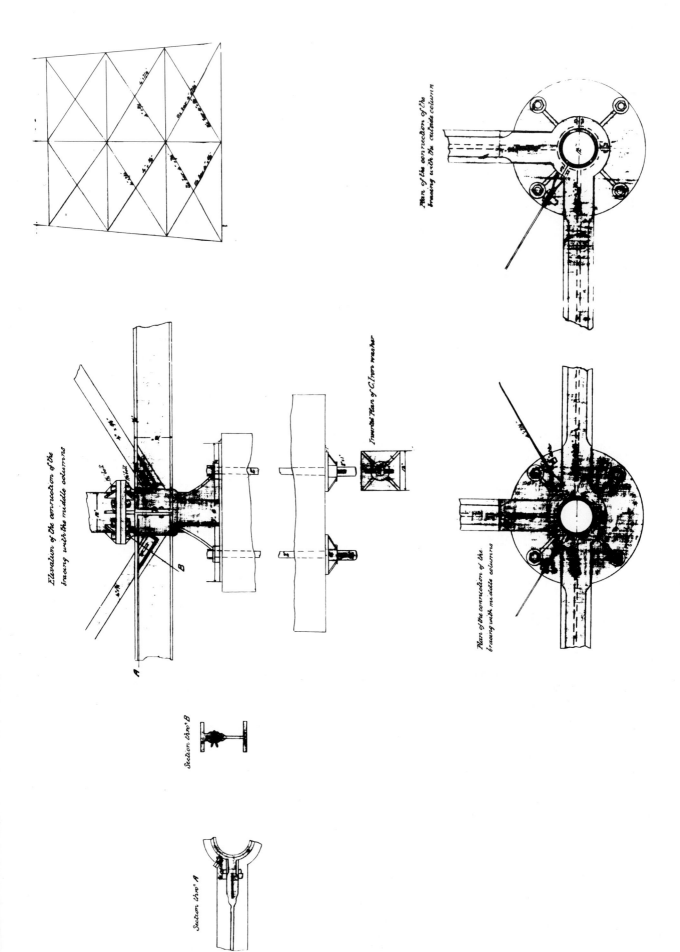

Belah Viaduct. Detail of ironwork. Reproduced by kind permission of the Public Record Office.

Belah Viaduct. Detail of proposed Strengthening of cast iron trestles on both Belah and Deepdale Viaducts. Reproduced by kind permission of the Public Record Office.

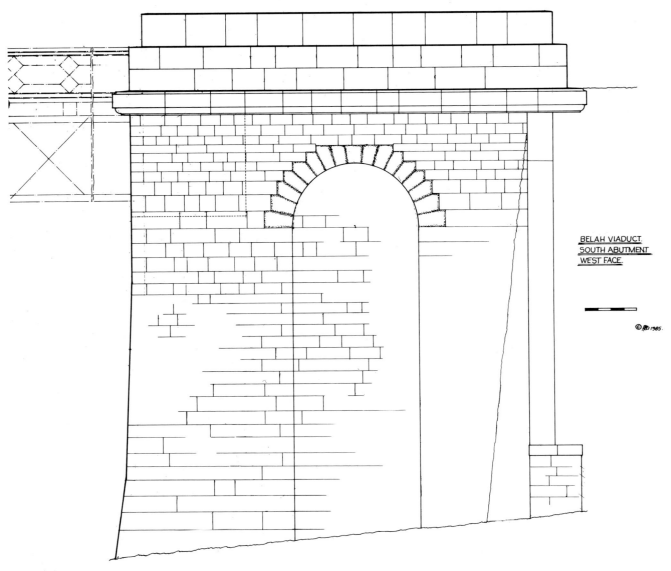

BELAH VIADUCT.
SOUTH ABUTMENT
WEST FACE

© PW 1985.

Belah Viaduct. Stone south abutment west fact detail.   *Author*

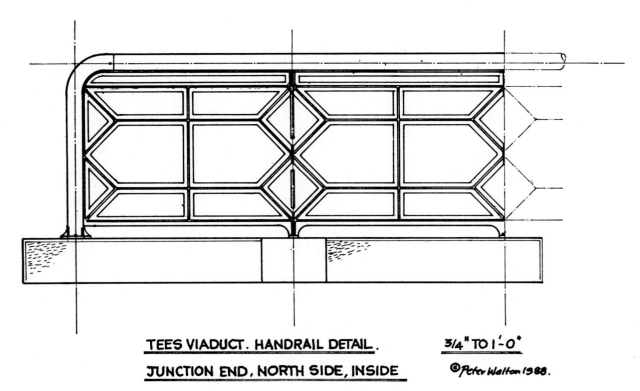

TEES VIADUCT. HANDRAIL DETAIL.

JUNCTION END, NORTH SIDE, INSIDE

3/4" TO 1'-0"

© Peter Walton 1988.

Tees Viaduct handrail detail – typical for Belah and Deepdale.   *Author*

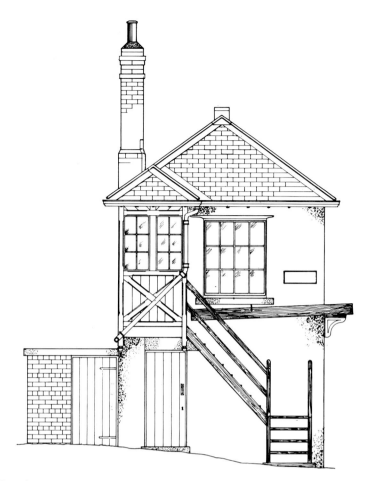

Belah Signal Box East Elevation.
Scale: 4mm = 1ft

Author

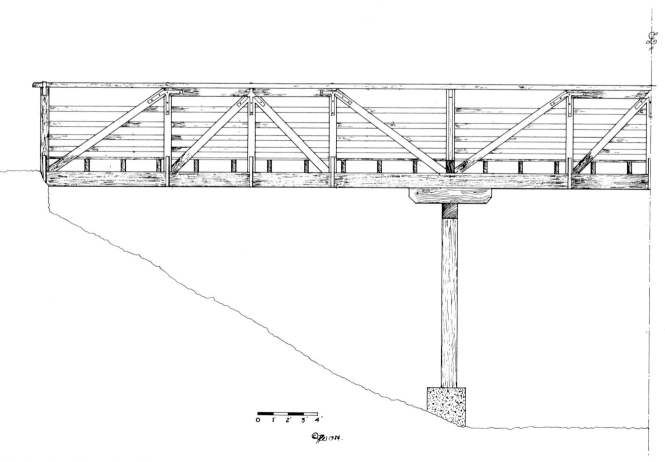

Timber Overbridge No. 120.
Scale: 4mm = 1ft

Author

107

Barras Station (surveyed 1912).

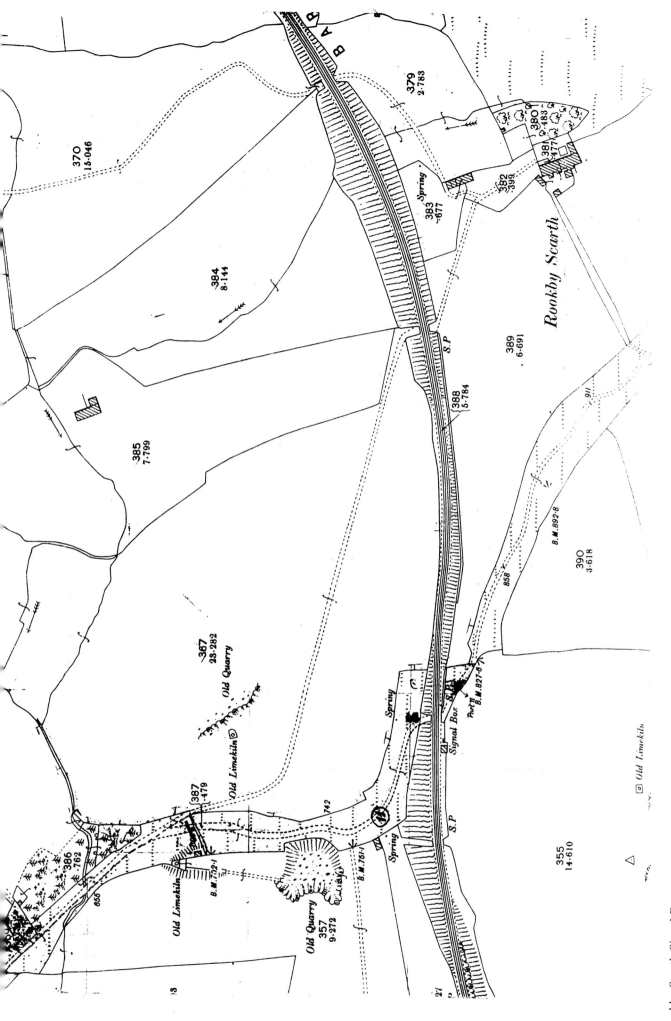

Rookby Scarth Signal Box.

The same signal in more pleasant conditions on 8th July 1959.
J. F. Mallon

Merrygill 'down' distant signal in the snow.
Neville Bousfield

Merrygill 'up' starting signal in the snow.
Neville Bousfield

Merrygill signal box.

Author

Merrygill Viaduct from the north-west with the signal box in the background.

Eddie Foster

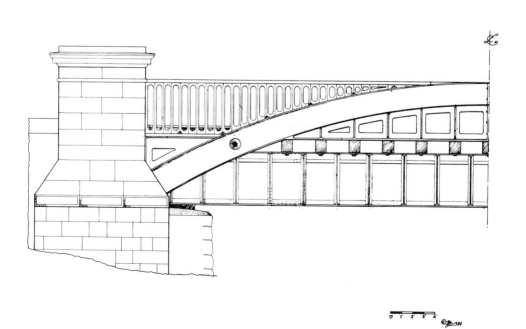

Stenkrith Bridge over the River Eden, Bridge No. 145.
Scale: 3mm = 1ft

Author

The goods shed at Kirkby Stephen from the north. This building still exists in use for light industrial purposes.

N. Haddow

The deserted but intact station building at Kirby Stephen East at the time of closure.

J. T. Hall

The station complex from the west in early 1962.　J. T. Hall

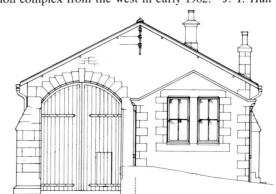

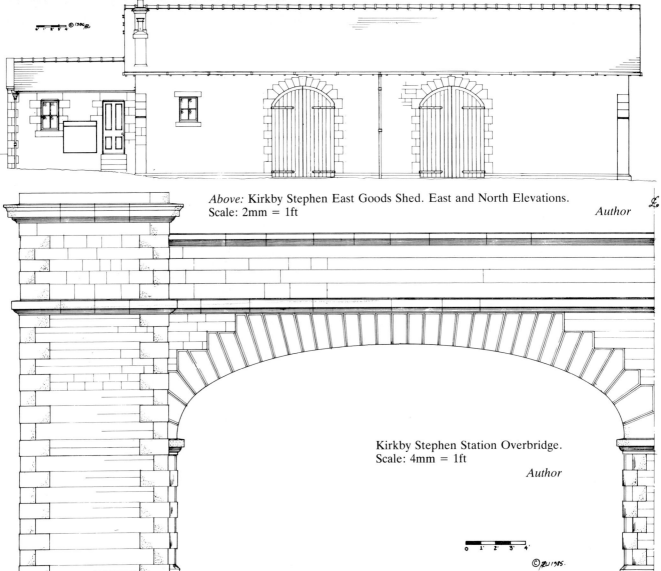

Above: Kirkby Stephen East Goods Shed. East and North Elevations.
Scale: 2mm = 1ft

Author

Kirkby Stephen Station Overbridge.
Scale: 4mm = 1ft

Author

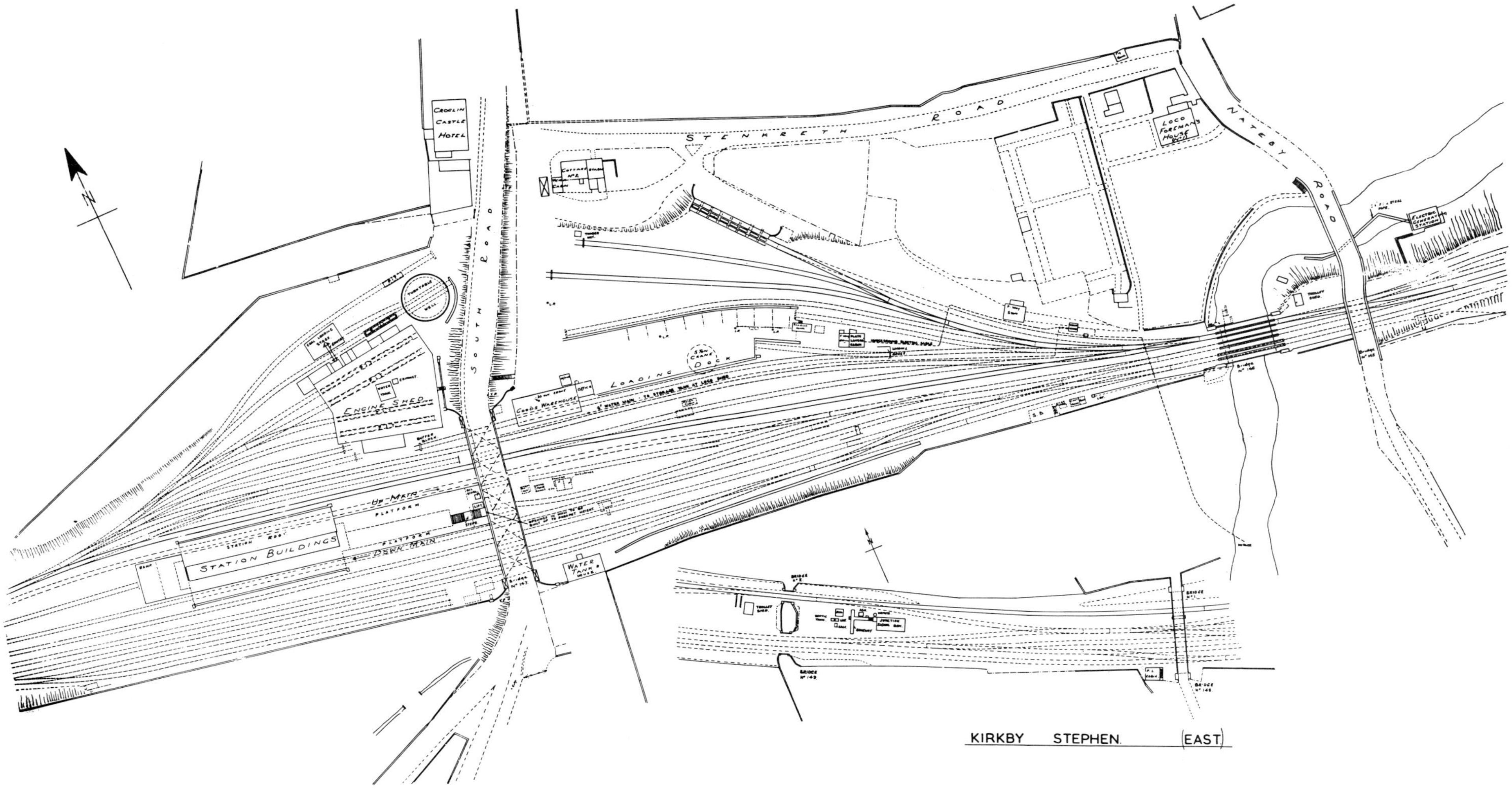

Kirkby Stephen East Station Plan. The rather depressing scheme for "rationalizing" the comprehensive station and junction area following closure to passengers in 1962. However, this plan indicates well the location of the many railway associated structures.

113

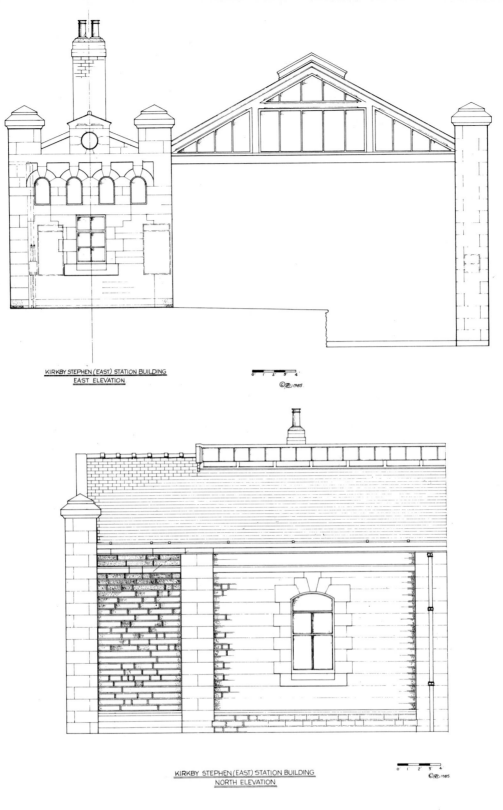

KIRKBY STEPHEN (EAST) STATION BUILDING
EAST ELEVATION

KIRKBY STEPHEN (EAST) STATION BUILDING
NORTH ELEVATION

Kirkby Stephen East Station Building. Part East Elevation at time of closure.
Scale: 3mm = 1ft

Author

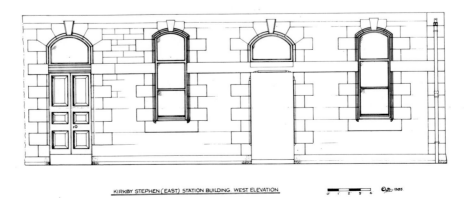

KIRKBY STEPHEN (EAST) STATION BUILDING. WEST ELEVATION

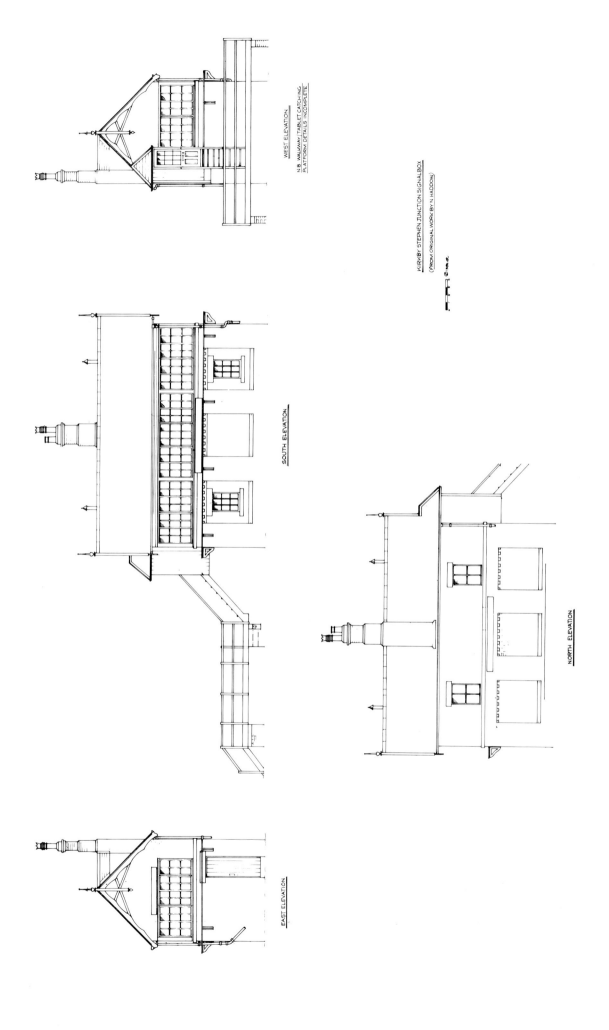

WEST ELEVATION

N.B. WALKWAY/TABLET CATCHING
PLATFORM DETAILS INCOMPLETE

SOUTH ELEVATION

EAST ELEVATION

NORTH ELEVATION

KIRKBY STEPHEN JUNCTION SIGNALBOX

(FROM ORIGINAL WORK BY N HADDOW)

Kirkby Stephen Junction Signal Box (formerly Kirkby Stephen West) at the time of closure. East, South, West and North Elevations.
Scale: 2mm = 1ft

N. Haddow/Author

115

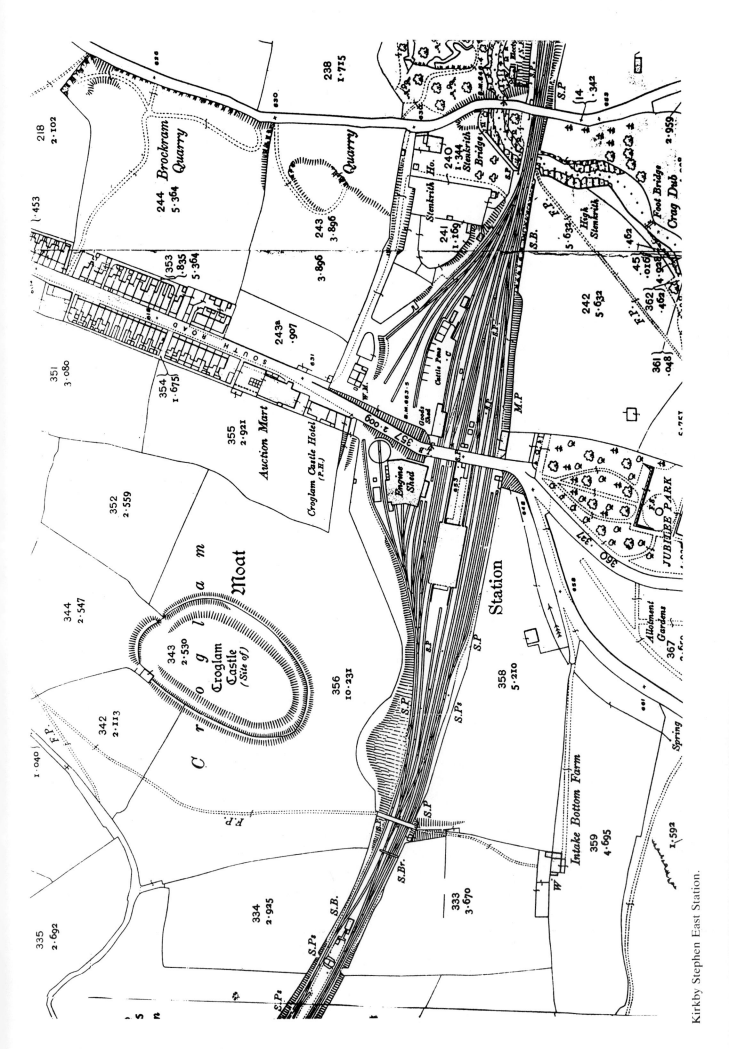

Kirkby Stephen East Station.

A closer look at the gantry and layout looking west at the junction. The Tebay line passes to the left of the box and the Eden Valley line to the right.

J. T. Hall

A detailed look at the typical North Eastern Railway Central Division signal box at Kirkby Stephen Junction. Seen here shortly after the Tebay lines had been removed.

Author

The gently rusting, but intact interior of Kirkby Stephen Junction box in 1966.

Author

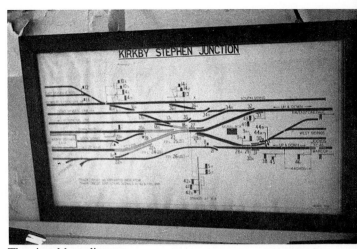

The signal box diagram.

Sid Steadman

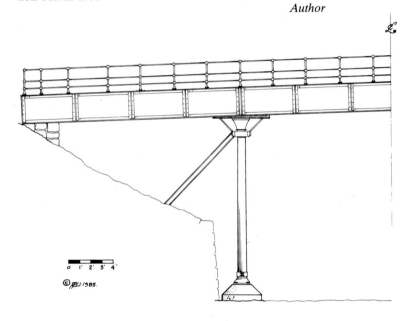

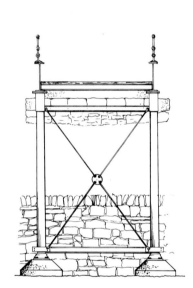

Metal Overbridge at Sandy Bank, West Elevation.
Scale: 3mm = 1ft

Author

Ravenstonedale station, looking west.

J. T. Hall

118

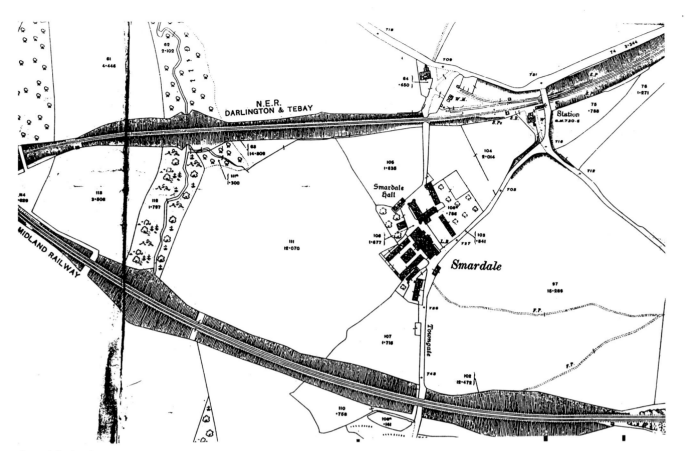

Smardale Station.

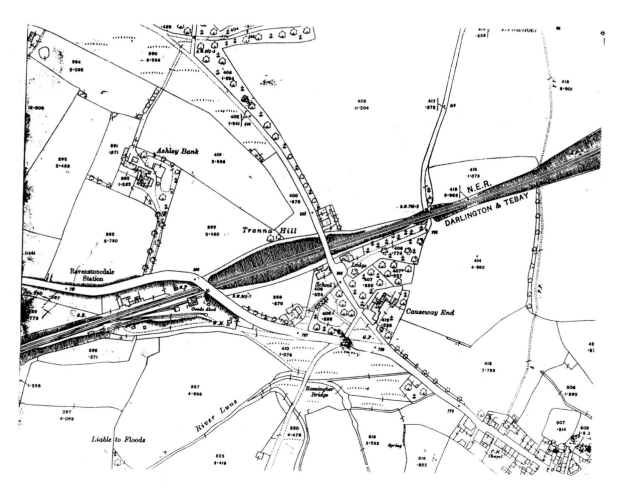

Ravenstonedale Station.

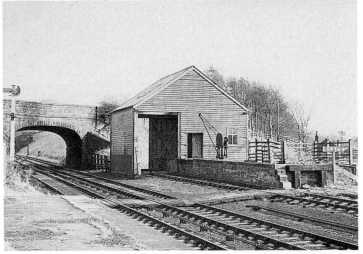

The timber goods shed at Ravenstonedale from the west, one week after complete closure.

Ron Herbert

The station building and platform in 1962.

Ron Herbert

A lovely picture taken at the turn of the century. Note the almost unchanged layout to the later views of Ravenstonedale.

K. L. Taylor collection

The immaculate gardens to the rear/eastern side of the station building at Ravenstonedale. Imagine passengers leaning over the fence and appreciating the layout, whilst waiting for their train, some eighty years ago.

Michael Gregson collection

The station and signal box from the west.

J. T. Hall

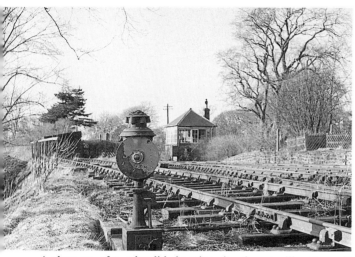

A close up of a splendid shunting signal controlling the exit from the yard. (Lever No. 7).

Ron Herbert

Ravenstonedale signal box from the east.

Ron Herbert

The station during the early part of this century from the west. Note the 'down' home signal. This was later moved to the other side of the bridge as seen on a number of previous pictures.

Jean Willan collection

Gaisgill in its prime, viewed from the east.

Jack Bell collection

Gaisgill's 'down' distant signal, located near Kelleth, on 19th August 1959.

J. F. Mallon

Gaisgill station, crossing and box from the east, gently decaying one week after closure in 1962.

Ron Herbert

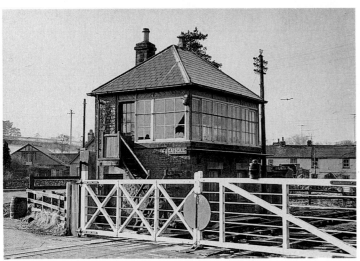

Gaisgill crossing box and trespass notice.

Ron Herbert

Gaisgill Station.

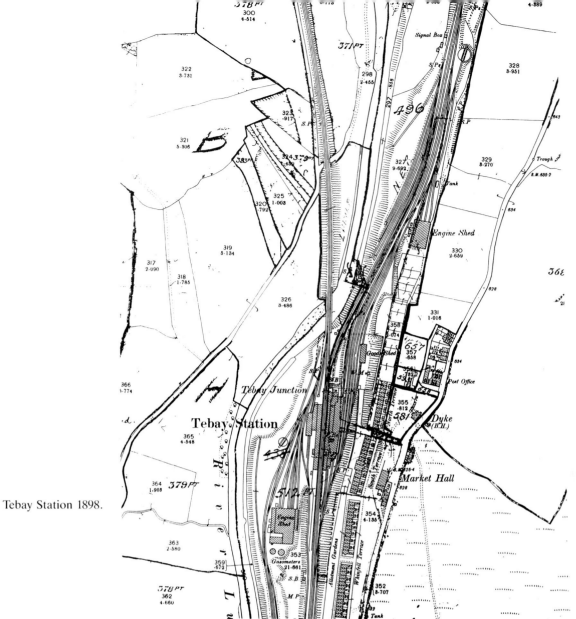

Tebay Station 1898.

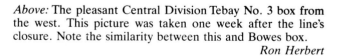

Above: The pleasant Central Division Tebay No. 3 box from the west. This picture was taken one week after the line's closure. Note the similarity between this and Bowes box.
Ron Herbert

Above right: The proximity of the NER and LNWR lines converging at Tebay is seen here. The modern signal box was Tebay No. 2.

Author

Right: Another view of the yard showing the fine 'up' distant signal for Tebay No. 3 box and the LNWR signalling which controlled the entrance to the West Coast Main Line.
J. F. Mallon

Musgrave Station (1915 edition).

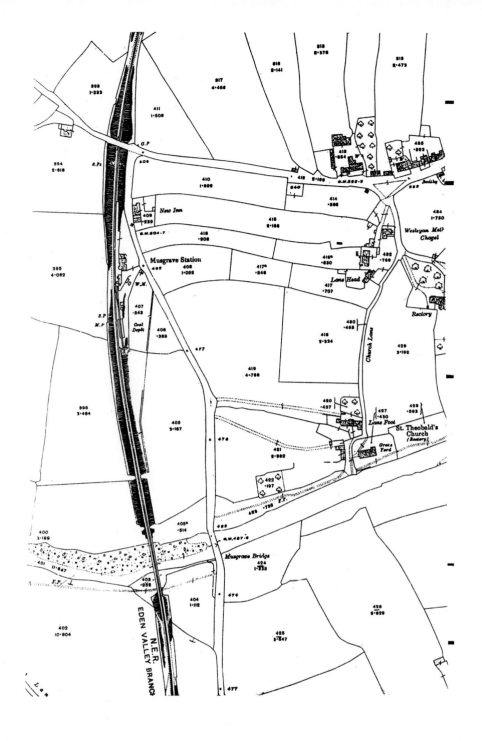

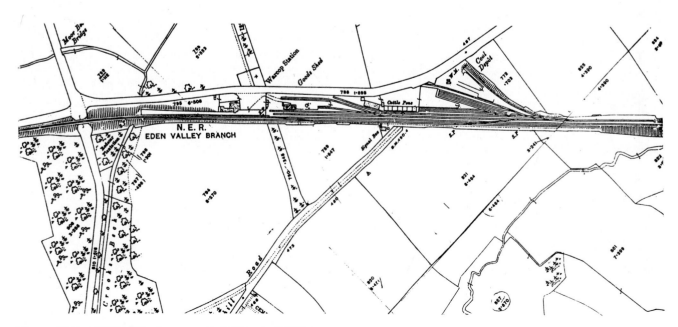

Warcop Station (1915 edition) surveyed in 1859 revised 1912.

Waitby Gate crossing, cabin and crossing keeper's cottage.

Author

The remains of Waitby Gate crossing's slotted post 'down' distant signal.

Author

Musgrave station closed completely in 1952. The platform was cut away and the sidings and equipment removed. Only the house still remains as a very pleasant private dwelling. This picture was taken from the north-west.

Author

Two views of the station at 'Musgrave for Brough' taken in LNER days. Notice the small, unique station house and the timber signal box on the Kirkby Stephen end of the platform.
Eddie Foster

The signal box sign at Musgrave.

Author

Station Gardens Competition 1955

This is to Certify that

Warcop Station

has been Commended in the

Station Gardens Competition

for the Year 1955

Chief Operating Superintendent.

For J.W. WATKINS,
General Manager.

BRITISH RAILWAYS

WARCOP SIGNAL BOX - NORTH ELEVATION

WARCOP SIGNAL BOX - WEST ELEVATION.

Warcop Station Platform Signal Box. North and West Elevations.
Scale: 4mm = 1ft

Author

Warcop Station. West Elevation.
Scale: 2mm = 1ft

Author

Warcop No. 13 'up' starting signal and Flitholme cabin.

Author

The very pleasant platform signal box at Warcop, which re-placed an earlier structure located on the other side of the line, a few hundred yards towards Kirkby Stephen. Notice the excellent lattice post bracket signal – No. 15 the 'up' home and No. 12 the advance starting signal.

Author

The interior of the signal box showing the compact layout. The box possessed two tablet machines, one for the section between Kirkby Stephen Junction and Warcop, and the other, between Warcop and Appleby Station box. The Kirkby Stephen machine can be seen in this picture.

Author

A rare view taken on the steps of the original signal box at Warcop. The railwayman to the left was Harry Watt, the signalman "Siggy Jim" Wilkinson and the children Arthur and Alice Metcalfe. Their father, Mr Metcalfe, was stationmaster at the time

Michael Gregson collection

Warcop station from the south-west, showing the loading dock yard crane. The small bracket signal was No. 9.

N. Haddow

The view south from Warcop, taken from the north-west. The NER bracket signal, No. 14, controlled movements "Up main from Siding" and the small arm – signal No. 3 formerly controlled access to the lifted siding ahead.

Author

BOOKING OFFICE FOR HORSES

The once-heavy Brough Hill Fair traffic handled at Warcop necessitated the provision of an exclusive 'Booking Office for Horses'. A separate ground frame to handle the fair traffic was also provided.

Author

Warcop station possessed an end-loading facility which enabled road vehicles to be moved on to or off railway rolling stock. With the continued development of diesel tractors and equipment, etc., in the 1950s many road locomotives, arrgricultural engines and steam rollers were scrapped.

The engine pictured here was used in Hellbeck Quarry, Brough and on various construction schemes, the council estate at Westgarth, Kirkby Stephen being one. The AEC 'Matador' loading the roller onto the rail vehicle was driven on the day by Mr Frank Jackson. The 'Matador' still survives at Brough.

G. Walton

Warcop station shortly after construction and still in its single storey form. Notice the absence of the waiting room screen. Of this type of station only Cliburn survived conversion into a double storey station/house.

Michael Gregson collection

The platform weighing machine, still in existence in 1986.
Author

The view to the north of the extensive yard at Warcop.
J. F. Mallon

The station building at Warcop.
Author

Two fine views of the platform at Warcop from the south. These show the building in its converted state, complete with 'half panelling'. The whole of the building was eventually concrete rendered, similar to the lower areas and chimney seen here.

Michael Gregson collection

The very substantial and elegant station building intact, some little while after closure. The building is very similar to that at Lartington. Appleby was constructed in 1861 without a waiting room screen and the rear upper storey house extension, (the rendered area).

Ron Herbert

The station at Appleby East in 1959.

J. F. Mallon

The level crossing and signal box at Appleby East.

J. F. Mallon

The large goods shed at Appleby.

Author

Signalman, the late Alf Smith, in Appleby East box shortly after the withdrawal of the passenger service. Alf was basically a Midland man but did work the East box for the passage of the thrice weekly freight which ran to Merrygill Quarry.

Author

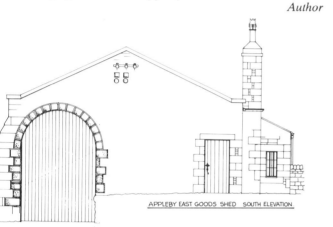

APPLEBY EAST GOODS SHED   SOUTH ELEVATION.

Appleby East Goods Shed.
South and East Elevations.
Scale: 2mm = 1ft

Author

APPLEBY EAST GOODS SHED · EAST ELEVATION.

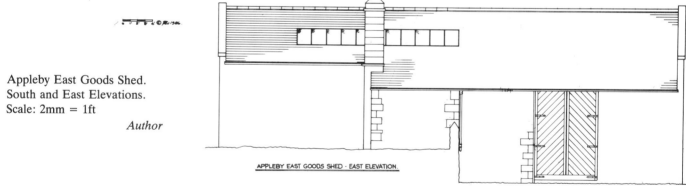

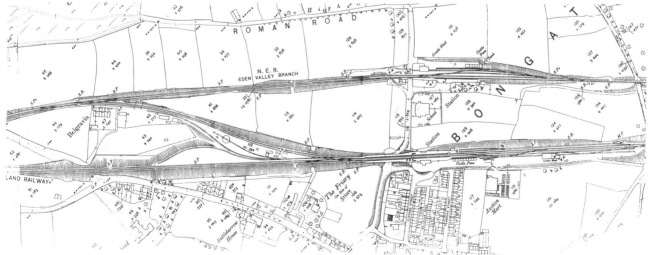

Appleby East (NER) and Appleby West (MR) Stations (1915 edition).

Appleby East Station. East Elevation.
Scale: 2mm = 1ft

Author

Appleby East Station. North Elevation.
Scale: 2mm = 1ft

Author

From the north-west

Three views of the station signal box. From the south-west.

From the south-east

Author

133

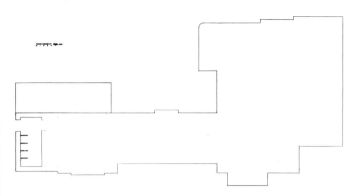

Appleby Junction signal box from the south in 1959. The short section of line between the junction and Appleby East (station) box was double track.

J. F. Mallon

Appleby East Station Plan.
Scale: 1mm = 1ft

Author

The coal cells at Appleby; typical of many throughout the system. In NER days the railway operated its own coal business from the relevant stations.

N. Haddow

Kirkby Thore signal box from the road overbridge. The signalling equipment was being dismantled when this picture was taken. Shortly afterwards all traces of the box, lamps, tablet catching platforms, etc., were removed. The main A66 road now passes over the site.

J. W. Armstrong

A 1918 photograph of the station box, complete with staff and horse-drawn float. The carter was Ted Thompson late of the Grapes Inn at Appleby; the signalman at the top of the steps is Joseph Watson, and railway staff behind the float; left to right: Jack Hinman, Joseph Holmes, the station clerk and the Station Master, Mr Blake who was at Appleby for many years. The building behind the box was the NER stable and was still standing in the late 1980s, converted to a private dwelling.

Ian Taylor collection

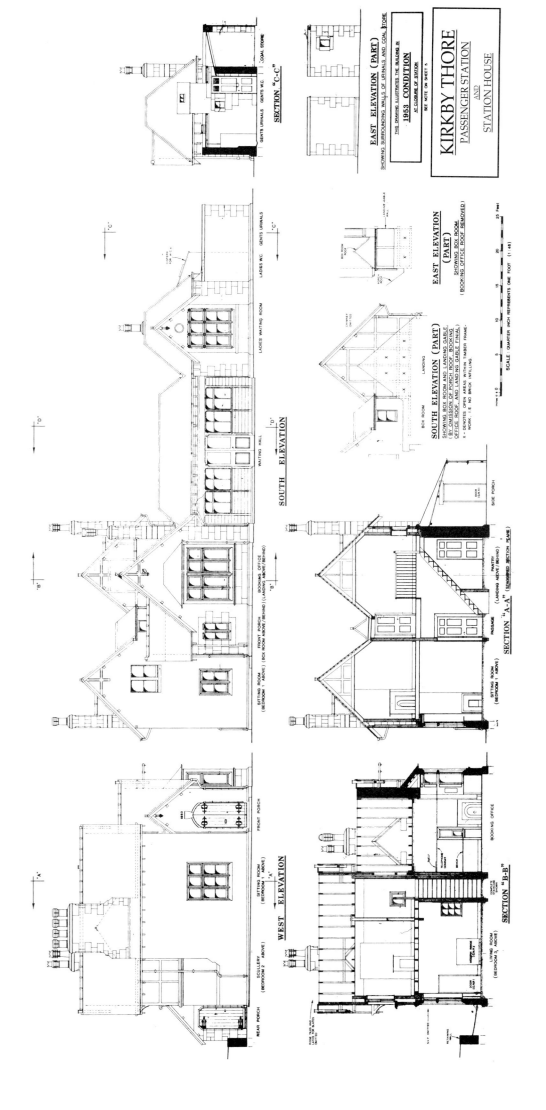

Kirkby Thore Station in 1953 condition fully detailed with notes.

Peter Singlehurst

A different world in 1895 as Kirkby Thore station, in its prime, poses for the camera. Savour the details of these splendid Victorian scenes. Of particular railway interest is the absence of the waiting room screen at this time. Note hyphenated name in second picture.

David Foster collection

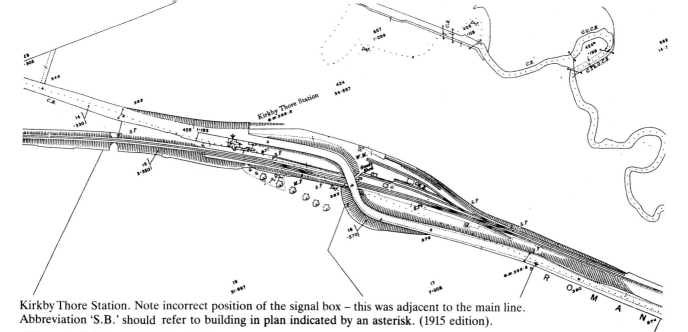

Kirkby Thore Station. Note incorrect position of the signal box – this was adjacent to the main line. Abbreviation 'S.B.' should refer to building in plan indicated by an asterisk. (1915 edition).

Temple Sowerby station and yard from the south in 1959. Notice the new concrete sleepers in the foreground. These, fresh ballast, new signalling equipment, etc., were all installed during the 1950s. *J. F. Mallon*

A closer look at the station building shortly after closure. Very similar to Kirkby Thore but opposite handed.

Ron Herbert

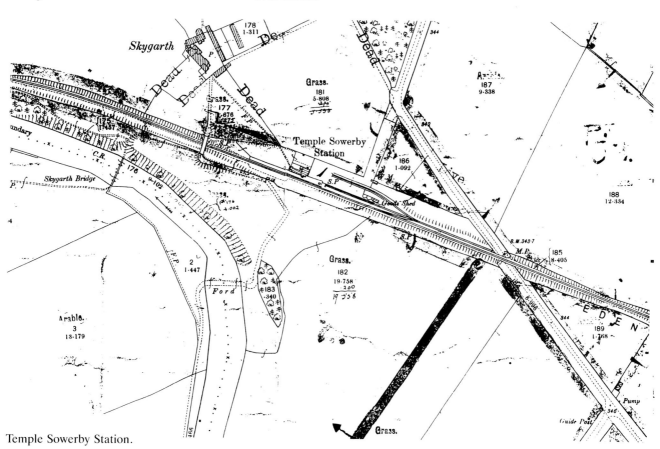

Temple Sowerby Station.

Temple Sowerby station showing part of the signalling arrangement controlled from the platform cabin, similar to the arrangement which applied at Musgrave.

Lens of Sutton

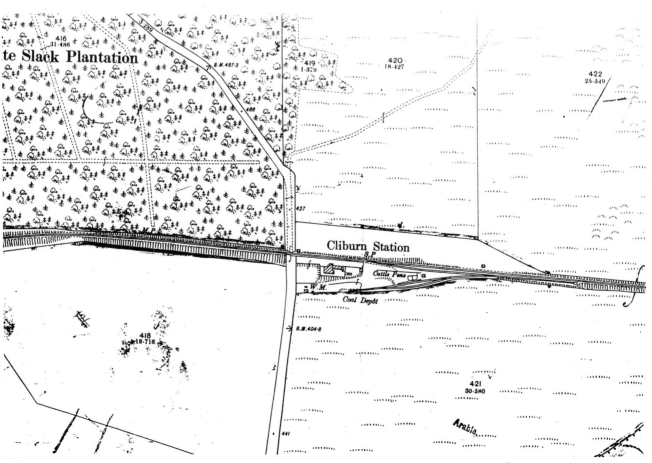

Cliburn Station

Cliburn station from the south-east.

J. F. Mallon

Cliburn station building from the north-east. The building remained to the end as a rather attractive single-storey structure. It may well be that many of the other buildings were actually built as single-storey and doubled later. The original contract prices compared between those at, for example Kirkby Thore, and Appleby would suggest this to be the case. Appleby was definitely built at two levels in 1861.

Ron Herbert

The crossing box at Cliburn. Latterly the only function of this box was to protect the crossing, the block posts being at Appleby East and Clifton Moor. Originally a yard and signalling was controlled by this box.

Ron Herbert

Cliburn Station East Elevation.
Scale: 2mm = 1ft

Author

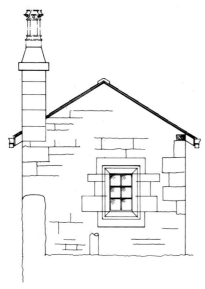

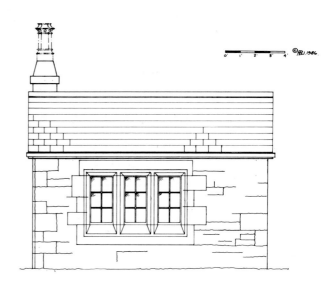

Cliburn Goods Office. South and East Elevations.
Scale: 4mm = 1ft

Author

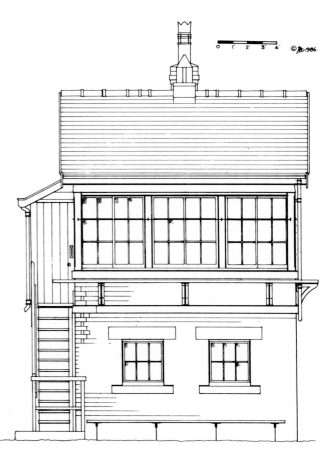

Cliburn Signal Box. North and West Elevations.
Scale: 4mm = 1ft

Author

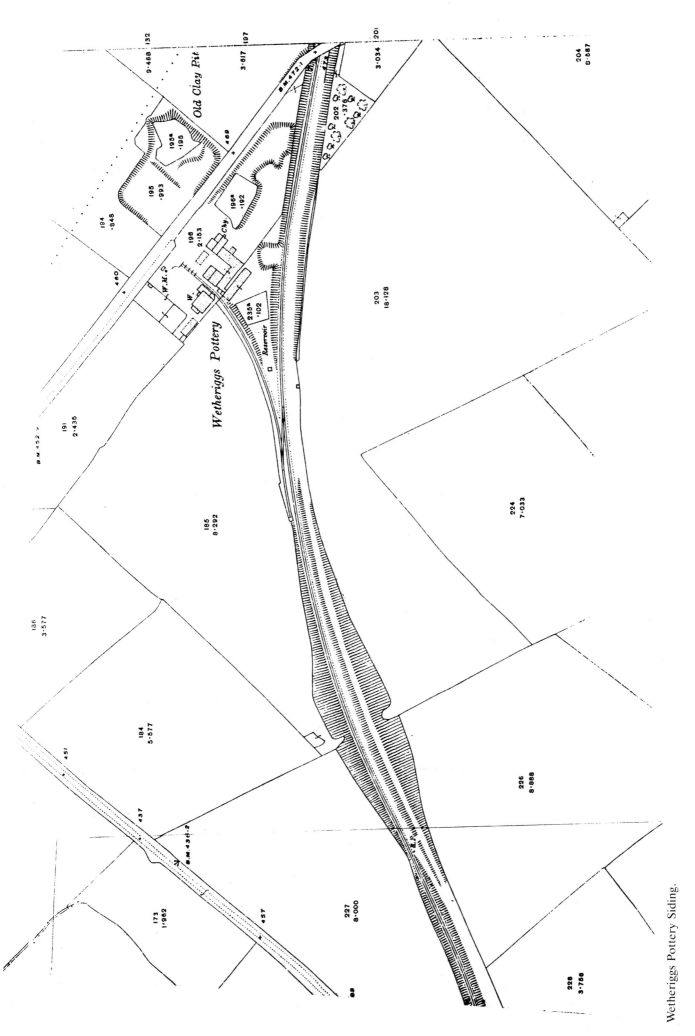

Wetheriggs Pottery Siding.

Two views of the semi-derelict station at **Clifton Moor** shortly after the remaining coal traffic was finally withdrawn. Notice the close proximity of the West Coast Main Line seen in the background of the first picture. The tiny platform signal cabin replaced an earlier box on the same side of the line to the south of the platform. The main station building, now minus the signal cabin and substantially modified, still exists as a private dwelling.

N. Haddow

A third view shows well the 'down' platform layout and the position of the goods shed. The stop blocks denotes the end of the coal drop siding.

Clifton Moor Waiting Room.
Scale: 4mm = 1ft

Author

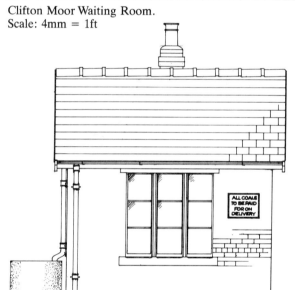

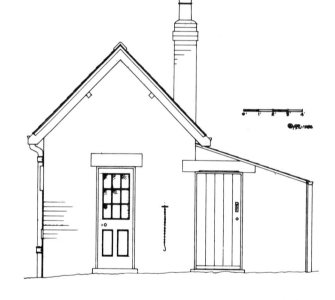

Clifton Moor Goods Office.
Scale: 4mm = 1ft

Author

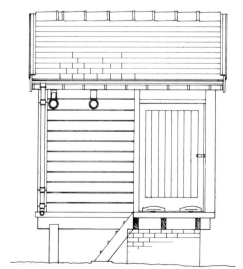

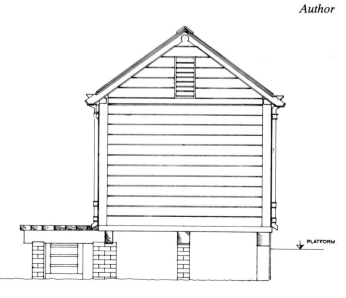

Clifton Moor Goods Shed.
Scale: 4mm = 1ft

Author

143

The station house at Clifton Moor.

N. Haddow

The 'up' side (southbound) platform with its ornamental private waiting room constructed for Earl Lonsdale (The Yellow Earl) resident of nearby Lowther Castle. *Author*

Two illustrations of details of the goods shed and goods office.

Author

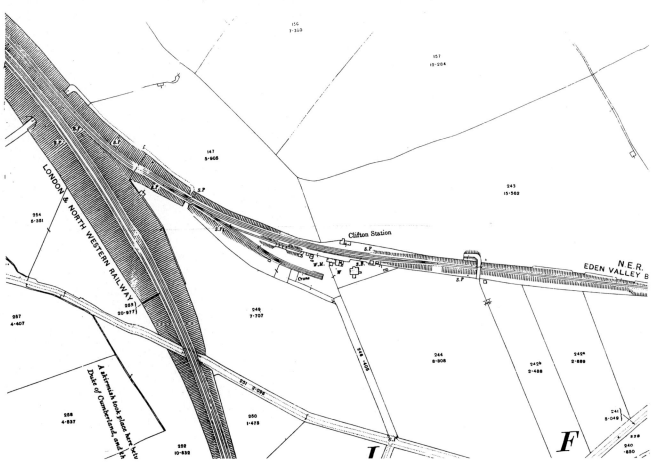

Clifton Moor.

Clifton station 'down' platform prior to the change in name from Clifton to Clifton Moor in 1927 and before the construction of the platform signal cabin.

G. Crisp collection

Clifton Moor station clock.

Author

One of the typical lever plates in the platform signal box at Clifton Moor.

Author

The signal box nameboard

Author

Eden Valley Junction signal box, when still controlling the West Coast Main Line after closure and removal of the Valley branch.

Author

A rare picture of ex-GNR Class D3 4-4-0 No. 4077 being serviced at Redhills.

Neville Bousfield

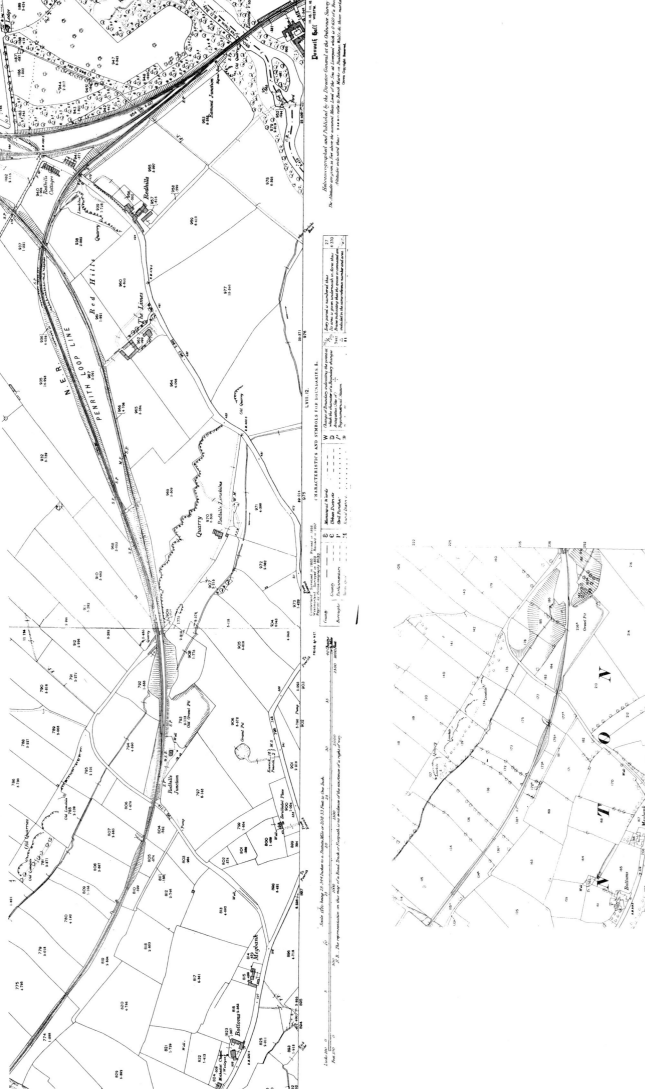

1900 edition showing The Redhills curve as built, and an extract from 1864 edition whilst under construction.

5

Working the Lines

The main line over Stainmore between Barnard Castle and Tebay was opened for mineral traffic on 4th July 1861 and for passenger traffic on 8th August 1861. It has been said that the line was opened from Barnard Castle to Barras rather earlier, on 26th March 1861 for mineral traffic only.

An official opening ceremony took place on 7th August 1861. The first mineral train from Darlington to Tebay was worked by S&DR 0-6-0 No. 156 *Herschel*. When the first passenger train ran, S&D locomotive *Edward Pease* ran in advance of the train and another, *Thomas Meynell* (named after the Chairman) was used to assist the train in the rear.

By October 1861 the directors were able to travel the whole length of the Eden Valley line with an engine and carriage and reported it nearly complete, but it was not until 8th April 1862 that it was opened for mineral traffic (although there is some evidence that coal reached Appleby by the line earlier). The Board of Trade inspection was carried out on 3rd May, and the inspecting officer considered Skygarth Bridge required some strengthening before permission could be given to run passenger trains.

The passenger service began at last on 9th June 1862 and there was evidently some kind of informal opening on 7th June, of which the *Cumberland and Westmorland Advertiser* reported, "There was not the least demonstration - No Lord Brougham to open it! No sod cutting treat! No contractor's visit! No extra officials!" The line was a single one except at the stations, which were at Musgrave, Warcop, Appleby, Kirkby Thore, Temple Sowerby and Cliburn. The earliest timetables suggest that no trains called at Musgrave at first.

At Clifton the train ran into the LCR station (later Clifton & Lowther) where traces of additional sidings then required may still be seen in an adjacent field. This junction, whereby LCR opposition had been avoided, was always considered a defect and fortunately did not last very long, for Penrith passengers had to change trains at Clifton and local traffic at the time of opening was said to be trifling.

It is significant to mention at this stage that the eastern feeder route from West Auckland to Barnard Castle was opened for mineral traffic in July 1863 and for passengers on 1st August 1863.

From the outset, the situation at the western terminus of the Eden Valley line at Clifton was not satisfactory and the passing of the Cockermouth, Keswick & Penrith Railway Act in 1861, and the obvious implications surrounding the proposed construction of this line, highlighted the defect.

The southward facing junction at Clifton resulted in inconvenience and delay for passengers travelling along the Valley branch for Penrith and the North. The possibility of organising through freight working northward over the branch and then west over the proposed railway from Penrith to Keswick, Cockermouth and the Workington area would have involved a variety of reversals and difficulties.

Possibly the Eden Valley Railway anticipated the direction events would take when the original line between Wetheriggs and Clifton was built. The one overbridge involved was not built to accommodate double track whereas all the other overbridges between Kirkby Stephen and Wetheriggs were built with future doubling in mind. Accordingly a bill was deposited in December 1861 for a deviation and extension from Wetheriggs towards Clifton Village and then parallel with the London & North Western Railway line to Penrith with a connection to the Cockermouth, Keswick & Penrith Railway.

In the event the London & North Western Railway Company gave the Eden Valley Railway running powers over the portion of its line, which was to run parallel with the extension, and provision was made in the bill for the necessary connection to the CKPR. The Act was passed on 7th July 1862 for the extension line from Wetheriggs Junction to Eden Valley Junction, this being about 1½ miles long and was opened to passenger traffic on 1st August 1863.

The LNWR's new found co-operation may well have been associated with the Company's revised view of the already-constructed South Durham & Eden Valley lines as a golden opportunity to invade the North East.

The LNWR had already made friends with the little West Hartlepool Railway and had even purchased land and warehouse accommodation in West Hartlepool in readiness for their occupation. The LNWR tried to obtain running powers from Tebay to West Hartlepool, but this was opposed by the North Eastern Railway and the high hopes of the LNWR disintegrated in 1863 as far as penetration of the North East was concerned.

The Connection arrangement to the proposed CKPR line was deferred by mutual consent between the relevant companies in the spring of 1862 and by the time the Valley branch extension was opened the Eden Valley line had become a part of the North Eastern Railway. The South Durham & Lancashire Union Railway and the Eden Valley Railway had been amalgamated with the Stockton & Darlington Railway on 30th June 1862 and on 13th July 1863 an Act received the royal assent amalgamating the S&DR with the North Eastern Railway.

A new North Eastern Railway Act on 23rd June 1864 provided for a connection from the London &

North Western Railway line at Eamont Bridge to Redhills Junction on the new Cockermouth, Keswick & Penrith Railway which opened for mineral traffic later in the year. It can be seen on the extract from the 1864 Ordnance Survey map that the CKPR line is essentially complete and that the tip of the North Eastern 'Redhills Curve' connection is already shown. The curve was opened shortly after the CKPR, probably in July 1866.

The earliest timetable for the 'South Durham Line' of the Stockton & Darlington Railway Company in September 1861 indicates that the service over the main line for passengers consisted of two trains daily each way with an extra train on market days (Wednesday). The timetable on page 155 precedes the opening of the Eden Valley branch and shows that connections from Tebay to Penrith and the North are given. Notice also that the time taken for trains between Barnard Castle and Tebay were a mere 1 hour 35 minutes.

The very first excursion train ran only three weeks after the opening of the line. The train from Darlington destined for Windermere carried 21 first class passengers, who paid 7s. 6d ($37^1/_2$p), and 154 second class passengers, who paid 4s (20p) return. Unfortunately, on the return trip the engine, *Fox*, was derailed on the downhill stretch near Bowes. The driver died later from the injuries he sustained. Several passengers were also injured.

Freight services following opening involved five mineral workings and two mixed freights, all from the Darlington area to the West. These were later supplemented by workings from the West Auckland area, on average about 15 trains per day.

At the turn of the century it would be perfectly normal to see about nineteen, twenty or more westbound freights in a day pounding towards the Summit, the majority consisting of a 'double load' of 32 wagons of minerals. These trains were split at the Summit and worked as 'single loads' to Kirkby Stephen where about two thirds of the freight services continued to Tebay and beyond and the remainder to Penrith and beyond.

A corresponding number of eastbound trains, goods and empties, also ran, again employing where relevant, the practice of 'double' or 'single' loads with a revised provision for empties, namely Tebay-West Auckland. A 'single load' consisted of 25 empties and a 'double load' 50 empties.

Eastbound trains were worked by two locomotives, the assisting engine detaching at the Summit and following in due course 'light' engine to Barnard Castle. Assistance was then further required for trains to West Auckland.

Also by the turn of the century, through workings in the summer from Darlington to Penrith had begun. The service was later extended to penetrate the Lake District at Keswick, travelling over the Cockermouth, Keswick & Penrith Railway.

The attractions of tourism increased prior to the outbreak of the First World War leading to comprehensive train connections from the East Coast Main Line into the Darlington to Keswick service. Through coaches from points of origin at York and Newcastle were arranged. It also seems likely that at some stage a through coach from King's Cross may also have been provided.

A variety of unusual services traversed the Stainmore route, notable amongst which was an

July 1872

experiment with a North East to Isle of Man 'boat train', running from Newcastle to Barrow to connect with a ship leaving Barrow's Ramsden dock. The service was withdrawn six years after its introduction in 1905.

The normal passenger service between Darlington and Tebay consolidated into the well tried three trains each way pattern with a similar service between Kirkby Stephen and Penrith. After the Grouping in 1923, relatively few changes occurred in the passenger timetable until 1932.

The 1928 timetable recorded the pattern of services during the late 1920s, namely: Eastbound passenger trains from Darlington at 6.50 am, 12.38 pm and 5.30 pm, all to Tebay. Westbound passenger trains from Tebay at 10.55 am, 4.32 pm and 8.12 pm.

Notice also the through service from Penrith to Darlington at 7.13 am, returning from Darlington at 2.59 pm and the seasonal Mondays only service between Kirkby Stephen and Barrow in Furness.

The Valley branch saw five trains each way each day including a through service from Darlington* departing from Kirkby Stephen at 8.30 am, 11.35 am, 2.25 pm, 4.31 pm* and 6.48 pm and departing from Penrith at 7.13 am,* 10.23 am, 1.20 pm, 4.22 pm and 8.12 pm. Of particular interest is the inclusion of the 3.40 pm Sundays only service from Penrith to Darlington.

In 1932 a number of alterations to the passenger timetable became evident, the 1933 timetable detailing these. There was still the 6.50 am, with the 12.30 pm, 3.00 pm and 5.30 pm departures from Darlington, with the corresponding returns from Tebay and Penrith. By now however there was an additional Saturdays only 2.00 pm Darlington to Penrith service with a through carriage from York and Saltburn to Keswick.

A nicely prepared Class G5 0-4-4 tank, No. 2089 waits at Penrith.

Neville Bousfield

Journey's end. Penrith station – the family of the late Bert Eden pose in front of his engine, former Great Eastern Railway class E4 2-4-0 No. 7478 waiting at the head of the Eden Valley branch passenger train.

Author's collection

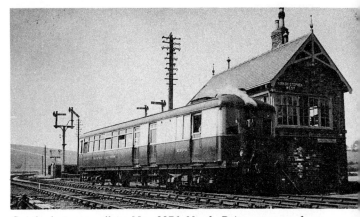

Sentinel steam railcar No. 2276 *North Briton* returns from Ulverston with a convalescent home working: possibly on 19th July 1936. This picture is taken shortly after the railcar had relinquished the single-line token at Kirkby Stephen West (later Junction) signal box.

J. L. Birkbeck collection

Also, it should be noted that the second year of the Newcastle to Blackpool service was advertised with a through coach to Southport, this service leaving Newcastle at 9.15.

The Newcastle to Blackpool specials, followed by similar excursions from Darlington, South Shields, etc., became famous over the Stainmore route and ran right up to the last summer of 1961. The services were interrupted temporarily during the Second World War.

The importance of the line between Kirkby Stephen and Tebay for local passenger use declined gently as the years went by, culminating in the withdrawal of the local service and passenger facilities at Smardale, Ravenstonedale and Gaisgill as from 1st December 1952. At the same time Barras became an unstaffed halt.

On the Valley branch Musgrave was the first casualty, closing completely on 3rd November 1952. This isolated station had been the scene of hectic activity during bridge replacement between Musgrave and Kirkby Stephen, when the branch was closed temporarily between these two points and passengers were conveyed by bus to connect with trains at each end.

Of particular interest was the 'not-advertised'

Durham to Ulverston service which ran from 1932 until 1962. In the early days of this service it ran on alternative Mondays changing in the spring of 1936 to alternative Fridays. The Sentinel steam railcar, No. 2276 *North Briton* worked this service on at least one occasion in the mid-1930s.

Many other unusual and interesting passenger and freight services used the route over the years, notable amongst which were the "Northern Belle" cruise excursions of the early 1930s, travelling from King's Cross to the North East, then over Stainmore to the Lake District via Penrith. The passengers were provided with sleeping and living accommodation on the train for the duration of the trip which lasted for one week.

The LNER also operated scenic circular tours outward via the Wensleydale branch from Northallerton through Hawes to Hawes Junction (Garsdale), part of the Settle-Carlisle line to Appleby (LMS), and then returning via Appleby (LNER), Kirkby Stephen and Stainmore.

It is interesting to note in this respect that the connection between the Midland Railway and the North Eastern branch at Appleby was only ever used for freight working, with the exception of an early short experiment whereby North Eastern trains ran from

Appleby (West) station to Penrith connecting from Midland expresses into London & North Western trains at Penrith, and of course the LNER circular tour mentioned. In the mid-1950s the then new dmus ran on circular excursions from Carlisle via the Settle-Carlisle route, Appleby West, Appleby Junction, Penrith the West Coast Main Line.

The connecting line was also used occasionally for diverting traffic from the Settle-Carlisle line, the West Coast Main Line and vice versa in the event of a problem on the S&C, north of Appleby West.

The last time the connection was used for a proper steam hauled passenger service was on the fateful 'last day', 20th January 1962, when the "Stainmore Limited" ran specially into Appleby West.

Other notable 'extra' workings on the Valley branch included a special milk train which ran on some Thursday evenings between Penrith-Appleby and Darlington, picking up both milk and rabbits from

As mentioned previously, certain stations became unstaffed and others began to share station masters prior to eventual closure.

The freight services continued the pattern first begun in the 19th century except that usage of the Valley branch for through mineral working began to decline from a relatively early date, ceasing to run shortly after the First World War, resuming for a short while in the spring of 1926 and possibly again in 1928 before ceasing altogether.

A typical main line freight working for the East by a Kirkby Stephen crew in the immediate post Second World War period, from start to finish for any of the regular freight turns would be as follows: Two engines would normally be required and both would be prepared and ready by the time the crew signed on. The guard for the trip would advise the locomotive crew before they left the shed from which siding the train should be drawn.

Appleby Junction box from the north-west showing a dmu excursion arriving over the connection with the Settle – Carlisle line from Appleby North. Originally this was a full double-track junction. Latterly the trackwork was rationalised to form a single-line junction and eventually, in the 1950s, the box was closed completely. The tablet machine for trains entering or leaving the Valley branch were located in a concrete hut on the west side of the line.

J. W. Armstrong

Cliburn as well.

Ammunition trains used the Eden Valley branch occasionally, as did special trains for Appleby New Fair and Brough Hill Fair. Temporary signalling arrangements were used at Warcop and Appleby to handle this traffic. On appropriate occasions Band of Hope "Demonstration Specials" ran between Tebay and Appleby, invariably packed with temperance supporters.

The working of the line from a signalling and general staffing point of view changed gradually as the fortunes of the line altered. The list of signal boxes previously included changed little over the years. As traffic began to decline, signal box opening hours were rationalised.

Loads from west to east at this time could include pig iron, steel rails and girders from the West Cumberland Steel Works or lime and limestone from the two local limeworks. Or of course trains could be composed of return workings of empty wagons.

The train engine would retrieve the train from the relevant siding and then proceed to Kirkby Stephen East signal box's starting signal. The banking engine would be attached to the rear of the train. When the signal was pulled to 'clear', the engines would indicate readiness to depart by whistling and the train would attack the vicious curving climb away from Kirkby Stephen past the engineers' sidings.

At Stainmore the train would stop to detach the banking engine, Rule 55 being observed. The guard would pin down approximately a quarter of the wagon brakes for the descent to Barnard Castle, the banking engine following 'light' when the train passed Bowes. Brakes would be unpinned at Barnard Castle, the banking engine being attached to the front of the train for the remainder of the run to either Fieldon Bridge box and sidings at West Auckland or possibly as far as Shildon. When the train was safely deposited in the appropriate siding the locomotives were released for turning, fire cleaning, watering and oiling at West Auckland shed. This accomplished, the locomotives would proceed to the 'ladenyard' for the return working after first collecting the brake van and guard.

Trains here were assembled with a locomotive at each end before departure up the heavy climb to Cockfield Fell.

Two superheater locomotives would be able to whistle to each other on the Barnard Castle approaches, thus eliminating the need to stop for water and achieving a slight run at the imminent climb to Stainmore from the East. Engines using saturated steam generally required a water stop at Barnard Castle.

The performance at Stainmore involving the detaching of the banking engine was similar to that for the eastbound run, only, in this instance about half of the wagon brakes were applied. It was possible for the guard to control the speed of the descending train by use of the handbrake alone.

The banking engine was often re-attached at Kirkby Stephen for the climb through Smardale Gill to Sandy Bank. The banking engine would leave the train at Ravenstonedale and return to Kirkby Stephen, or occasionally it remained with the train for the run to Tebay and returning 'double-headed' later.

This typical working practice experienced many alterations throughout the life of the line. Sometimes banking engines would run round the trains they had assisted to the Summit and then pilot the train for the remainder of the journey. On other occasions the banking engine would be detached at Stainmore and allowed to precede the train they had assisted.

Experiments to detach the banking locomotives without completely stopping the train being assisted were also tried with mixed success. This uncoupling was achieved by a rope from the coupling to the cab over the boiler.

The situation regarding freight working slightly later, in 1956 and 1959, is well illustrated by the following locomotive and train crew diagrams and associated literature. Note particularly the explanation of 'single' and 'double' loadings, the restrictions on locomotives of certain classes and the arrangements for banking assistance, slip coupling, etc., as they were in the 1950s.

Class 1463 'Tennant' 2-4-0 at speed passes under the occupation bridge to the west of the cottages, returning light engine to Kirkby Stephen.

Iain Smith collection

BR Standard Class 2 2-6-0 No. 78013 slows to a standstill at the Summit banked by No. 78017.

Gavin Morrison

The eastbound freight from Barras has now breasted the Summit and has stopped so that train engine, No. 78013, can be joined by its banker, No. 78017, which will continue the journey as a pilot. Both these views are from 16th August 1958.

Gavin Morrison

Locomotive and Train Crew Diagrams Freight Trains – 1956

Kirkby Stephen Depot
Diagram KN 1–3 – Two Engines

	Arr.	Dep.	
Shed		5.45am (LEs coupled)	**K.S. 1**
Kirkby Stephen	5.50	6.00 Turn No. K.S. 1	1st set enginemen sign on at 5.30am
Stainmore	b		Guard sign on at 5.30am
Barnard Castle	w		
St Helens	D	A (8.55am)	**K.S. 5**
Stainmore	b&w		2nd set enginemen sign on at 2pm.
Kirkby Stephen	–		Guard sign on a 2pm.
Tebay	D	A (12.45pm)	**K.S. 1**
Kirkby Stephen	D	– LEs	Assisted in rear K. Stephen to Stainmore.
Shed	–	2.15pm (One Engine)	Doubled headed B. Castle to St Helens and
Kirkby Stephen	2.20	2.30 Turn No. K.S. 5	St Hellens to K. Stephen.
Merrygill	2.35	3.00	Assisted in rear K. Stephen to Tebay.
Kirkby Stephen	3.05	3.30 (Two Engines)	Assisted in rear St Helens to Stainmore by
Stainmore	b		W. Auckland No. 2 banker.
Barnard Castle	w		
St Helens	D	A (6.30pm)	**K.S. 5**
Stainmore	b&w		Assisted in rear K. Stephen to Stainmore.
Kirkby Stephen	D	– LEs	Doubled headed B. Castle to St Helens.
Shed	–		Assisted in rear St Helens to Stainmore. Doubled-headed Stainmore to K. Stephen.

Diagram KN 4 (1st Part)
One Engine

	Arr.	Dep.	
Shed		6.35am LE	**K.S. 2**
Kirkby Stephen	6.40	7.15 Turn No. K.S. 2	Enginemen sign on 5.50am
Appleby		*	Guard sign on 6.20am
Clifton Moor		*	
Penrith	D	A (9.45am)	Conveys water cans between Appleby and
Clifton Moor		*	Cliburn and also between K. Stephen and
Weatheriggs		*	Smardale.
Temple Sowerby		*	
Appleby		*	
Kirkby Stephen	D	A (10.45am)	
Ravenstonedale		*	
Tebay	D	A (12.05pm)	
Gaisgill		*	
Ravenstonedale		*	
Kirkby Stephen	D	– LE	
Shed		– Then works Turn K.S. 9 (Dia. KN4-2nd Part)	

Note – A diagram number refers to one locomotive, whereas a turn number refers to a train.

A	– attaches traffic	Q	– when required
D	– detaches traffic	W	– stops for water
*	– shunts as required	b	– stops to pin down wagon brakes

Diagram KN 5 – Assisted by Loco or Diagram KN. 6
One Engine (KN. 5)   One Engine (KN. 6)

	Arr.	Dep.	
Shed		7.00am (LEs coupled)	**K.S. 3**
Kirkby Stephen	7.05	7.15 Turn No. K.S. 3	Assisted in rear K. Stephen to Stainmore.
Stainmore	b		Double-headed B. Castle to St Helens and
Barnard Castle	w		St Helens to K. Stephen.
St Helens	D	A (10.15am)	Assisted in rear K. Stephen to Tebay.
Stainmore	b&w		Double-headed Tebay to K. Stephen.
Kirkby Stephen	–		Assisted in rear St Helens to St Helens to
Tebay	D	A (2.10pm)	Stainmore by West Auckland No. 1. Banker.
Kirkby Stephen	D	– LE	
Shed	–	4.35pm (LEs coupled)	**K.S. 7**
Kirkby Stephen	4.40	4.50 Turn No. K.S.7	Assisted in rear K. Stephen to Stainmore
Stainmore	b		Double-headed B. Castle to St Helens to K. Stephen.
Barnard Castle	w		Assisted in rear K. Stephen to Tebay.
St Helens	D	A. (7.45pm)	Double-headed Tebay to K. Stephen.
Stainmore	b&w		Assisted in rear St Helens to Stainmore by West Auckland No. 3 banker.
Kirkby Stephen	–	–	
Tebay	D	A (11.30pm)	
Kirkby Stephen	D	– LE	

Diagram KN 4 (2nd Part)
One Engine (Assisted by Loco Diagram KN7)

	Arr.	Dep.	
Shed		5.30pm (LE)	**K.S. 9**
Kirkby Stephen	6.35	5.45 Turn No. K.S. 9	Enginemen sign on 4.45pm.
Stainmore	b		Guard sign on 5.15pm.
Barnard Castle	w		
Darlington (Up Sidings)	D	– (LE)	**K.S. 9**
Darlington (West Yard)	–	A (8.45pm)	Assisted in rear K. Stephen to Stainmore. Double-headed B.
Stainmore	b		Castle to Darlington.
Kirkby Stephen	D	– LE	Assisted in rear Darlington to Stainmore.
Shed	–		

Diagram KN 7.
One Engine

	Arr.	Dep.	
Shed		6.30am (LE)	**K.S. 4**
Kirkby Stephen	6.35	6.45 Turn No. K.S. 4	Enginemen sign on 5.45am.
Warcop	–		Guard sign on 6.15am

Works trips as required between Warcop and Kirkby Stephen
Then assists KN 4 to Darlington and return No. K.S. 9

K.S. 9
Enginemen sign on 4.45pm.

West Auckland Depot
Diagram WA 1 (One Engine) Assisted by WA. 4 (One Engine)

	Arr.	Dep.	
Shed		6.10am (LEs coupled)	**WA. 20**
Van Sidings	6.15	6.20 (Engine & Brake Van)	Enginemen sign on 5.55am.
St Helens	6.25	6.45 Turn No. WA20	Guard sign on 5.50am.
Barnard Castle	w(Q)		Double-headed and assited in rear St Helens
Stainmore	b&w		to Stainmore.
Kirkby Stephen	–	–	Double-headed Stainmore – K. Stephen.
Tebay	D	A (10.25)	Assisted in rear K. Stephen to Tebay.
Kirkby Stephen	–	–	Double-headed Tebay to K. Stephen.
Stainmore	b&w		Assisted in rear K. Stephen to Stainmore.
Barnard Castle		–	
St Helens	D	– LE	Double-headed Barnard Castle to St Helens.
Shed	–	4.05pm (LEs coupled)	
Van Sidings	4.10	4.15 (Engines & Brake Van)	**WA. 21**
St Helens	4.20	4.40 Turn No.WA 21	Enginemen sign on 3.50pm Guard sign on.
Barnard Castle	w(Q)		Double-headed and assisted in rear at WA.
Stainmore	b&w		20 (above).
Kirkby Stephen	–	–	
Tebay	D	A (8.30 pm)	
Kirkby Stephen	–	–	
Stainmore	b&w		
Barnard Castle	–	–	
St Helens	D	– LE	
Shed	–		

Diagram WA 7 One Engine

	Arr.	Dep.	
Shed	–	6.30am LE No. 1 Banker	**No. 1 Banker**
			Enginemen sign on 5.45am.

Assists WA.20 in rear from St Helens at 6.45am, and KS. 3 in rear from St Helens at 10.15am to Stainmore.

	Arr.	Dep.	
Shed	–	4.25pm LE No. 3 Banker	**No. 3 Banker**
			Enginemen sign on 3.40pm.

Assists WA.21 in rear from St Helens at 4.40 pm, and KS. 7 in rear from St Helens at 7.45pm to Stainmore.

Diagram WA 8 One Engine

	Arr.	Dep.	
Shed	–	8.40am LE No. 2 Banker	**No. 2 Banker**
			Enginemen sign on 7.55am.

Assists KS. 1 in rear from St Helens to Stainmore at 8.55am, then works to Wear Valley, etc.

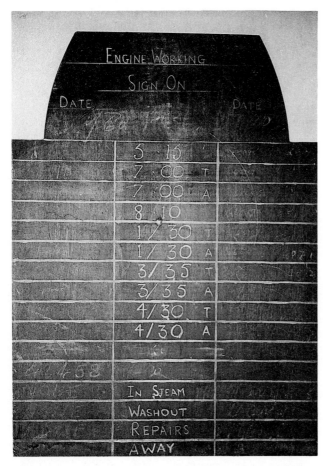

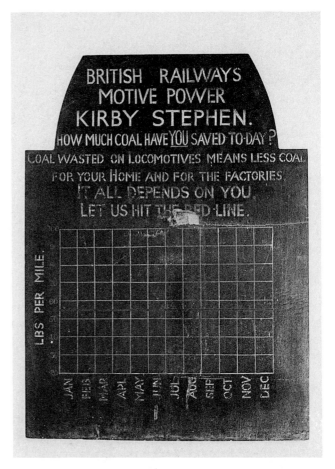

The Eden Valley pick-up operated from Kirkby Stephen travelled to Penrith each morning and then shunted at most locations on the return trip, the majority of siding facilities being arranged on the east side of the route. In addition to conveying water cans, all sorts of interesting traffic was handled, including coal, timber, oil, gas oil, etc. Many stations became collection and delivery points for traffic such as milk.

Appleby East in particular offered a fully integrated passenger and freight facility. The original horse and cart delivery system to and from the station to connect with the pick-up and other trains was replaced by motor lorries.

In the 1950s a blue Ford lorry handled the traffic. In addition to traffic received and despatched via the pick-up, Appleby also received cattle from Cockermouth on Monday nights and despatched loaded cattle vans (fully fitted) by attaching them to the rear of the passenger trains on Thursday mornings as required for Preston. There was a considerable amount of lime traffic from Kiesley Quarry to Dorman Long. The coal businesses all along the routes were handled by the railway - the station masters effectively acting as agents, selling coal to the distributing coal merchants. Coal cells and offices existed at most stations. During the last decade of operation, traffic of this sort was still considerable, even Wetheriggs Pottery required a wagon load every month. It is very unfortunate that very few photographs record the activities of the various 'pick-ups' during their heyday of operation.

In addition to the Eden Valley pick-up freight, similar arrangements applied at the eastern end of the route where a similar train ran to Bowes from Darlington, and on the Kirkby Stephen-Tebay section, where a pick-up ran to serve Tebay, Gaisgill, Ravenstonedale and Smardale. As can be seen from

The Engine Working Sign On board at Kirkby Stephen Shed. Notice faint evidence of engine numbers, particularly on the left hand side: 3.35T 62045, 4.30T 65669, 4.30A 65673 and four spaces from the bottom 46458. On the right hand side 5.15 65695, 7.00T 65717, 7.00A 65655, 8.10 65673, 1.30T 65103, 3.35T 43128, 3.35A 43130, 4.30T 46470, 4.30A 46474.

The really noteable entry is No. 62045. If this is correct then this would have been the second recorded appearance of a Class K1 2-6-0 at Kirkby Stephen, the other being of No. 62060 on 27th April 1956 westbound at Kirkby Stephen at 4.32 pm, returning east light passing at 6.22. It seems probable that No. 62045 worked between Kirkby Stephen and Tebay in the late 1950s following the derailment of the two Q6s in 1955.

the train crew diagram, the Tebay pick-up was effectively an extension of the Eden Valley turn. The Bowes pick-up working is detailed as Darlington working D36.

When the celebrated last trains had travelled east over the line on 20th January 1962, the only sections of the route remaining in use were as follows:

Eden Valley Junction to Clifton Moor (freight). Appleby North to Appleby Junction to Merrygill Quarry (freight). Barnard Castle – Middleton-in-Teesdale (passenger & freight).

The passenger service from (Darlington) Barnard Castle – Middleton-in-Teesdale was withdrawn from 30th November 1964. The freight service lasted until 5th April 1965. The freight service to Clifton Moor was withdrawn from 6th July 1964.

The Merrygill Quarry rail traffic and the residual traffic to Kirkby Stephen East goods ceased on 31st October 1974 and the line was cut back to Flitholme Permanent Way Cabin to the south of Warcop.

At the time of publication, the only section of the Stainmore and Eden Valley lines remaining is the

Appleby Junction – Warcop branch – at present disused. The last freight to use the line was hauled by Class 31 No. 31217 on 16th March 1989.

Hellbeck Quarries at Brough were important users of the railway via the loading facilities at Warcop. It is a source of amazement that when the Valley branch was 'rationalised' after the closure of 1962, that the remaining siding facility at Warcop was arranged with one track removed from the major loading dock to prevent any future usage! In the same way the entire station area at Kirkby Stephen was effectively destroyed with the exception of the station building and goods shed as the only road left in situ was No. 1, being one track removed from the platform edge, no doubt to deter use of the remnants of the branch for rail tours etc!

Speed Limits and Speed Restrictions on Running Lines. (See also page 61 of General Appendix.)
Engine Turntables, Water Columns or Troughs.
Catch Points and Spring or Unworked Trailing Points on Running Lines.

TABLE A—LINE No. 49—continued.

BARNARD CASTLE.

WEST SIGNAL BOX—Method of Cautioning. Rule 41 :—After an Up train has been brought quite or nearly to a stand at the Home signal in accordance with Rule 41 the Starting signal will be lowered before the green hand signal is exhibited, and the Driver must keep a sharp look-out for this hand signal when passing the signal box.

BETWEEN BARNARD CASTLE AND KIRKBY STEPHEN.

DEEPDALE VIADUCT, BETWEEN LARTINGTON AND BOWES, AND BELAH VIADUCT, BETWEEN BARRAS AND KIRKBY STEPHEN :—When Passenger or Freight trains are assisted from Barnard Castle to Stainmore, the assistant engine must be attached on the rear at Barnard Castle and detached at Stainmore.

When Passenger or Freight trains are assisted from Kirkby Stephen to Stainmore, the assistant engine must be attached on rear at Kirkby Stephen and detached at Stainmore.

...

BETWEEN BOWES AND BELAH SIGNAL BOXES :—In the event of a severe snowstorm occurring and a block taking place on the line traffic may be worked on a Single line between Belah and Bowes, viz.: on the DOWN line between Belah and Stainmore, and on the UP line between Stainmore and Bowes, it being necessary to work the single line in this way owing to there being several sets of catch points between Belah and Bowes.

APPLEBY.

STATION SIGNAL BOX :—Drivers must be prepared to deliver or receive the token either at the signal box or at the platform.

KIRKBY THORE.

STATION SIGNAL BOX : Drivers of Down trains must be prepared to deliver and receive the token either at the signal box or at the platform.

LINE No. 50.—BARNARD CASTLE (TEES VALLEY) TO MIDDLETON-IN-TEESDALE.

	SPEED LIMIT
Middleton-in-Teesdale	Engine Shed and Turntable line.

LINE No. 51.—KIRKBY STEPHEN WEST TO TEBAY.

TABLE J—continued.

Line No.	From	To	Condition	Trains Authorised and Remarks.
33	Grosmont	Goathland	A	*Passenger and Freight trains.
	Goathland	Summit	A	*Passenger and Freight trains.
	Pickering (Bridge Street)	Goathland (Summit)	A	*Freight trains.
36	Whitby (Bog Hall)	West Cliff	A	Passenger and Freight trains.
	Loftus	Grinkle	A	Freight trains.
	Carlin How	Brotton	A	Freight trains.
	Brotton	Carlin How	A	Freight trains, provided train does not convey timber, castings or other articles on two or more bolster wagons.
37	Guisborough Jct.	Nunthorpe	A	Freight trains.
	Saltburn West	Brotton	A	Freight trains. Provided train does not convey timber, castings or other articles on two or more bolster wagons.
39	Battersby	Castleton	A	Freight trains.
40	Redcar (Upleatham)	Saltburn West	A	Freight trains. Provided train does not convey timber, castings or other articles on two or more bolster wagons.
42	Bedale	Garsdale	A	Freight trains.
43	Northallerton East	Northallerton	A	Freight trains.
	West Hartlepool (Church Street)	Clarence Road	D	Passenger trains—slip couplings at West Hartlepool Stn.
	Greenland	Clarence Road	A	Freight trains.
48	Catterick Bridge	Catterick Camp	A	Military trains.
I, 52	Darlington (Croft Yard)	Stainmore	A	Freight trains.
& 49				
49	Barnard Castle West	Stainmore	D	Passenger trains—slip couplings at Barnard Castle. During snow storms or in stormy weather the assisting engine must be coupled with the screw instead of the slip coupling, and the Automatic brake pipes connected.
	Kirkby Stephen West	Stainmore	D	Passenger and Freight trains—slip couplings at Kirkby Stephen. When it is necessary to attach assisting engine to the rear of a Passenger train during snowstorms or in stormy weather, the assisting engine must be coupled with the screw instead of the slip coupling, and the Automatic brake pipes connected.
51	Kirkby Stephen West	Ravenstonedale	D	Freight trains—slip couplings at Kirkby Stephen.
52	Shildon South	Fieldon Bridge	A	Freight trains.
	Wear Valley	Crook West	A	Freight trains.
	HOPE TOWN	SHILDON NORTH	A	Freight trains—assisting engine may have brake van in front of or behind it.
	SHILDON NORTH	FIELDON BR.	A	
	Crook West	Tow Law	A	Freight trains.
54	Bishop Auckland (North or West)	Spennymoor (Dean & Chapter)	A	Freight trains.
55	Bishop Auckland North	Barnard Castle East	A	Freight trains.
58	Dearness Valley	Brancepeth	A	Freight trains.
& 57	Baxter Wood No. 2	Waterhouses Goods	A	Freight trains.

* See also Local Instructions herein.

LOCAL WHISTLES—continued

Line No.	Signal Box at which Whistle to be given		Meaning of Whistle	Code
46	Port Clarence—			
	Station		To or from Station Sidings	1 short, 3 long
			To or from Up Main and Empty Sidings	2 short, 3 long
			To or from Up Main and No. 1 Siding	2 short, 4 long
			Down Main to No. 1 Siding	1 short, 4 long
			To and from Foundry	1 short, 1 long
			To and from Down Sidings	1 short, 2 long
49	Barnard Castle—			
	East		To Goods Station or Station Yard	3 short, 1 long
	Kirkby Stephen—			
	Junction		To or from Engine Shed or Goods line and Tebay	2 short, 2 long
			To or from Engine Shed or Goods line and Penrith	1 short, 1 long
52	Shildon—			
	Simpasture		No. 1 Reception line to Simpasture Branch	2 long, 1 short, 1 long
			No. 1 Reception line to Main	2 long, 2 short, 1 long
			No. 2 Departure line to Simpasture Branch	3 long, 1 short, 1 long
			No. 2 Departure line to Main	3 long, 2 short
			Shunting line to Simpasture Branch	4 long, 1 short, 1 long
			Shunting line to Main	4 long, 2 short
			No. 1 Reception line to Down Main to Shildon	2 long, 1 crow
			No. 2 Departure line to Down Main to Shildon	3 long, 1 crow
	South		Down Main to Goods Yard	1 short, 1 long
			Down Main to Shildon Works	1 long, 1 short, 1 long
			Empty Sidings to Down Main	2 short, 1 long
			Empty Sidings to Goods Yard	1 long, 1 long
			Goods Yard to Up Reception	2 long, 3 short
			Goods Yard to Shildon Works	1 short, 1 long
			Goods Yard to Empty Sidings	2 long, 1 short, pause 1 short
	Crook—			
	Thistleflat		Up Reception to Down Main	2 long, 1 crow
	East		Up Main to and from Carriage Siding	1 short, 1 long
	West		Up train out of control	1 continuous
54	Spennymoor—			
	Dean and Chapter		From Colliery requiring to attach or detach at Ferryhill	1 long, 1 long
			From Colliery inward road	1 long, 1 crow
55	Willington—			
	Brancepeth Colliery		To or from Laden Sidings	2 short, pause, 1 short, pause, 1 short
			To or from "C" Pit	1 short, 1 crow
58	Durham—			
	Baxter Wood No. 1		Consett Branch to Down Goods line	3 short, 1 long
			Down Goods line to Down Main line	3 short, 1 long
	Consett—			
	South		To or from Main line and Engine Shed	2 short
			To or from Goods Yard and Engine Shed	1 short, pause, 2 short
			Main line and Reception Sidings	1 short, 1 long
			Yard to Main line	1 short, 3 long

Extracts from
LNER
Appendix
1947
&
from Whistle Code
Book.

Ivatt Classs 4MT 2-6-0 No. 43049 of Carlisle Kingmoor depot accelerates the thrice weekly train away from Warcop, past signal No. 13 and towards Kirkby Stephen on 30th December 1966. By this time the splendid NER slotted post signals stood only to serve as gaunt reminders of better days. A 'one engine in steam' system applied which still required tablet possession, but unfortunately not operation of signalling, even though this was operationally intact.

Author

Ivatt Class 4MT 2-6-0 No. 43000 on the thrice weekly freight to Carlisle, prepares to pass the tablet pouch to the Warcop signalman. Shortly after this picture was taken the box was closed completely and the signal arms were sawn off. Some while later the signals were destroyed.

Author

The view from the brake van as a Kirkby Stephen freight passes through the platform.

Author

Foretaste of gloom. Barnard Castle station, still safe for another year, provides accommodation, right, for trackwork lifted from the Stainmore line.

Maurice Burns

Above right: Business as usual at Barnard Castle on the morning of 20th January 1962. The saddest day in the history of the line. The 10.52 on Penrith–Darlington DMU calls on this, the last day of the 'Stainmore Railway'.

Ron Herbert

Right: English Electric Type 1 Bo-Bo Diesel No. D8085 passes through Appleby East with the branch freight in the mid-sixties. These diesels were very much a rarity over the Settle – Carlisle line and even rarer still on the Eden Valley branch.

Author

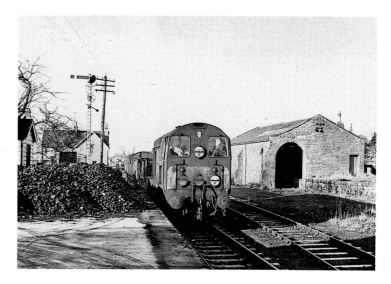

One of Carlisle Upperby's Ivatt 2MT 2-6-0s, No. 46455 removes an empty wagon from the overgrown branch. As mentioned previously, the short stretch of line between the junction and Clifton Moor was retained for coal traffic until July 1964.

Derek Cross

The interior of the train shed at Barnard Castle in 1964.

Maurice Burns

View looking west from the train shed in October 1964. The West box of 1906 replaced an earlier structure on the same site.

Maurice Burns

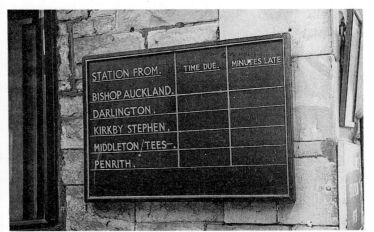

The train arrival board at Barnard Castle in November 1964.

Maurice Burns

Still a healthy service on the remaining Darlington-Middleton-in-Teesdale branch, shown on the Departure Board in November 1964. The line closed completely from 28th November 1964.

Maurice Burns

The Eden Valley branch is disturbed on 20th May 1987 by Class 40 diesel No. 40118, on one of the very infrequent troop specials to Warcop. This view is taken looking towards Appleby Junction from the north. The train is just arriving empty stock from Warcop. The locomotive will reverse the train into the loop behind Appleby North (Settle and Carlisle) signal box and onto the Settle–Carlisle main line.

The bridge in the foreground carried the Eden Valley branch over the Long Marton Road. This bridge has since been demolished and the 'head shunt' further shortened. The concrete cabin in the background housed the Eden Valley branch tablet machine after the Junction box closed.

Author

One of the celebrated Class 40s, No. 40024 *Lucania* returns to Appleby through New Hall with empty flats after depositing armoured cars at Warcop.

Author

The very last Class 40 diesel in normal service. No. 40122, (D200) shunts the remnants of the yard at Warcop on 26th February 1986.

Author

The Wickham inspection trolley, complete with gang, at Bowes.
Ian Robinson

Transferring the mail for the last time at Appleby East on the night of 20th January 1962. The guard is Mr Steve Lamb from Darlington.

J. T. Hall

A view of Tebay shed circa 1893. Although printed from a much deteriorated negative it was considered this rare view should be included. The exact opening date of the shed in this form is a little confused. Original operations of the line were primarily from Shildon. The Tebay shed, built circa 1866, was closed again shortly afterwards and re-opened in 1878. It finally closed in 1902. The deteriorating remains of the shed then stood for over fifty years before being eventually demolished.

J. W. Armstrong

A J21 in smart external condition bids farewell to the lovely bracket signals at the east of Tebay Yard. The roof of No. 3 box can be just detected behind the nearest signal.

J. W. Armstrong

Jack Hall, now retired, was the signalman who offered the "Stainmore Limited" – the last Stainmore passenger train – onto the Eden Valley branch as signalman at Eden Valley Junction on 20th January 1962.

About 1927, the staff at Clifton pose on the 'down' platform.

G. Crisp collection

Many of the Stainmore line pictures in this book were taken by the late Eddie Foster, a resident of the area and a very keen enthusiast. Eddie enjoyed the delights of the line, often accompanied by his friend Owen Jackson. Eddie took almost all of the pictures, but one day managed to be photographed himself standing here on the running plate of Worsdell Class Q5 0-8-0 No. 443 inside the shed at Kirkby Stephen.

Owen Jackson

During the Second World War, lady cleaners were employed in Kirkby Stephen shed. In this 1944 picture the people gathered on and around the locomotive footplate were, left to right: J. S. Wharton, unknown, J. Johnstone, Mrs Bennett and Miss B. Watson. Standing: A. G. Braithwaite, W. Jackson and H. Elliot.

T. Hunter Collection

Farewell. The "Stainmore Limited" at Tebay on 20th January 1962.

G. W. Morrison

Two Kirkby Stephen railwaymen pose for Eddie's Camera outside the shed. The 0-6-0 locomotives in the background were: left Class J25, probably No. 1726 and Class J21 No. 1801 of 1894 vintage, which was withdrawn in 1938.

Eddie Foster

The late Charlie Metcalfe stands proudly on the runningplate of his engine – G5 0-4-4T No. 1916. Charlie collapsed and died in the arms of his fireman Jack Rutter, whilst working the branch pasenger at Waitby Crossing.

D. Metcalfe collection

A fine gathering on the footplate of an E4 2-4-0 at Kirkby Stephen shed *c*1942. The staff are left to right on the locomotive: Top row, both unknown. Unknown, A. G. Braithwaite (fitter's mate), John Metcalfe (fireman) Albert Dodson (fireman), unknown, Laurie Walker (fireman), Robert Trilk, Unknown. Standing, left to right: two labourers from Darlington, Jack Satterthwaite, unknown.

A Sayer collection

A happy gathering of train crews on the platform at Kirkby Stephen East in the 50s. The chaps standing are: Alec Davis, now a cafe owner in Kirkby Stephen and Colin Walker, now a postman in Kirkby Stephen. Seated are, left to right: Eugene Moore, Tommy Morris, Len Greeve and David Binks.

J. E. Askew

6

Locomotives of the Stainmore Line

Locomotive working over the Stainmore and Eden Valley lines was handled from the date of opening in 1861 by the Stockton & Darlington Railway.

Prior to the formal opening on 7th August 1861, two locomotives had already been built with working the Stainmore Line in mind. These two locomotives were designed by William Bouch (brother of Thomas) of the Stockton & Darlington Railway.

The numbers and names of the locomotives were 160 *Brougham* and 161 *Lowther*. Both engines were built in 1860 by Robert Stephenson & Co. They were advanced for their time in as much as they employed a true bogie type 4-4-0 wheel notation with 6 ft diameter coupled driving wheels, as opposed to the more common 2-4-0 and 2-2-2 types. Other advanced features included an extraordinarily well protected, large windowed cab (the first British engines with side windows?) to combat the often inclement Stainmore weather.

Principal Dimensions
Cylinders: 16 in x 24 in
Boiler dia: 4 ft
Boiler length: 10 ft 6 in (Tomlinsons *North Eastern Railway*)
　　　　　 or 11 ft 6 in (J. McLean *North Eastern Railway Locomotives 1854-1905*)
　　　　　　 (176 iron tubes)
Heating surface: 1,128 sq ft
Weight of engine: 32 tons 4 cwt
Price each: £2,050

Four more 4-4-0 locomotives were designed by William Bouch and produced in the early part of 1862: No. 162 *Saltburn*, No. 163 *Morecambe*, No. 164 *Belfast* and No. 165 *Keswick*. These early names are particularly interesting. *Lowther* and *Brougham* of course

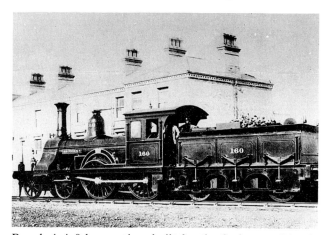

Bouch 4–4–0 locomotives built for the Stainmore Line in 1860, weighing 32 tons 4 cwt, cylinders 16in x 24in. No. 160 *Brougham*. Note the large cab.

have Westmorland associations. *Morecambe* and *Belfast* indicate the ambitions of the Stockton & Darlington Railway to serve the West Coast of England with a view to shipping coal from Morecambe to Northern Ireland. *Keswick* was so named at least two years before the railway got there! Nos 162-165 were inside-cylindered 4-4-0s with coupled driving wheels of 7 ft diameter.

No. 165 *Keswick*

K.L. Taylor collection

William Bouch locomotives of the Stockton & Darlington Railway
The second batch of four 4–4–0s, built 1862, weight of engine 32 tons 4 cwt, cylinders 16in x 24in.
No. 163 *Morecambe*

K.L. Taylor collection

No. 164 *Belfast*

K.L. Taylor collection

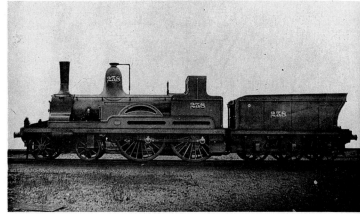

Most surprisingly the large cabs of *Brougham* and *Lowther* were purported to be unpopular with enginemen and this feature was omitted from the four later engines, a low weatherboard being substituted. The price per locomotive was in the region of £2,500. A steam brake was fitted.

Principal Dimensions for No. 162 *Saltburn* as quoted by J.McLean:
Cylinders: 18 in x 24 in
Boiler dia: 4 ft 3 in
Boiler length: 10 ft 3 in
Weight of engine: 54 tons 4 cwt
Total Weight of engine and tender: 71 tons 6 cwt
Cylinders enlarged to 17 in dia in 1880.

Ten further 4-4-0s were built between 1871 and 1874. These were not completely dissimilar to *Brougham* and *Lowther* in appearance, being outside-cylindered, but these locomotives incorporated a variety of rather novel features including 13 in dia brass piston valves and a piston stroke of at least 30 in. The driving wheels were 7 ft 1 in dia and boiler pressure

"Ginx's Baby"
Nos 238, 239, 240, 241, 1265/6/7/8/9 and 1270 4–4–0, designed by William Bouch for S&DR, driving wheel dia. 7ft 1in, piston stroke 30in, with piston valves. Rebuilt by NER as 2–4–0s.
No. 238.

K.L. Taylor collection

was 140 lbs. These locomotives were numbered 238, 239, 240 and 241 (appearing in 1871) and Nos 1265, 1266, 1267, 1268, 1269 and 1270 (appearing in 1874) and designated as Darlington Section engines. The class was not successful in original form. The piston valves were particularly troublesome.

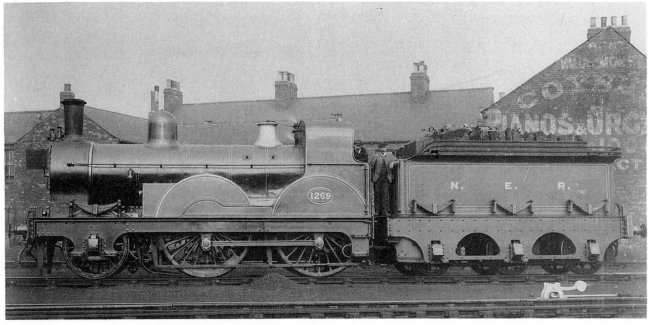

No. 1269, as rebuilt as a 2–4–0, photographed at Hull Botanic Gardens.

A. Wilson/K.L. Taylor collection

The engines became known as "Ginx's Babies", a name which puzzled North Eastern enthusiasts for years until it was found that a book advocating poor law reform had been written by Edward Jenkins, MP for Dundee in 1872. The fictional pauper who was the main character in the book was called Ginx. In the story Ginx apparently vowed that when his next child was born he would drown Same in the water butt! The "Ginx's babies" were rebuilt from 1875 onwards at Gateshead into a form identifiable with that of the Class 901.

The majority of mineral working during the early years of the lines' existence was handled by Stockton & Darlington Class 1001 locomotives, the first of which appeared in 1852 built by Gilkes Wilson & Co. with 4 ft 2½ in dia coupled wheels.

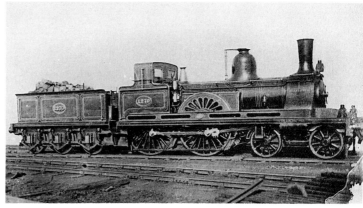

No. 1270

Locomotive and General Railway Photographs

Class 1001 0–6–0
No. 1275, the preserved example in the fine railway museum at Darlington North Road in 1986. No. 1275 was part of the last batch of 60 locomotives to be built. Designed by William Bouch and built prior to 1875. Boiler pressure 140 lb/sq in, cylinders 12in x 26in, tractive effort 14,779 lb.
This locomotive was withdrawn in 1923 after completing 908,984 miles in service and retained for preservation in the old York Railway Museum.

Author, courtesy Darlington Borough Council

The early locomotives had 17 in 18 in cylinders. Subsequent locomotives had 5 ft 0½ in dia coupled wheels with 17 in 24 in cylinders. Fifty-four of these engines were built between 1860 and 1868, the final total of 125 being achieved in 1875.

The last 60 locomotives had principal dimensions as follows:

Cylinders: 17 in x 26 in

Grate area: 12.6 sq ft
Heating surface: 1,268 sq ft
Boiler pressure: 140 lbs/sq in
Boiler dia: 4 ft 0¾ in
Boiler length: 14 ft
Tractive effort: 14,779 lbs
Total weight of engine and tender: 52 tons

These were numbered 1221-1237, 1246-1264 and 1271-1290.

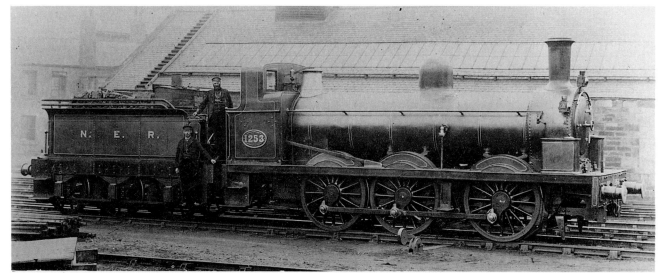

No. 1253, another of the last batch of 60 locomotives, and one which did not make it to the grouping. Photographed at Shildon.
K.L. Taylor collection

The North Eastern Railway-designated 1001 class, known by some as "long-boilered" locomotives, but perhaps more accurately described as "short-coupled", became common over the Stainmore line. These locomotives became more or less standardised from 1860 onwards. Many had names of local interest, eg S&D No. 168 was *Clifton*, and No. 169 was *Tufton*. Some were named after animals, birds and planets. The distinctive appearance of these engines was partially due to the short-coupled rear four driving wheels which resulted in the cab overhanging by a considerable distance.

The very deep buffer beam was a link with the earliest days when a separate set of buffers was required at a lower level to handle coal conveyed in chaldron wagons. The long boiler was particularly suited to working coal trains where a long, uninterrupted run was rarely possible. The boiler could provide a good supply of steam when starting away but kept the 'stand by' losses to a minimum.

They worked 'double loads' over the Stainmore route which involved two locomotives to a train - one assisting in the rear on rising gradients and then attached in front on falling gradients, this practice

Class 1068 2–4–0
Six locomotive built at Darlington Works 1875/6 with slight variations. Details for No. 1068: weight in working order, 33 tons 18 cwt, boiler pressure 140 lb/sq in, cylinders 17in x 24in, driving wheel dia. 6ft 6in.
No. 1068 at Wearhead station (not on the Stainmore Line).
D. Hoseason/K.L. Taylor collection

No. 1109, one of the earlier batch of locomotives. Notice the outside tender springing.
Locomotive and General Railway Photographs

becoming common and well-known on the Stainmore route right up to the end of freight working.

Predecessors of the final development of the Stockton & Darlington 0-6-0 designs associated with the Stainmore and Eden Valley lines were No. 134 *Kendal* and No. 156 *Tebay* built by Gilkes Wilson and Robert Stephenson respectively in 1858. Subsequent locomotives included No. 156 *Herschel* which worked the first mineral train through from Darlington to Tebay.

The 0-6-0 locomotives of Stockton & Darlington Railway origin continued to handle the majority of the Durham coke to Barrow traffic until the advent in 1886 of the North Eastern Railway B class 0-6-2Ts (LNER Class N8). The 1001 class still handled trains of haematite ore from Whitehaven to Kirkby Stephen travelling via the Cockermouth, Keswick & Penrith Railway, the Redhills curve and the Eden Valley branch.

On the passenger side, six 2-4-0 locomotives were built at Darlington in 1875 and 1876 for the Stainmore line. These were designated as Class 1068 and were numbered 1035, 1050, 1062, 1066, 1068 and 1098. Fourteen of these 2-4-0s were eventually built, commencing with No. 1068. They were nicknamed "Gamecocks". No. 1068 was displayed at the fiftieth anniversary celebrations of the Stockton & Darlington Railway in 1875 but was scrapped in 1909.

Principal Dimensions of the 1068 class, according to J. McLean:
Cylinders: 17 in x 26 in
Boiler barrel dia: 4 ft
Boiler barrel length: 11 ft
Boiler pressure: 140 lbs/sq in
Weight of engine in working order: 33 tons 18 cwt

Improvements to the basic concept of the S&D 0-6-0 1001 and other designs were being considered by Edward Fletcher, the Locomotive Superintendent in the early 1870s. In 1875 the locomotive engineer, William Bouch, was ill and rumours suggested he was being assisted or deputised for by John Kitching (Darlington's Divisional Locomotive Superintendent). A variety of experiments were undertaken upon the 1001 class at this time, particularly lengthening the wheelbase. These experiments resulted in the Fletcher Class 398 which became a collection of locomotives and rebuilds with many detail differences between manufacturers.

The 398s began to appear over the Stainmore Line at about the turn of the century. The last to be withdrawn from normal traffic was No. 1412 in 1928. The numbering sequence, or lack of it, is too diverse to describe in this book!

Locomotives of the Stockton & Darlington Railway

When the Stockton & Darlington Railway became part of the North Eastern Railway in July 1863, about 160 locomotives were transferred, but as the line was worked by a separate committee for ten years, the engines were not renumbered until 1873. Below is an inventory of them. In most cases the renumbering was effected by the simple and ingenious expedient of adding 1,000 to the existing number. The number of engines owned by the NER at that time was less than one thousand, so that duplicate numbering was thereby avoided.

No.	Name	No.	Name	No.	Name	No.	Name	No.	Name
1.	Locomotion	42.	London (sold)	83.	Victoria	124.	Brookside	165.	Keswick
2.	Hope	43.	Sunbeam	84.	Albert	125.	Gazelle	166.	Oswald Gulkes
3.	Black Diamond	44.	Sun	85.	Hardinge	126.	John Wakefield	167.	Newlands
4.	Stockton	45.	Gannymede	86.	Zetland	127.	Polam	168.	Clifton
5.	Hopetown	46.	Antelope	87.	Fryerage	128.	East Mount	169.	Tufton
6.	Dispatch	47.	Unicorn	88.	Deanery	129.	Stanley	170.	Reliance
7.	Prince	48.	Active	89.	Huddersfield	130.	Hutton	171.	Gladstone
8.	Leader	49.	Raby Castle	90.	Merchant	131.	Longhull	172.	Barrow
9.	Middlesbrough	50.	Meteor	91.	Australia	132.	Appleby	173.	London
10.	Auckland	51.	Arrow	92.	Yarm	133.	Kirkby Stephen	174.	John Dixon
11.	Bee	52.	Comet	93.	Uranus	134.	Kendal	175.	Contractor
12.	Trader	53.	Manchester	94.	Neptune	135.	Eden	176.	Windsor
13.	Ocean	54.	Tyne Side	95.	Elephant	136.	Tebay	177.	Osborne
14.	Tees	55.	Wolsingham	96.	Middleton	137.	Deepdale	178.	Balmoral
15.	Tory	56.	Tow Law	97.	Gainford	138.	Beelah	179.	Edinburgh
16.	Stanhope	57.	Shotley	98.	Pierremont	139.	Crossfell	180.	Dublin
17.	Whig	58.	Woodlands	99.	Ayton	140.	Penrith	181.	Malton
18.	Etherley	59.	Hall Garth	100.	Stobart	141.	Excelsior	182.	Elton
19.	Darlington	60.	Cleveland	101.	Marske	142.	Wycliffe	183.	Acklam
20.	Adelaide	61.	Star	102.	Cotherstone	143.	Windermere	184.	Lark
21.	Earl Grey	62.	Southend	103.	Darlington	144.	Ulleswater	185.	Swallow
22.	Lord Durham	63.	Birkbeck	104.	Durham	145.	Panther	186.	Union
23.	Wilberforce	64.	Larchfield	105.	Teesdale	146.	Ostrich	187.	Ironage
24.	Magnet	65.	Stephenson	106.	Staindrop	147.	Leopard	188.	Lily
25.	Derwent	66.	Priam	107.	Barnard Castle	148.	Zebra	189.	Spring
26.	Pilot	67.	Orion	108.	Eagle	149.	Fox	190.	Summer
27.	Witton Castle	68.	Brunswick	109.	Falcon	150.	Mastiff	191.	Autumn
28.	Conside	69.	Clarendon	110.	Hawk	151.	Mercury	192.	Winter
29.	Miner	70.	Alarm	111.	Stag	152.	Venus	193.	Princess
30.	Wear	71.	Hackworth	112.	Lion	153.	Mars	194.	Alice
31.	Redcar	72.	Peel	113.	Camel	154.	Jupiter	195.	Helena
32.	Eldon	73.	Aberdeen	114.	Edward Pease	155.	Saturn	196.	Whitby
33.	Shildon	74.	Emperor	115.	Meynell	156.	Herschel	197.	Kildale
34.	Driver	75.	Baring	116.	Lartington	157.	Planet	198.	Roseberry
35.	Commerce	76.	Prince of Wales	117.	Nunthorpe	158.	Lune	199.	Escomb
36.	Guisbro'	77.	Alexander	118.	Elm Field	159.	York	200.	Eskdale
37.	Gem	78.	Lonsdale	119.	Greta	160.	Brougham	201.	Carlton
38.	Rokeby	79.	Carlisle	120.	Brough	161.	Lowther	202.	Ireland
39.	Ruby	80.	The Duke	121.	Tiger	162.	Saltburn	203.	England
40.	Queen	81.	Miller	122.	Kestrel	163.	Morecambe		
41.	Dart	82.	Hawthorn	123.	Bellevue	164.	Belfast		

Principal Dimensions of the 398s were:
Cylinders: 17 in x 24 in
Grate area: 17 sq ft
Heating surface: 107 sq ft
Boiler pressure: 140 lbs/sq in
Boiler barrel dia: 4 ft 3 in
Boiler length: 10 ft 7 in
Tractive effort: 15,722 lb
Total weight of engine and tender (full): 66 tons

In 1886/8 the then new Worsdell-von Borries principle compound Class B 0-6-2 tanks and the Class B1 simple expansion versions began to appear from Darlington North Road Works. The Class B compound tanks took over some of the Stainmore freight working in about 1889. (See the appendix referring to Tebay shed's locomotive allocation of 1878 which indicates this development). The Class B and B1s were essentially tank locomotive variants of the Class C and C1 tender locomotives which appeared at approximately the same time. At the Grouping of 1923 all the compound locomotives had become Class B1s, having been rebuilt to the simple form.

Sixty-two locomotives became LNER Class N8, eleven of these being the original compound design now rebuilt. The B1 were joined in 1893/4 by 20 Darlington built Class Ns which became N9s at the Grouping, and in 1902/3 by 20 class Us which became LNER Class N10.

As indicated in the appendix of Tebay shed allocations, the Worsdell tanks began to be replaced by Class T 0-8-0s c1902.

The tender locomotives of Classes C and C1 also began to appear in 1886. Again designed by T.W. Worsdell, Class C were compounds, while the Class C1 were simples. These were designated Class J21 at the Grouping. They were designed to supplement the Class 59 McDonnell engines of 1882. Some Class 59s worked over the Stainmore route, the class becoming LNER J22s.

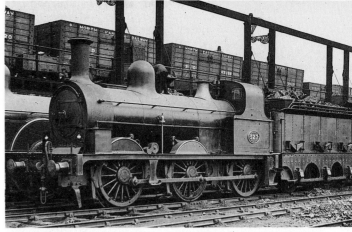

Class 398 No. 327. The class ultimately totalled 325 examples, but there were many detail variations including wheel sizes etc.

Locomotive Publishing Co.

Class B 0–6–2T
Designed by T.W. Worsdell as a compound locomotive with quantity production commencing in 1888. High pressure cylinder 18in x 24in, low pressure cylinder 26in x 24in. Driving wheel dia. 5ft. From 1902 they were rebuilt as single locomotives.
No. 523 in NER guise. It was driven by Joseph Armstrong and was the locomotive which replaced S&D 0–6–0 No. 1213 at Tebay shed circa 1889.

K.L. Taylor collection

Class 398 0–6–0
Designed by Fletcher, built between 1872 and 1883, weighing 37 tons 6 cwt (nominal). Boiler pressure 160 lb/sq in. Cylinders 17in x 24in, tractive effort (85%) 15,733 lb, driving wheel dia. 5ft.
No. 1087 on Kirkby Stephen shed, between 1923 and its withdrawal in 1927. Built at Gateshead in 1883.

Eddie Foster/Iain Smith collection

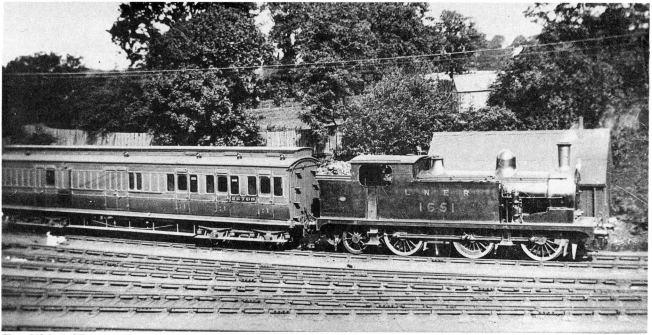

Class N9 0–6–2T
Designed by W. Worsdell, built between 1893 and 1894, weighing 56 tons 10 cwt, boiler pressure 160 lb/sq in, cylinders 19in x 24in/19in x 26in, tractive effort 19,237 lb/20,840 lb. Driving wheel dia. 5ft $1^1/_4$in.
No. 1651 seen here in Kirkby Stephen East goods yard.

Eddie Foster

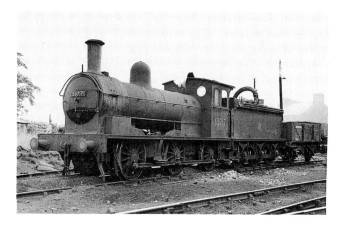

Class J25 0–6–0
Former North Eastern Railway Class P1 designed by W. Worsdell, built between 1898 and 1902, rebuilt variously. Weighing 39 ton 11 cwt, boiler pressure 160 lb/sq in, cylinders $18^1/_2$in x 26in, tractive effort 21,904 lb, driving wheel dia. 4ft $7^1/_4$in.
No. 65717, formerly Nos 5617 (1946) and 2130 (1923), on Kirkby Stephen shed 28th June 1952. This was one of the relatively few superheated J25s. It was withdrawn in 1958, the last J25 being withdrawn in 1962.

J.F. Aylard

Hard to resist the temptation to include this side study of J25 No. 2051 shunting in Kirkby Stephen goods yard, boasting its 1923 number (later No. 5704). Notice the private owner wagons.

J.F. Mallon collection

Class J21 0–6–0

Former North Eastern Railway Class C, designed by T.W. Worsdell, built between 1886 and 1895, rebuilt by W. Worsdell and Raven variously. Weighing 42 tons 1 cwt/43 tons 15 cwt, boiler pressure 160 lb/sq in, cylinders 18in x 24in/19in x 24in and 19in x 26in. Tractive efforts 17,266 lb, 19,237 lb and 20,840 lb respectively. Driving wheel dia. 5ft 1$\frac{1}{4}$in.

No. 30 is seen here, from Kirkby Stephen East box. This is its 1923 number, the 1946 allocated number being 5065. No. 30 was actually withdrawn in 1946 and in its final form was non-super-heated and possessed Westinghouse and vacuum brakes.

J.F. Mallon collection

The Class C and C1 locomotives became synonymous with the Stainmore and Eden Valley routes. The building rate of these tremendously successful engines was particularly prolific, 201 being built between 1886 and 1895. The entire class remained intact until 1929. The last locomotive to be withdrawn was No. 876 (65033) in April 1962 - ironically the same year the Stainmore line closed. The end of an era indeed.

Also associated with the Stainmore line were the slightly later Wilson Worsdell designed Class P1 locomotives which became J25s at the Grouping. These locomotives worked over the Stainmore route until the 1950s when, like the J21s, they were replaced by LMS and BR Standard designs.

The principal dimensions at the Grouping of the J21s/J25s were:
Cylinders: 19 in x 24 in/18$\frac{1}{2}$ in 26 in
Grate area: 17.2 sq ft/17.2 sq ft
Heating surface: 108 sq ft/108 sq ft
Boiler pressure: 160 lbs/sq in/160 lbs sq in
Tractive effort: 19,237 lbs/21,904 lbs
Total weight of engine and tender: 79 ton 4 cwt/78 tons

The compound Class Cs began to be rebuilt as simples in 1901 with many of the rebuilt engines fitted with superheaters after 1914.

In about 1890 two 2-2-2 single drivers were kept at Penrith, Nos 1692 and 1693. Originally Nos 161 and 280 of Class 447 built in 1862 and withdrawn in 1897, these worked the Eden Valley line until about 1895 when they were replaced by "Ginx's Babies" Nos 1268 and 1269, by then rebuilt as 2-4-0s.

Principal dimensions of Nos 161 and 280, as given by J. McLean: Built 1862 by Fletcher, the last withdrawn in 1899.
Cylinders: 16 in x 22 in
Boiler pressure: 130 lbs/sq in
Driving wheel dia: 6 ft 6 in

By the mid-1880s a more stable approach to the working of the Stainmore line was being considered. The earliest available data suggest that McDonnell Class 38 No. 426 was allocated to Kirkby Stephen shed in 1885. At about this time trials took place over the Stainmore route to determine which locomotives were most suitable for passenger work.

No. 65089, formerly Nos 5089 (1946) and 1561 (1923), on Kirkby Stephen shed 28th June, 1952. She finished her days superheated, with steam and vacuum brakes and was withdrawn in 1954.

J.F. Aylard

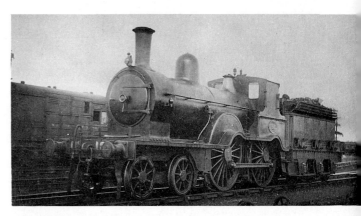

Class 38 4–4–0

Designed by McDonnell, built 1884. Weight of engine 39$\frac{1}{2}$ tons, boiler pressure 140 lb, cylinders 17in x 24in.

No. 158, sister engine to No. 126, which worked over Stainmore in about 1885.

W.H. Whitworth/K.L. Taylor collection

A sister engine, No. 126, was involved in the trials along with Class 1463 'Tennant' No. 1467 and a Class 901, No. 154. These comparisons culminated in the choice of the Fletcher Class 901 locomotives being the most suitable for the Stainmore and Eden Valley line passenger services.

For a variety of reasons the locomotive crews disliked the 38s, and one of their few claims to fame involving the Stainmore line was the occasional use of No. 1318 in its later years with modified cab to offset the weather, when working the Darlington stores van over the route.

The splendid 901 class locomotives were built between 1872 and 1882, 45 in all. A few were still in service albeit in rebuilt form, after the Grouping. They were probably the best of Fletcher's locomotives, and became particularly famous for their work on the East Coast Main Line during the great 'Railway races to the North' in the late 1880s.

Principal dimensions of the 901s were:
Cylinders: 17 in x 24 in
Grate area: 16 sq ft
Heating surface: 98 sq ft
Boiler pressure: 140 lbs sq in
Boiler barrel dia: 4 ft 3 in
Boiler length: 10 ft 3 in
Total weight: 39½ tons

Arguably the most famous J21 of all, No. 65033: the last engine to use the turntable at Tebay NE, and the last J21 to travel over Stainmore.

Formerly Nos 5033 (1946) and 876 (1923) it was in fact withdrawn in 1939 but was reprieved and repaired due to the outbreak of war and went on to become the last J21 to be withdrawn, in 1962. Nos 65033 and 65099 lay at Darlington awaiting a decision as to their fate, from 1962 to 1966 when 65099 was cut up. No. 65033 was saved at the last minute and was later restored as No. 876 at the North of England Open Air Museum, Beamish, where it can be seen in immaculate condition today.

No. 65033 pauses at Kirkby Stephen East with the last J21-hauled Stainmore train.

John Mallon

No. 65033 – its future in the balance at Darlington Works in 1965.

Author

In pristine condition ex-NER Class G1 (LNER Class D23) 4-4-0 No. 679 of 1887 vintage, rebuilt as a 4-4-0 in 1902, and ex-NER Class 1463 'Tennant' 2-4-0 No. 1477, bask in the sunshine at Kirkby Stephen shed. The 'Tennants' replaced earlier Fletcher Class 901 locomotives and then, as the years passed, were themselves replaced by the G1s.

Eddie Foster

No. 135, again at Penrith, in September 1921.

Locomotive and General Railway Photographs

Another Fletcher locomotive associated with the Stainmore and Eden Valley routes was his BTP type (Bogie Tank Passenger), 130 of which were built between 1874 and 1883. Some of these tanks boasted driving wheel diameters as great as 5 ft 6 in and cylinders 16 in-17 in 22 in. A respectable number survived beyond the Grouping when they became Class G6. The 1885 Kirkby Stephen allocation included Nos 591, 693 and 1020.

In the early 1900s the powerful Worsdell 0-8-0 Class T and TIs began to appear. The Class Ts had piston valves and the TIs slide valves. The first ten Class T, Nos 2116-2125 emerged from Gateshead Works in 1901.

Principal dimensions were:
Cylinders: 20 in x 26 in
Grate area: 21 sq ft
Heating surface: 130 sq ft
Boiler pressure: 175 lbs sq in
Boiler barrel dia: 4 ft 9 in
Boiler length: 15 ft
Tractive effort: 28,100 lbs
Total weight of engine and tender: 102 tons

Class 901 2–4–0
Designed by Edward Fletcher, built 1872 onwards, weighing approximately 40 tons.
No. 905 at Penrith circa 1895. The locomotive men include John Tomlin and George Armstrong. The regular 901 was in the shops at the time. The locomotive is being prepared for the afternoon (1.15pm) shift.

J.W. Armstrong collection

No. 911 on shed at Kirkby Stephen, circa 1908.
Locomotive and General Railway Photographs

Class BTP later Class G6 0–4–4T
Designed by Edward Fletcher, built 1874–1883, cylinders, 16/17in x 22in, driving wheel dia. 5ft 6in.
No. 1020 a Kirkby Stephen engine, poses in front of the fine stone-built signal box at Kirkby Stephen East.

John Mallon collection

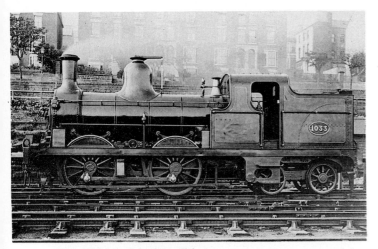

No. 1033 in original condition.

Locomotive and General Railway Photographs

No. 1431 in rebuilt condition.

Locomotive Publising Co.

Class Q5 0–8–0

Former North Eastern Railway Class T designed by W. Worsdell built between 1901 and 1991, weighing 58 ton 8 cwt. Boiler pressure 175 lb/sq in. Cylinders 20in x 26in, tractive effort 28,000 lb, driving wheel dia. 4ft 7$\frac{1}{4}$in.

Two studies of the class with No. 444 (No. 646 in the background) and No. 2118 at Kirkby Stephen shed. The later Nos for 444 and 2118 were 3295 and 3252 respectively. Notice the superb NER water crane alongside No. 2118. This locomotive replaced No. 443 at Kirkby Stephen in 1931.

J.F. Mallon collection and Eddie Foster

'Tennant' No. 1477.

Locomotive and General Railway Photographs

Four Class TIs Nos 527, 1002, 1704 and 1708 replaced Class B 0-6-2 tanks at Tebay c1902. The T and TI class locomotives, later to become LNER Class Q5, worked over the route until 1914 when they were transferred elsewhere because of weight restrictions imposed over Belah Viaduct. This weight restriction also applied to the Class B/B1 tanks and, surprisingly, to the 1463 'Tennant' 2-4-0s. The Class B tanks were able to bank westbound rains to the Summit. The restriction west of the Summit was relaxed between 1923 and 1929.

A further effect of the relaxation of the weight restriction over Belah in 1923 was the appearance of the 'Tennant' 2-4-0s which gradually supplanted the faithful 901s on passenger turns.

The 1463s were built under the direction of the NER General Manager Henry Tennant in 1885 to replace earlier McDonnell 4-4-0s on the East Coast Main Line. They gave successful and reliable service on the crack East Coast expresses until replaced by more modern motive power which released the forty 2-4-0s for use on routes such as the Stainmore line.

Principal dimensions of the 'Tennants' were:
Cylinders: 18 in x 24 in
Grate area: 18 sq ft
Heating surface: 114 sq ft
Boiler barrel dia: 4 ft 3 in

The 'Tennants' themselves gave way to Class GI 4-4-0s (LNER Class D23) in the late 1920s. The GIs, introduced in 1887 (the suffix disappeared in 1914), were essentially rebuilds of earlier Class G 2-4-0 locomotives. By the time they appeared as Stainmore regulars they were nearing the end of their careers but nevertheless they handled passenger services for a number of years. Relatively few engines were involved but these obviously became regular performers.

Class 1463 'Tennant' 2–4–0

Edward Fletcher retired as Locomotive Superintendent in 1882. Archibald McDonnell occupied the position between 1882 and 1884 when he resigned, and T.W. Worsdell was appointed in 1885. Between the resignation and the new appointment, the NER was without a locomotive superintendent and it was during this period that the general manager, Mr Henry Tennant suggested the construction of a similar class of engine to the Fletcher 901 class, but with a longer wheelbase and larger cylinders. In February 1885 the first of twenty Class 1463 locomotives was ready for service.

No. 1477 is seen here at Kirkby Stephen. The footplateman on the left is Mr Johnathan Burton who later became the mayor of Newcastle.

Eddie Foster

Principal dimensions of the G class locomotives were:
Cylinders: 18 in x 24 in
Grate area: 15.16 sq ft
Heating surface: 98 sq ft
Boiler barrel dia: 4 ft 3 in
Total weight of engine and tender: 78 tons 15 cwt

No. 258 in LNER days at Harrogate in July 1927, as Class D23.

Locomotive and General Railway Photographs

Class G 4–4–0
Designed by Wilson Worsdell, built 1887/8 as 2–4–0 Class G1. Rebuilt 1901–1904 as 4–4–0, reclassified G and became LNER Class D23.
No. 472, a Stainmore regular, is seen leaving Merrygill Viaduct. Notice the horse boxes preceeding the fine clerestory-roofed coaches.

Eddie Foster

Class E4 2–4–0
Former Great Eastern Railway locomotives designed by J. Holden, built between 1891 and 1902. Weighing 40 tons 6 cwt, boiler pressure 160 lb/sq in, cylinders $17\frac{1}{2}$in x 24in tractive effort, 14,700 lb, driving wheel dia. 5ft 8in.
No. 7411 takes water at Kirkby Stephen.

Eddie Foster

In 1929 Q5 class locomotives were again required to work the western section of the line between Kirkby Stephen and Tebay. As the weight restriction over Belah Viaduct still applied for these locomotives, special dispensation was given for No. 443 to travel to Kirkby Stephen from Shildon, split and separate from its tender, with an empty boiler and part of its motion dismantled. It was exchanged for No. 2118 shortly afterwards to enable a works visit to be made. In 1931 a further Q5 was transferred to Kirkby Stephen, No. 444. Kirkby Stephen shed maintained a pair of Q5s until 1942 when they were eventually transferred away. Shortly after the Q5s had become established at Kirkby Stephen, the elegant Class Gs (D23s) succumbed to the unsuitable former Great Northern

Railway D3 4-4-0s for use on passenger services.

The D3 Nos 4075, 4077, 4347/9/50/4 appeared variously between 1930 and 1931, the first D23 being withdrawn in 1929. Some of the D3s were modified to combat Stainmore conditions, notably by the introduction of a single side window in the cabs.

Continuing unpopularity preceded the eventual replacement of the D3s over Stainmore by an equally unusual but considerably more successful locomotive, the Holden designed former Great Eastern Railway Class E4 2-4-0s.

The late Bert Eden, driver from Shildon and latterly Kirkby Stephen, recounted that these locomotives also had inadequate cabs and pressure from the locomen resulted in speedy modifications. The E4s which arrived at Kirkby Stephen from 1935 onwards were Nos 7408, 7411, 7416, 7478 and 7496. No. 7411 was the first to arrive and 7478 being the last to return to its East Anglian homeland in April 1942. In between 1935 and 1942 a variety of transfers of E4s took place between the sheds at Penrith, Kirkby, Middleton, Darlington and Barnard Castle.

Wilson Worsdell designed his Class O 0-4-4 tank engines for manufacture between 1894 and 1901 - a total of 110 engines being built. These engines became Class G5 at the Grouping and they became particularly involved in the working of the Eden Valley branch passenger trains from about 1927 onwards. At this time No. 1916 became the Penrith engine for the next eight years before it was transferred to Kirkby Stephen where No. 1334 resided. No. 1916 would work the majority of the four daily return trips from and to

Penrith over the Valley branch. For quite a while the regular driver of this locomotive was the late Charles Metcalfe of Kirkby Stephen. Other G5s were obviously involved at Kirkby Stephen as the accompanying pictures of Nos 1737 and 2100 illustrate. One early Kirkby Stephen working diagram indicates the use of G5s to Tebay.

Principal dimensions of the G5 class were:
Cylinders: 18 in x 24 in
Grate area: 15.6 sq ft
Heating surface: 98 sq ft
Boiler pressure: 160 lbs/sq in
Boiler dia: 4 ft 3 in
Boiler length: 10 ft 3 in
Tractive effort: 17,200 lbs (85%)
Weight (full): 54 tons 4 cwt

No. 7416 receives major attention underneath the excellent lift on Kirkby Stephen shed.
Eddie Foster

No. 7478 turns on the table behind the shed
Eddie Foster

Class G5 0–4–4T
Designed by W. Worsdell, built between 1894 and 1901, weighing 54 tons 4 cwt, boiler pressure 160 lb/sq in, cylinders 18in x 24in, tractive effort 11,607 lb. Driving wheel dia. 5ft 1¹/₄in.
No. 1737 on shed at Kirkby Stephen.

No. 2100 in the goods yard at Kirkby Stephen.

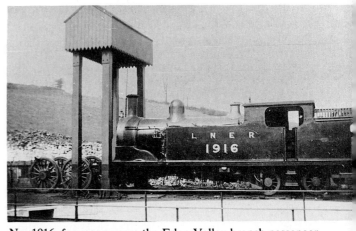

No. 1916, for many years the Eden Valley branch passenger engine, receiving attention on shed at Kirkby Stephen.

From 1886 onwards and throughout all the varied and interesting motive power changes which occurred up until the outbreak of the Second World War, the fine little J21s and J25s supplemented the other classes of locomotive as necessary.

With the transfer away from the North of the E4s in 1942 the faithful J21 and J25 0-6-0s were on their own again until the emergence after the war of the Ivatt 2MT and 4MT 2-6-0 designs, later supplemented by British Railways Standard designs. Class 4MTs of the 76xxx series, Class 3MT 77xxx series, Class 2MT 78xxx series and Class 3MT tanks, 82xxx series all became commonplace as the 1950s progressed. The 82xxx tanks worked the Penrith-Darlington trains until the arrival of the dmus in 1958.

The J21s and J25s gradually disappeared after a long and distinguished career, the last working of a J21 being the celebrated railtour of 1960 involving No.

65033, also believed to be the last NER engine to use the turntable and yard at Tebay on the date of the occasion, 7th May 1960. The last J21s and J25s in normal service had drifted gently over Stainmore Summit to the east for the last time some years earlier.

The final exciting development involving a new class of North Eastern Railway locomotive occurred in April 1955 when two Class Q6 locomotives - former NER Class T2 0-8-0s BR Nos 63355 and 63373 (NER Nos 1283 and 2216)˙ were transferred to Kirkby Stephen to work trains to and from Tebay. Whilst working double-headed tender first to Kirkby Stephen on 20th May 1955 they became derailed near Smardale. The incident was blamed on a combination of speed and a broken tender spring. However, the opinion of local railwaymen suggested that the track had recently been subject to permanent way work and had not been properly secured. Either way the Q6s,

Class 4MT 2–6–0
Ivatt design, introduced 1947 with taper boiler. Weight 59 tons 2 cwt, boiler pressure 225 lb (superheated), cylinders 17½in x 26in, tractive effort 24,170 lb, driving wheel dia. 5ft 3in.
No. 43130 resting at the rear of Kirkby Stephen shed. This was one of the few engines fitted with a stovepipe chimney.

Neville Bousfield

No. 43056 provides assistance for an eastbound freight at Merrygill.

Neville Bousfield

The famous railtour of 7th May 1960 after arrival at Barnard Castle behind No. 65033. This was the last run of a J21 class 0-6-0 over Stainmore.

J. F. Mallon

The last locomotive to use the turntable at Tebay NE was Class J21 0-6-0 No. 65033.

J. F. Mallon

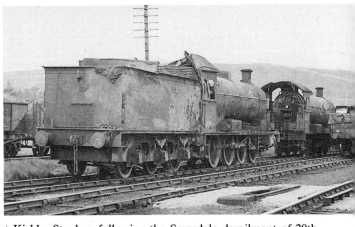

The two Q6s Nos 63355 and 63373 stored in the West sidings at Kirkby Stephen following the Smardale derailment of 20th May 1955. They were transferred back to the North East following this incident.

J. W. Armstrong

The famous derailment at Smardale on 20th May 1955. Two ex-NER Class Q6 0-8-0s, Nos 63355 and 63373 left the tracks whilst running tender first with a train of empties towards Kirkby Stephen.

J. W. Armstrong

both badly damaged, were transferred back to the North East - a class never to reappear until some more were used on demolition trains in 1962/3 when the line and structures were dismantled with indecent haste. This class even worked over Belah Viaduct during this period.

The line's locomotive history would not be complete without mention of the diesel multiple units which took over the Penrith-Darlington passenger services in 1958 and continued to work these until closure. Many other locomotives made appearances over the line during its hundred year history, notably including *Aerolite* and the Sentinel steam railcars which worked the fortnightly Durham Miners' trip to their convalescent home at Ulverston. For these workings a conductor was taken on at Tebay and after arrival at Ulverston the railcars complete with crew, ran empty to Barrow where the LNER crew lodged overnight, returning home the next day.

Class 59s, Class Q 4-4-0s and also Class M 4-4-0s worked over the line at about the turn of the century; Class Ms on a fairly regular basis. Class 686, 1440 and other 2-4-0s all made appearances in the early days. A similar locomotive to the Class M, Class M1 No. 1621 is preserved in the National Railway Museum at York. A Class D 4-4-4 tank was tried over the route in 1914 but was said to be too heavy. This was a Vincent Raven design of 1913.

Seven Class J10 0-6-0s of Great Central Railway origin were transferred from Springs Branch (Wigan), Chester (Northgate) and Trafford Park to Darlington in November 1956 but were withdrawn the following month. This transfer occurred via Kirkby Stephen and it is known that one of these, No. 65162, passed over Stainmore in steam.

Sentinel steam railcar almost certainly No. 2276 *North Briton*, wreathed in steam departs from Kirkby Stephen towards Tebay and the West.

Eddie Foster

A rare picture of the now-preserved locomotive No. 66 *Aerolite* leaving the Eden Bridge at Musgrave. The train would be an officer's inspection special.

Eddie Foster

Class J22 0–6–0

Former NER Class 59, designed by McDonnell, built between 1883 and 1885, weighing 36 tons 12 cwt. Boiler pressure 160 lb/sq in, cylinders 17in x 26in, tractive effort (85%) 15,195 lb–16,753 lb. Driving wheel dia. 5ft 1in and 5ft 7$^1/_4$in.

No. 369, built at Darlington in 1884, shunts the goods shed road at Kirkby Stephen. Twelve of the class were built by R. Stephenson & Co. and had longer frames than the others and had straight running boards. No. 369 received its Worsdell boiler in 1899 and was withdrawn in 1926.

J.F. Mallon collection

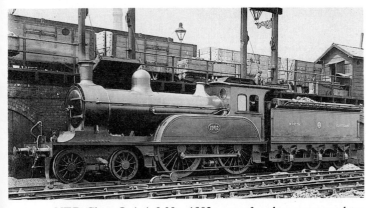

NER Class Q 4–4–0 No. 1902, one of a class rumoured to have worked over the route, along with Class Ms, at about the turn of the century.

Locomotive Publishing Co.

A rare view of Class 686 No. 694 approaching Ravenstonedale.

Lens of Sutton

It is speculated that a troop special on Friday 27th April 1956 travelled over Stainmore behind K1 class 2-6-0 No. 62060, passing Kirkby Stephen at 4.32 pm. The engine returned light, passing at 6.22 pm.

In 1947 at the time J21 No. 5090 was stranded near Belah for approximately eight weeks, a Hull (Botanic Gardens) G5 was sighted at Penrith.

It is on record that London & North Western Railway locomotives occasionally worked excursion trains to Warcop for Brough Hill Fair and it is known that one of the famous DX 0-6-0s ran through from Tebay to Barnard Castle on a special. A LNWR "Cauliflower" once worked the afternoon passenger from Penrith to Kirkby Stephen when the North Eastern engine had failed.

The ex-LMS Fowler 4MTs were also rumoured to have made trips over the line in the 1950s, Nos 44016, 44060 and 44081 (all with tender cabs) being involved. One such locomotive managed to cause considerable damage inside Kirkby Stephen shed when the water

Class K1 2–6–0 No. 62045 runs light over Tees Viaduct on 12th August 1964.

J.L. Birkbeck

The 'Ghost Station' of Kirkby Stephen East on 31st July 1963. Fowler 4F class 0–6–0 No. 44451 rests in the platform of the almost intact station as the crew use the former porter's room for lunch. The train is the thrice weekly pick-up freight to Merrygill Quarry which continued until October 1974.

J.L. Birkbeck

'Jubilee' class 4-6-0 No. 45657 *Tyrwhitt* exchanges tokens at Kirkby Thore in March 1953. The train is the southbound, diverted "Thames – Clyde Express", travelling over the valley branch due to engineering work on the Settle – Carlisle line. The train would rejoin the Settle – Carlisle route via Appleby Junction and Appleby North.

Geoff Jackson

scoop was mistakenly screwed down instead of the tender brake. When the locomotive was moved it did a grand job gathering sleepering, etc. for quite a few yards until the problem was isolated! A WD 2-8-0 is known to have worked down the Eden Valley branch to Kirkby Stephen for servicing in the 1950s.

As can be seen from one of Ron Herbert's excellent pictures, a Stanier Class 4MT 2-6-0, No. 42962 worked to Kirkby Stephen on a railtour.

The Eden Valley branch more than once provided a diversionary route for both West Coast and Settle-Carlisle main line trains. Many interesting trains will have crept quietly between Eden Valley Junction and Appleby Junction before rejoining the Settle-Carlisle line at Appleby North. The unique picture of the 'Jubilee' 4-6-0 on the "Thames-Clyde Express" at Kirkby Thore by Geoff Jackson is one of the very few photographic records of such Eden Valley diversions.

'Jubilees', "Black 5s", 8Fs and WDs were all employed when the dumping of surplus 16-ton mineral wagons on the former NER main line near Tebay and the Eden Valley branch between Clifton Moor and Appleby was taking place.

The last train was worked by BR Standard locomotives Nos 76049 and 77003 on 20th January 1962.

Kirkby Stephen Shed Allocation 1885
Class 38 4-4-0: No. 426
Class BPT 0-4-4T: Nos 591, 623 and 1020
Class 1068 2-4-0: No. 1066
Class 1001 0-6-0: Nos 1176, 1178, 1179, 1181, 1182, 1184 and 1225

Stanier Class 5MT 2–6–0 No. 42962 at Kirkby Stephen, on the SLS/MLS "Northernfells Railtour."

Ron Herbert

British Railways Class 3MT 2-6-0 No. 77003 pilots Class 4MT 2-6-0 No. 76049 on the "Stainmore Limited", the last steam-hauled train to travel over the route at Kirkby Stephen East on 20th January 1962.

Gavin Morrison

The "Stainmore Limited" prepares to relinquish the tablet for the very last time at Ravenstonedale, 20th January 1962.

Gavin Morrison

The last train steams through the January sunshine past milepost 7, between Warcop and Appleby, behind BR 2-6-0s Nos 77003 and 76049.

R. H. Leslie

The shed at Kirkby Stephen in its final operational form on 16th August 1958. The shed was variously enlarged in the 1860s. At the time this picture was taken the former NER 0-6-0s had gradually disappeared from the scene. The motive power for the Stainmore line being dominated by various British Railways' Standard classes and former LM Class 2MT and 4MTs. BR Class 4MTs 2-6-0s Nos 76020 and 76047, both smartly prepared, wait for their next turn of duty.

Gavin Morrison

In earlier LNER days, the shed is packed with ex-NER 0-6-0s. To the right of the picture is No. 147, a J21 later to become No. 5072 and then 65072, being finally withdrawn in 1950. The shed, like so many others of the time, was not only home for the Kirkby Stephen allocation of locomotives, but was also able to undertake many repair and fitting jobs.

The building adjoining the shed on the left-handside housed joiners, the mess room, brick store, the furnace and the iron store. The four-road shed was effectively a 'V' shape which surrounded a central fitting shop towards the rear of the building. The original shed was a two-road structure. The 1865 extension nearest the station had larger doors. Notice the fine array of ventilators which later disappeared.

Eddie Foster

Of additional interest is the wages sheet from Kirkby Stephen shed from 1885 which lists twelve drivers and twelve firemen (in pairs), beside the locomotive allocated to each, plus seven mineral guards and thirty engine cleaners.

In 1986 a survey was made and it was found that many railway families and relatives of railwaymen lived in the Kirkby Stephen area. It is interesting to identify how many surnames are common with the 1885 list.

The list read:

Drivers:
J. Stephenson
J. Tomlin
G. Sowerby
G. Snaith
W. Archer
B. Dobson

Firemen:
T. Hodgson
A. Smith
W. Burrows
J. Dawson
T. Danby
J. Chapman

Guards:
C. Bousfield
W. Brodrick
S. Chapman
J. Moss
G. Smith
R. Smith
W. Tengate
R. Hewitson
T. Raine
D. Hunn
J. Welsh
R. Bushby
J. Thompson
A. Richardson
H. Wright
R. Whitfield

J. Burrell
E. Horsley
J. Horsfield

Cleaners:
T. Bushby
J. Furness
R. Dobson
A. Blake
W. Watson
W. Dickinson
J. Whitehead
G. Murray
S. Alderson
C. Cooper
T. Brodrick
A. Hodgson
T. Birtle
W. Wilkinson
R. Dobson
W. Hutchinson
H. Raine
J. Proud
C. Thexton
S. Atkinson
J. Robinson
W. Muckelty
J.M. Sykes
J.G. Willey
T. Wright
J. Thompson
H. Thompson
J. Horsfield
R. Stephenson

Tebay Shed Allocation c1878

S&D 0-6-0s No.	Driver	Wordsell tank replacement 1889 Compound No.
1177	Robert Jackson	238
1213	Joseph Armstrong	523
1212	Matthew Willey	351
1224	Joseph Balmer	215
1222	James Glendinning	346
1032	Miles Robinson	345
1180	Robert Laidlaw	1145
1186	Thomas Miller	1072

The Wordsell tanks were replaced by Class T 0-8-0s c1902:

1708	R. Jackson
527	M. Willey
1704	R. Laidlaw
1002	M. Robinson

Tle Class Ts were allowed 40 empty wagons Tebay – West Auckland and 27 loaded wagons on the return trip. The compound 0-6-2 tanks they replaced were allowed 25 and 16 respectively.

Former Great Central Railway Class J10 0–6–0 No. 65176, on Kirkby Stephen shed, 5th December 1956.

Geoff Jackson

Penrith Shed Allocation c1900

Fletcher Class 901 2-4-0 No.	Driver	Fireman
167	J. Tomlin	J. Dawson (later George Armstrong)
911	J. Stephenson	Robert Armstrong

The Kirkby Stephen passenger engine was:

1066	W. Archer

Class 1001

1179	J. Raine
1181	J. Birrell
1182	J. Tweddle
1183	R. Busby
1184	J. Nicholson
1185	G. Smith

(Used on various goods and mineral trains.)

In the 1890s the Penrith engines included 2-2-2 engines Nos 190 and 1679, Fletcher 0-4-4WT No. 1020 (The first passenger firing turn in 1892 for Robert Armstrong), and in the mid-1890s rebuilt S&D 2-4-0s Nos 1267 (J. Stephenson/Robert Armstrong) and 1268 (J. Tomlin/G. Armstrong).

Nos 1267 and 1268 were replaced relatively quickly by the Fletcher 901s Nos. 911 and 167 these being far more suitable for handling the newly introduced Darlington – Penrith expresses. The two 2-4-0s, Nos 1267 and 1268 were poor steamers while the 901s were described by J. W. Armstrong as "grand little engines" and were the regular passenger power for 25 years.

Barnard Castle Shed

Smaller but similar to Kirkby Stephen, Barnard Castle shed closed very early in 1937, by which time its allocation had dwindled to one locomotive, Class E4 2-4-0 No. 7463.

Like Kirkby Stephen, the shed was later extended, the original one road shed being built in 1865 and doubled ten years later.

Amidst considerable controversey, extensive sections of both the Eden Valley branch and the Ravenstonedale – Tebay line were used after closure for the storage of 'seasonal surplus' mineral wagons. Here, "Austerity" 2-8-0 No. 90157 assembles wagons on 6th May 1962. Since then the whole section of the line between Ravenstonedale and Tebay has become a main road, obliterating almost all signs of the railway.

Ron Herbert

7

The Decline and Fight Against Closure

The gradual change in social travel and transport patterns, and the emergence of fairly widespread family vehicle ownership after the Second World War led to a gradual decline in many of the marginal services that the railway over Stainmore and through the Eden Valley offered.

Withdrawal of freight traffic services from local stations began in 1952 with the loss of Musgrave on 3rd November and Smardale, Gaisgill and Barras on 1st December 1952. Musgrave, Smardale, Ravenstonedale and Gaisgill also lost their passenger service on the same dates. Barras became an unstaffed halt on 1st December 1952, with Lartington becoming unstaffed in February 1953 and losing its freight service.

Kirkby Thore closed completely on 7th December 1953 on which date Temple Sowerby lost its passenger service. Cliburn struggled on until 17th September 1956 when it was closed completely.

However, the route continued to carry a steady and considerable freight traffic between East and West and was still popular as a summertime excursion route between the North East and Blackpool. In addition a significant number of local people used the service, particularly from Kirkby Stephen where the station was considerably more conveniently sited than many of those which had already closed such as Ravenstonedale, Musgrave, Kirkby Thore, Temple Sowerby, and Cliburn.

In the regional boundary alterations in the early 1950s the lines were divided to the east of Kirkby Stephen between the London, Midland Region and the North Eastern Region. Perhaps this could be viewed as the first ominous move in terms of the line's long term future. Nevertheless, at first little seemed to change, the freights still ran, although the traditional industries which they served were beginning to decline. Even so, westbound services in 1958 included consignments from Brancepeth, Derwenthaugh, Lambton, Marley Hill, Trimdon Grange, and Horden, and eastbound from the Westmorland quarries where tonnages despatched by rail were increasing.

The passenger services still operated with the various revisions already described. The whole national railway network made a profit in 1953 and as the '50s progressed it seemed as though the Stainmore line might well benefit.

The Conservative government of the day seemed content to allow the British Transport Commission to install quantities of concrete sleepers on the Valley branch, erect concrete cabins, and repaint Belah Viaduct in 1956, together with widespread signalling modifications, signal box rebuilding and refurbishing, etc.

On Monday 3rd February 1958, amidst limited pub-

Class 2MT 2-6-0 No. 46480 prepares to leave Tebay with the last service passenger train to Kirkby Stephen on 30th November 1952.

J. W. Armstrong

licity, the passenger services between Darlington, Barnard Castle and Penrith were handed over to the then relatively new diesel multiple units. The dmus could breast Stainmore Summit at 40 mph and the improved ride available was praised by many passengers. There were suggestions made that these trains could run all the way through from the North East to Keswick.

Hardly had the word spread regarding the attractions of the new dmu operations before the service was substantially decimated on 15th September. The most valuable trains of all to local users, the 7.34 am Kirkby Stephen to Darlington and the 10.34 pm return were withdrawn. Then approximately one year later, the bombshell of a closure proposal was dropped on 2nd December 1959, after a year in which the BTC said the passengers carried figures were "disappointing" (but the 1958 passenger revenue figures had shown an increase of £1,400 p.a.).

It is unfair to blame the rail user of the time for not fully anticipating what was going on behind the scenes. By the 1980s we had become accustomed to the deceit surrounding most rail closure issues. Any present day timetable alteration on any line which may be threatened with closure is viewed with justifiable, deep cynicism, as is any expense which may create an administrative case for closure. The now standard type of adage, "If they paint your station, they must be going to close it", holds more than a suggestion of truth.

In 1959 the trusting conservative community of Kirkby Stephen was suddenly faced with the prospect of a railway closure which would lead to the loss of hundreds of jobs, and the subsequent depopulation of

Bill 1 (top left)

BRITISH RAILWAYS

EXCURSIONS TO
Barnard Castle
Kirkby Stephen   Appleby
Penrith and Keswick

SUNDAYS

18th June to 3rd September 1961

OUTWARD		SECOND CLASS RETURN FARES					RETURN:	
		Barnard Castle	Kirkby Stephen	Appleby East	Penrith	Keswick		
	am	s. d.	s. d.	s. d.	s. d.	s. d.		pm
†Saltburn ... ...dep	8 55	A 9/6	13/-	15/-	17/-	21/-	Keswick ... ...dep	6 30
†Marske ... ... ,,	8 59	A 9/-	12/6	14/6	17/-	20/6	Penrith ... ... ,,	7 20
†Redcar East ... ... ,,	9 3	A 8/10	12/-	14/-	16/6	20/-	Appleby East ... ... ,,	7 44
†Redcar Central ... ,,	9 8	A 8/10	12/-	14/-	16/6	20/-	Kirkby Stephen ... ,,	8 7
†Grangetown ... ... ,,	9 17	A 7/10	11/6	13/-	16/-	19/6	Barnard Castle ... ,,	8 50
†South Bank ... ... ,,	9 21	A 7/8	11/-	13/-	15/6	19/-	North Road ... arr	9 17
†Cargo Fleet ... ... ,,	9 24	A 7/6	10/6	13/-	15/6	19/-	Darlington ... ... ,,	9 23
†Middlesbrough ... ,,	9 29	A 7/4	10/6	12/6	15/-	18/6	Eaglescliffe ... ... ,,	9 57
†Thornaby ... ... ,,	9 34	A 6/8	10/-	12/-	14/6	18/-	Stockton ... ... ,,	10 17
*West Hartlepool ... ,,	8 35	A 9/-	12/-	14/-	17/-	20/6	Billingham ... ... ,,	10 25
*Billingham ... ... ,,	8 48	7/6	11/-	12/6	14/6	19/-	West Hartlepool ... ,,	10 35
*Stockton ... ... ,,	8 57	A 6/8	10/-	12/-	14/6	18/-	Thornaby ... ... ,,	10 4
†Eaglescliffe ... ... ,,	9 41	A 6/-	9/6	11/6	14/-	17/6	Middlesbrough ... ,,	10 9
Darlington ... ... ,,	10 2	A 4/-	7/6	10/-	12/6	16/-	Cargo Fleet ... ... ,,	10 15
North Road ... ... ,,	10 7	A 3/10	7/-	9/6	12/-	15/6	South Bank ... ... ,,	10 18
Barnard Castle ...arr	10 38	—	—	4/6	6/6	9/6	Grangetown ... ... ,,	10 22
Kirkby Stephen ... ,,	11 22	—	—	—	—	—	Redcar Central ... ,,	10 33
Appleby East ... ... ,,	11 45	—	—	—	—	—	Redcar East ... ... ,,	10 36
	pm						Marske ... ... ,,	10 41
Penrith ... ... ,,	12 10	—	—	—	—	—	Saltburn ... ... ,,	10 45
‡Keswick ... ... ,,	1 6	—	—	—	—	—		

†—Change at Darlington in each direction   ‡—Change at Penrith in each direction
*—Change at Thornaby and Darlington in each direction   A—Cheap Day Fare—Any Train—Any Day

Children under three years of age, free; three years and under fourteen half fares.

(Fractions of a 1d. reckoned as 1d.)

TICKETS CAN BE OBTAINED IN ADVANCE
at the stations or accredited rail ticket agencies

Further information will be supplied on application to the stations, agencies, or to the District Commercial Superintendent, British Railways, Zetland House, Middlesbrough, Tel. 45481 (Ext. 252)

NOTICE AS TO CONDITIONS
These tickets are issued subject to the Regulations and Conditions in the Commission's Publications and Notices applicable to British Railways.
Luggage allowances are as set out in the conditions.

Published by British Railways (N.E. Region) 5/61   Printed in Great Britain   Dick Bros. Ltd. M'bro.—C 4

Bill 2 (top right)

Half-day Excursions
TO

CARLISLE

WEEKDAYS

FROM 15th JUNE TO 12th SEPTEMBER 1959

FROM	TIMES OF DEPARTURE	RETURN FARE SECOND CLASS
	am	s d
KIRKBY STEPHEN EAST	10-21	6/3
WARCOP ... ... ,,	10-29	6/-
APPLEBY EAST ... ... ,,	10-39	5/6
CLIFTON MOOR ... ... ,,	10-53	3/6
	SX SO	
CARLISLE ... ... arr.	11-32 11-37	

Passengers go forward from Penrith by the 11-13 am (SX), 11-18 am (SO) train to Carlisle.   Return same day from Carlisle at 7-55 to connect with the 8-30 pm from Penrith.   Appleby and Kirkby Stephen passengers may if they so desire return to Appleby West and Kirkby Stephen West by the Services shown overleaf.

(SX)—Saturdays Excepted.   (SO)—Saturdays Only.

Children under three years of age, free ; three years and under fourteen, half-fares.

NOTICE AS TO CONDITIONS
These tickets are issued subject to the British Transport Commission's published Regulations and Conditions applicable to British Railways exhibited at their stations or obtainable free of charge at station booking offices.

TICKETS CAN BE OBTAINED IN ADVANCE AT STATIONS AND OFFICIAL RAILWAY AGENTS.

Further information will be supplied on application to the Stations, Official Railway Agents, or to Mr. J. A. K. GRAY, District Traffic Superintendent, Citadel Station, Carlisle. Telephone 25411 (Extn. 6).

TRAVEL IN RAIL COMFORT

June 1959   PX.350/52   BR 35000

PLEASE TURN OVER

LONDON MIDLAND

J. Wadsworth Ltd., Printers, Grange-over-Sands   Q.9

Bill 3 (bottom left)

DAY EXCURSIONS
TO

CARLISLE

DAILY EXCEPT SUNDAYS

UNTIL FURTHER NOTICE

OUTWARD AND RETURN BY ANY TRAIN

FROM	Third Class Return Fare
	s d
Kirkby Stephen East ...	8 9
Warcop ... ... ,,	7 9
Appleby East ... ... ,,	7/-
Cliburn ... ... ,,	5 3

TICKETS ARE VALID FOR RETURN ON DAY OF ISSUE ONLY

Children under three years of age, free : three years and under fourteen, half-fares.

CONDITIONS OF ISSUE OF EXCURSION AND OTHER TICKETS AT LESS THAN ORDINARY FARES

These tickets are issued subject to the British Transport Commission's published Regulations and Conditions applicable to British Railways exhibited at their stations or obtainable free of charge at the station booking offices.

TICKETS CAN BE OBTAINED IN ADVANCE AT STATIONS AND AGENCIES

Further information will be supplied on application to the Stations, Agencies, or to Mr. E. LORD, District Traffic Superintendent, Citadel Station, Carlisle. Telephone 25411 (Extn. 6)

June, 1954   P. 354/52   B.R. 35000

BRITISH RAILWAYS

Barrow Printing Co. Ltd.   Q 376

Bill 4 (bottom right)

ATTRACTIVE EXCURSIONS
TO

KESWICK

BASSENTHWAITE LAKE

WEEKDAYS

13th JUNE TO 11th SEPTEMBER 1960

FROM	TIMES OF DEPARTURE	TO	
		Keswick	Bassenthwaite Lake
	pm	s d	s d
KIRKBY STEPHEN EAST ...	12-4	6/9	7/6
WARCOP	12-13	6/3	7/-
APPLEBY EAST	12-21	5/3	6/6
CLIFTON MOOR	12-37	3/9	5/-
		pm	pm
ARRIVAL TIMES		2-3	2-21

Passengers change at Penrith and connect with the 1-30 pm train from Penrith.

RETURN ARRANGEMENTS
Passengers return on day of outward journey from Bassenthwaite Lake at 7-14 pm SX and 7-35 pm SO, Keswick 7-50 pm, to connect with the 8-30 pm from Penrith.
SO—Saturdays only.   SX—Saturdays excepted.

Children under three years of age, free ; three years and under fourteen, half-fares.

TICKETS CAN BE OBTAINED IN ADVANCE AT THE STATIONS AND OFFICIAL RAILWAY AGENTS.

Further information will be supplied on application to the Stations, Official Railway Agents, or to Mr. J. A. K. GRAY, District Traffic Superintendent, Citadel Station, Carlisle. Telephone 25411 (Extn. 6).

TRAVEL IN RAIL COMFORT

June 1960   PX.350/52   BR 35000

LONDON MIDLAND

J. Wadsworth Ltd., Printers, Grange-over-Sands   Q.10

TRAIN SERVICE
Tees-side with the Lake District
via Darlington and Penrith

13th JUNE to 11th SEPTEMBER 1960

		WEEKDAYS			SUNDAYS
		a m 4g 25	a m 9h 51	p m 2 57	a m E
York ... ... dep.		4g 25	9h 51	2 57	E
Saltburn ... ... dep.		4 55	9 25	2 55	8 55
Redcar Central ... ... ,,		5 8	9 38	3 8	9 8
Middlesbrough ... ... ,,		5 29	9 59	3 29	9 29
West Hartlepool ... ... ,,		—	9m 1	3B 3	8B 35
Stockton ... ... ,,		—	9m 20	3B 22	8B 57
Thornaby ... ... ,,		5 34	10 4	3 34	9 34
Darlington ... ... dep.		6 23	10 50	4 34	10 2
North Road ... ... ,,		6 27	10 54	4 38	10 7
Piercebridge ... ... ,,		6 34	11 1	4 45	—
Gainford ... ... ,,		6 41	11 8	4 52	—
Winston ... ... ,,		6 45	11 12	5 0	—
Broomielaw ... ... ,,		6 52	11 19	5 7	—
Barnard Castle ... ,,		7 1	11 24	5 13	10 43
Lartington ... ... ,,		7 6	11 29	5 18	—
Bowes ... ... ,,		7 14	11 37	5 26	—
Barras ... ... ,,		7 30	11 53	5 42	—
			p m		
Kirkby Stephen East ... ,,		7 42	12 4	5 54	11 27
Warcop ... ... ,,		7 50	12 13	6 2	11 37
Appleby East ... ... ,,		8 0	12 21	6 11	11 45
Clifton Moor ... ... ,,		8 14	12 37	6 26	—
					p m
Penrith ... ... arr.		8 23	12 45	6 35	12 10
Keswick ... ... arr.		10P 52	2P 3	8kP52	1P 6
Carlisle ... ... ,,		8P 47	1P 33	7P 18	12P 51

		WEEKDAYS					SUN-DAYS
		SX a m 9P 52	SO a m 9P 52	SO p m 1P 47	SX p m 1P 47	p m 7P 55	E p m 4 20
Carlisle ... ... dep.		9P 52	9P 52	1P 47	1P 47	7P 55	4 20
Keswick ... ... ,,		7Pz 49	9P 38	2P 12	2P 12	7Pb29	6 30
Penrith ... ... dep.		10 55	10 55	3 10	3 17	8 30	7 20
Clifton Moor ... ... arr.		11 2	11 2	3 17	3 28	8 38	—
Appleby East ... ... ,,		11 20	11 20	3 35	3 45	8 55	7 44
Warcop ... ... ,,		11 27	11 27	3 42	3 53	9 2	7 52
Kirkby Stephen East ... ,,		11 38	11 38	3 53	4 3	9 13	8 2
Barras ... ... ,,		11 51	11 51	4 7	4 17	9 26	—
		p m	p m				
Bowes ... ... ,,		12 6	12 6	4 22	4 32	9 41	—
Lartington ... ... ,,		12 13	12 13	4 29	4 39	9 48	—
Barnard Castle ... ,,		12 17	12 17	4 33	4 43	9 52	8 48
Broomielaw ... ... ,,		12 25	12 35	4 50	4 50	10 5	—
Winston ... ... ,,		12 30	12 41	4 57	4 57	10 11	—
Gainford ... ... ,,		12 35	12 45	5 1	5 1	10 15	—
Piercebridge ... ... ,,		12 42	12 52	5 8	5 8	10 22	—
North Road ... ... ,,		12 49	12 59	5 17	5 15	10 29	8 17
Darlington ... ... ,,		12 53	1 3	5 27	5 22	10 33	9 23
Thornaby ... ... arr.		1 34	1 34	6 4	6 4	11 4	10 4
Stockton ... ... ,,		1B 47	1B 47	6B 47	6B 47	11r 11	10B 17
West Hartlepool ... ... ,,		2B 8	2B 8	7B 5	7B 5	11r 30	10B 35
Middlesbrough ... ... ,,		1 39	1 39	6 9	6 9	11 9	10 9
Redcar Central ... ... ,,		2 3	2 3	6 33	6 33	11 33	10 33
Saltburn ... ... ,,		2 15	2 15	6 45	6 45	11 45	10 45
York ... ... arr.		2 17	2 6	6 38	6 28	1a 12	12a 43

B—Change at Thornaby
E—Not after 4th September
P—Change at Penrith
g—On Mondays departs York 4.41 a.m.
h—On Saturdays departs York 9.30 a.m.
k—Monday to Fridays 4th July to 2nd Sept. arrives Keswick 7.28 p.m.
a—a.m.

b—On Saturdays departs Keswick 7.50 p.m.
m—On Mondays to Fridays departs West Hartlepool 9.31 a.m. and Stockton 9.50 a.m. change Eaglescliffe
r—Change at Eaglescliffe
Z—From 4th July to 2nd Sept. departs Keswick 9.54 a.m.

C3   See other side for details of Fares and Excursions   B6/40

EXAMPLES OF DAY FARES
TO

From	Appleby East	Barnard Castle	Carlisle	Keswick	Kirkby Stephen	Penrith
	s d	s d	s d	s d	s d	s d
Barnard Castle	7/6	—	12/6	12/6	5/9	10/-
Billingham	14/-	7/3	15/-	17/6	13/-	15/-
Darlington	11/-	4/-	15/-	16/6	10/-	14/-
Middlesbrough	14/-	7/3	15/-	17/6	13/-	15/-
Redcar Central / Redcar East }	15/-	8/6	15/-	17/6	13/6	15/-
Saltburn	15/-	9/6	15/-	17/6	14/6	15/-
Stockton / Thornaby }	13/6	6/7	15/-	17/6	12/6	15/-
West Hartlepool ...	15/-	8/6	15/-	17/6	13/6	15/-

DAY LINE TICKETS
The 15/- Day Line ticket (Northern District) enables you to travel all day, any day via the Darlington—Penrith Line, and to Keswick on payment of 3/7d. extra. See special folder for details.

HALF DAY EXCURSIONS
Half day excursions at reduced fares are available from certain stations by selected trains. For particulars see handbills.

COMBINED RAIL—ROAD—STEAMER EXCURSIONS
Combined Rail—Road—Steamer Excursions are available on certain days from selected stations. For particulars see handbills.

Further information will be supplied on application to stations, Railway Ticket Agencies, Mr. D. S. Lewis, District Commercial Superintendent, Middlesbrough, Telephone 45481 (Ext. 252), Mr. E. I. Boyd, District Traffic Superintendent, Barrow, Telephone 1445 (Ext. 13), or to Mr. J. A. K. Gray, District Traffic Superintendent, Carlisle, Telephone 25411 (Ext. 6).

Published by British Railways (North Eastern Region). 6/60 Printed in Gt. Britain. Jowett & Sowry Ltd. Leeds 1   C3

PLEASE RETAIN THIS BILL FOR REFERENCE

Attractive Excursions

DARLINGTON

WEEKDAYS

13th JUNE TO 11th SEPTEMBER 1960

	OUTWARD TIMES	RETURN FARES SECOND CLASS
	am	s d
APPLEBY EAST .... depart	11-20	8/3
WARCOP ,,	11-27	7/-
KIRKBY STEPHEN EAST .... ,,	11-38	6/3
	pm	
DARLINGTON .... arrive	12-53 SX / 1-3 SO	
Return same day from DARLINGTON at	4-34 pm	

SX—Saturdays Excepted.   SO—Saturdays Only.

Children under three years of age, free ; three years and under fourteen, half-fares.

TICKETS CAN BE OBTAINED IN ADVANCE AT STATIONS AND OFFICIAL RAILWAY AGENTS

Further information will be supplied on application to the Stations, Official Railway Agents, or to Mr. J. A. K. GRAY, District Traffic Superintendent, Citadel Station, Carlisle. Telephone 25411 (Extn. 6).

TRAVEL IN RAIL COMFORT

June 1960   PX 350/52   BR 35000

LONDON MIDLAND

J. Wadsworth Ltd., Printers, Grange-over-Sands   Q 7

what was essentially an isolated area, particularly in winter. All credit to many of the stalwarts of the communities likely to be affected by the proposed closure, they managed with limited means to group and begin the fight to try to save their railway.

They analysed the closure proposal document issued by the British Transport Commission of the day which was riddled with inaccuracy and written in the usual platitudinous vein. By early 1960 the objectors to the proposed closure had managed to become a considerable irritant to the steam rollering tactics employed by the BTC.

The respective Transport Users' Consultative Committees were of course involved and from reading through the now archival material, which circulated at the time, it would seem that they were unsure whether to laugh or cry regarding which way they should present their reports to the minister. The joint North Eastern and North Western committees heard 51 objectors to the proposed closure on 24th February 1960 at Carlisle. (Notice the distance of about 45 miles from Kirkby Stephen, the loss of a day's pay if you wish to attend, etc.). The objectors included MPs, in particular the Labour MP for Bishop Auckland, Mr. H.J. Boyden, the relevant county councils, borough councils, parish, rural and urban district councils, plus the Ramblers' Association, Youth Hostels Association, cyclists' touring clubs, and representatives from commerce, industry and a number of private individuals.

An investigation into the memorandum submitted by the BTC and the assessment of all the objectors' statements led the joint TUCCs to recommend to the Central TUCC that freight traffic should be re-routed via Newcastle and Carlisle as proposed by the BTC in their memorandum on 2nd December 1959. They further recommended that passenger receipts should be increased by attracting tourist traffic.

Had the joint TUCC's report been heeded we may well have had a single lined, radio-signalled Stainmore line in the 1990s to enjoy, but it was not to be. The freights began to run via Newcastle and Carlisle, an extra 77 route miles in some cases, on 4th July 1960.

The North Western TUCC informed objectors on 10th November 1960 that the BTC considered the diversion of freight traffic via Newcastle and Carlisle was now satisfactory - and that the passenger service should now be withdrawn.

The estimated net saving by withdrawal of the passenger service was over £36,000 after allowing for an estimated loss of receipts of £19,147. These figures bore little relation to the original BTC memorandum disclosures which stated that net revenue could be improved by £103,274 if the line were to close, and that recovery of redundant materials would realise a net credit of £257,000. In the event the meeting of 9th December decided to postpone the decision for another year.

The North Western and North Eastern TUCCs invited objectors to attend a meeting at the Royal Station Hotel, Newcastle on Friday 9th at 11.30 am for the TUCC to explain the reasons for the various decisions that had been taken about the future of the line, and to give an indication as to the final recommendations.

Just how people who wished to attend, like Mr F.W. Parrott of Kirkby Stephen, a non-driver, was expected to get there when the first train of the day from Kirkby Stephen to the North East left at 11.37 am is not known!

Another meeting between the TUCCs in January 1961 could not agree on an eventual decision. The North West voted for closure, the North East voted for retention. The Central TUCC bounced the decision back to the area TUCCs without submitting the matter to the Minister of Transport.

In June 1961 the North East TUCC announced that it had agreed to the closure. The matter was then submitted to the Conservative Minister of Transport, Ernest Marples, who approved the closure on 7th December 1961.

With miraculous speed both London, Midland and North Eastern regions of British Railways announced less than a fortnight later that the last train would run on Saturday 20th January 1962.

The objectors still fought on bravely and before this

BRITISH RAILWAYS

WITHDRAWAL OF PASSENGER TRAIN SERVICE

Barnard Castle

Penrith Branch

from 22nd January 1962

AMENDED SERVICES BETWEEN
DARLINGTON, BARNARD CASTLE and
MIDDLETON-IN-TEESDALE

(replacing Table No. 39 in North Eastern England Time Table dated 11th September, 1961 to 17th June, 1962, inclusive).

CLOSURE OF KIRKBY STEPHEN TO TEBAY BRANCH FOR FREIGHT TRAFFIC

On and from 22nd January, 1962, the passenger train service will be withdrawn between Barnard Castle and Penrith. The stations affected are as follows:—

Lartington Halt	Kirkby Stephen East
Bowes	Warcop
Barras Halt	Appleby East
	Clifton Moor

Alternative facilities for passengers

The area affected by the closure is served by buses operated by the following:—

Durham District Services Ltd.	G.N.E. Motor Services
Ribble Motor Services Ltd.	Maudes Bus Services
United Automobile Services Ltd.	Primrose Deluxe Coaches

Alternative arrangements for Parcels and other Passenger Rated Merchandise.

Facilities exist at Barnard Castle, Kirkby Stephen West, Appleby West and Penrith stations for dealing with parcels and other passenger rated merchandise for the affected area.

Alternative arrangements for Freight Train Traffic
Barnard Castle—Penrith Branch

Freight traffic will continue to be dealt with at Kirkby Stephen East, Warcop and Appleby East and at Clifton Moor under unstaffed goods depot arrangements. Existing arrangements for the collection and delivery of small consignments throughout the area will continue.

Bowes and Temple Sowerby goods depots will be closed and the alternatives will be Barnard Castle and Kirkby Stephen East Goods stations respectively.

Kirkby Stephen—Tebay Branch

Freight facilities will be withdrawn from Ravenstonedale and the alternative depot will be Kirkby Stephen East.

The District Commercial Superintendent, Middlesbrough (Telephone Middlesbrough 45481) or the District Traffic Superintendent, Citadel Station, Carlisle (Telephone Carlisle 25411) will provide further information on application or, if desired, arrangements will be made for a Railway Service Representative to call.

sordid chapter about rail closure manipulation is brought to a close, their last ditch attempt to prevent closure is worthy of mention and great praise.

A meeting of the objectors at Barnard Castle early in January 1962 decided to ask the minister to receive a deputation before the closure date of 20th January.

Mr H.J. Boyden MP presided over a meeting which included:
Alderman J.F. Whitehead (Mayor) Appleby Borough Council.
Mr H.A. Jones (Town Clerk)
Mr F.W. Parrott, North Westmorland RDC and Kirkby Stephen Parish Council.
Mr F. Wilson, NWRDC
Nr R.C. Howell (Clerk) NWRDC
Mr A.M. Fell, Kirkby Stephen Chamber of Trade
Mr F.H. Rogers (Dep. Clerk) Westmorland County Council
Mr P. Sanderson, Keswick UDC
Mr Watson Sayer of Kirkby Stephen.
etc.

The Deputation intended to present evidence to the minister which would highlight alleged errors, misleading omissions, etc., which had been made in the submissions by the BTC. They would also have liked to have pointed out to the minister that the method of conduct at the TUCC inquiry in Newcastle gave no opportunity to objectors to question the commission's witnesses.

The Deputation also intended to inform the minister that the proposed closure would cause damage to the community out of all proportion to anything the BTC would save.

Amongst the people present at the Barnard Castle meeting was Mr W.E. Sayer, a local businessman who maintained that the BTC case for closure was so inac-

curate that he would like to buy the line and operate it himself! His offer was of course refused, but nevertheless his down to earth interpretation of the situation makes interesting reading. (I wonder why they did not give him a chance? They could not possibly have feared that he might have succeeded, could they?).

The sort of errors and misleading omissions in the BTC memorandum the Deputation were concerned about are detailed as follows:

Objectors had already observed:

1. The BTC were committed by the findings of the original TUCC hearings to publicise the new dmu operated passenger services and to generally try to increase tourist usage of the route. The Deputation felt that very little had been done in this respect.

2. If the revenue from conveying minerals from the quarries at Brough and Hartley were taken into consideration the total receipts on the line would exceed the cost of maintaining the service as submitted by the BTC.

In this respect the administration of the line by two separate regions added to the difficulties and costs. The objectors maintained that the line should be considered as a whole and not merely as it affected the London, Midland or the North Eastern regions. Further it was considered that the matter should be regarded as the responsibility of the BTC as a whole and that the closing of an allegedly unremunerative line should not be permitted on the grounds submitted in the BTC memorandum.

3. It was further recommended by the objectors that consideration be given to running passenger services at more convenient times, etc., and that additional effort to attract more freight to the route should be made. (An important beef exporter from the Eden Valley and possible new traffic between Teesside and Shap for slag traffic for Tarmac were two such possibilities at the time.)

4. It was claimed that it was the duty of the BTC to provide a public service and whilst it was appreciated that any service should endeavour to pay its way, this should be achieved by more efficient and economic working, thereby reducing costs and simultaneously seeking additional revenue.

It was not accepted that the only option was effectively complete closure.

More specifically the following further points were considered. All relate to the original BTC memorandum containing "The Case for Closure".

a) The revenue particulars did not include receipts from Hartley Quarries and Brough Quarries. Hartley Quarries paid £83,951 to British Railways for the year ending November 1959.

The Hartley Quarry freight bill was continuing at the rate of about £10,000 per month.

The figures from Brough Quarry (W.E. Sayer) were in the region of 3,000 tons per week, ie about £3,000 per week.

b) No allowance was made for increased costs which would undoubtedly be incurred trailing freight round via Newcastle and Carlisle.

c) No assurance was given that new freight traffic would be charged at the same rate/ton travelling via Newcastle and Carlisle compared with the Stainmore rate. Similarly, no assurance was given that a Barnard Castle-Kirkby Stephen passenger would be able to travel via Newcastle and Carlisle at the same fare as that over Stainmore.

d) A figure of £257,000 was disclosed by the BTC as the amount which would be realised by recovering redundant assets. This should have no bearing on any proposal, as this credit was a capital asset already paid for. This figure was inserted purely for effect.

e) A splendid non-sensical figure was also included for a new engine shed roof at Kirkby Stephen of £45,000/£50,000. Just eight years later steam locomotives had disappeared from the railway lines of Britain. The roof at Kirkby Stephen shed could surely have waited, or been removed in similar manner to those on many other deteriorating steam sheds of the day.

f) The BTC had already spent £9,000 on additional sidings at Millom to cater for the diversion of freight via Newcastle and Carlisle before the Minister's decision of the fate of the Stainmore line. Therefore this figure was irrelevant.

g) The populations served by the stations on the Stainmore route were disclosed in the BTC memorandum as follows:

	BTC Figure	1951 General Census Figure (The correct one!)
Barras station		
Stainmore	NIL	587
Brough	NIL	651
Kirkby Stephen East		
Kirkby Stephen	1,200	1,718

In fact these figures continue in this vein concluding that only 4,550 people could be construed as being in the Stainmore line catchment area. The real figure was in excess of 13,000.

h) No figure for revenue for freight from Kirkby Stephen East, Warcop or Appleby East was included.

j) The total revenue for traffic and freight for the twelve months ended 31st December 1958 was stated by the BTC to be:

Passenger		£ 4,915
Traffic from NE		£17,940
Traffic from NW		£ 3,502
Parcels		£ 2,713
Freight		£17,252
	Total	£47,322

This figure excludes the £83,951 from Hartley Quarry, the revenue from Brough Quarry (Warcop) and freight from Kirkby Stephen East, Warcop and Appleby East.

The original BTC estimated net savings from closing the route would only be £103,274. Therefore if all the figures were taken into account the line was making a handsome profit!

k) The figures for staff levels etc. were grossly exaggerated. By the time January 1962 had arrived, the staff levels had already been pruned from 170 to about 75. This economy did not appear in the BTC report. All in all the whole closure proposal appears to have been a contrived disgrace.

The brave objectors had already written to the Minister pointing out *all* the above and many more salient facts. The Deputation asked to meet the

Minister after their meeting in Barnard Castle on 5th January 1962, but they received a reply addressed to the Clerk of the Barnard Castle Rural Council, Mr G. Guyll, intimating that the Minister, Mr Ernest Marples, was not prepared to receive a deputation.

He pointed out that the closure proposals had been under consideration by the Transport Users' Consultative Committees for about two years, his letter continued, "During that period users had ample opportunity to make representations about the proposals. There is no doubt that full advantage was taken of those facilities".

He concluded that he had examined all the evidence and saw no reason to disagree with the Committee's views that any hardship to users would be outweighed by the financial savings arising from the closure. He was unable to agree that the committee machinery had proved in anyway defective and in his view no useful purpose would be served by his receiving a deputation. And so it ended with great bitterness and disappointment.

The Press accounts of the last train just three weeks later serve as a reminder of the fight to save this marvellous route. Now thirty years on from the closure the folly of the BTC and Ernest Marples, the TUCCs and the government of the day is there for all to see.

American tourists include visits in their itinerary to see the gaunt remaining stone splays of Belah Viaduct and marvel that a viaduct once stood there. One wonders what tourist potential there would be in trips on the line if it still existed?

All the while, heavy road transport slogs its way over the A66 within sight of the ruined trackbed where millions of tons of coke and limestone and millions of passengers - local people, holidaymakers, etc. - once passed without significantly disturbing anyone.

The approach to Stainmore Summit, looking east as shown in this sad picture taken in May 1962 after demolition had begun. The haste with which the Stainmore line was destroyed caused great concern and considerable regret.

Ron Herbert

Mineral wagons stored on the line in May 1962.   *Ron Herbert*

The final protest at Kirkby Stephen. Local people display their justifiable disgust at the closure of their railway. The man second from the right was Mr Watson Sayer a local quarry owner and businessman who offered to buy the whole line from British Railways, so convinced was he that operated and managed properly it could have been successful. (See the copy of one of his many letters of informed protest.) His offer was of course dismissed. I wonder what would have happened if he'd been given a chance?

T. Walsh

Quite literally this time, the very last train makes its slow progress towards the Summit from Bleathgill, taking up the track behind it on 4th July 1962.

Alec Corder

Above and below: The very end at Ravenstonedale. The track is removed – after 101 years progress is reversed.

Alec Corder

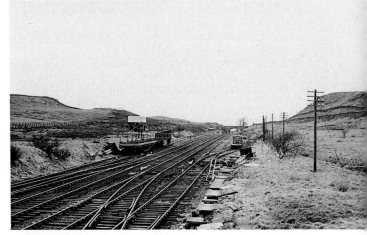

The approach to the Summit from the west, photographed in May 1962.

Ron Herbert

8

Stainmore

by J.W. Armstrong

So now in 1992, all that remains of the Stainmore and Eden Valley lines is a short branch to Warcop and the earthworks which thus far have not succumbed to 'progress' in terms of road construction. A few of the stone viaducts remain as do various bridges and ruined signal boxes, platelayers' huts, etc. An appendix prepared in September 1986 lists some of the more interesting items still remaining. Here and there remain stations, some tastefully renovated as private dwellings. It is difficult to imagine that just over thirty years ago the situation was vastly different.

Of all the 'Stainmore' enthusiasts, Mr J.W. Armstrong must surely be the most famous. The Armstrong family were associated with the route since the time of opening and JWA's account of a journey over Stainmore – interspersed with anecdotes – serves as a tribute to the memory of this now defunct route.

Robert Richardson, J. W. Armstrong's great-grandfather took the first passenger trains from Barnard Castle to Tebay, Clifton & Lowther, Penrith and Middleton-in-Teesdale. His engine was No. 111 *Stag*. Joseph Armstrong, J.W. Armstrong's grandfather drove Class B compound No. 523 from Tebay between 1889 and 1903 having started at Tebay in 1878. Joseph Armstrong had four sons, the eldest being J.W. Armstrong's father Robert who also worked on the footplate, as did J.W. Armstrong's Uncle George!

I have resisted the temptation to edit J.W. Armstrong's article "Stainmore", instead it is included in full, as it is a splendid account of the line in its heyday.

To any lover of the old NER, the line across the Pennines, with the wild and romantic country it traversed, was a magnet that could not be resisted and, long before rail tours were thought of, one could often come across some enthusiast making the trip as a matter of interest rather than an essential business trip.

My own interest in the line dates back to very early days of boyhood, with holidays in the Kirkby Stephen-Penrith areas, when the 901s were in practically sole charge of the passenger trains, and a few old "Quakers" ambled along the Eden Valley to Cockermouth. But the family tradition dates much further back than that, as I belonged to a family of footplatemen going back to the first days of the traffic over Stainmore, and was extra fortunate in that my father was a keen loco enthusiast apart from his job, and any type of loco that he came across was of great interest to him. He had great loyalty to the NE and their engines, and to him there was nothing as good!

All this stemmed way back to 1859, when a young miner was laid off work owing to a labour dispute, and spent his spare time watching some of those ungainly Stockton & Darlington products performing near the Mason's Arms crossing at Shildon. One day a driver shouted down to him, in the broad Shildon dialect, "If thou thinks thou can fire one of these, away down to t'shed and sign on". Without more ado, the young miner, who was Joseph Armstrong, my grandfather made his way to the old shed at Shildon, and easily passed the medical standard required, and as he was a good writer (no mean feat in those days) he was soon fixed up as a cleaner. Things were booming at Shildon in those days, collieries in the area were busy, and the line over Stainmore was well on the way to completion, which would mean an outlet to the West for Durham coke, and return loads of iron-ore for Teesside.

The new line, which was to be called the South Durham & Lancashire Union Railway, would be worked by the Stockton & Darlington Company from the start and it was opened in sections as follows, mostly in single line. The original line from Darlington to Barnard Castle, which had been opened by a separate Company in July 1856, and worked by the Stockton & Darlington Railway, was diverted to a new through station at Barnard Castle, and the existing terminus made into the goods depot. Just slightly east of this diversion, having commenced at Spring Gardens Junction, on the Haggerleases branch from Bishop Auckland. Goods traffic began running from this point to Barras on 26th March 1861, and goods and mineral traffic through to Tebay on 4th July of that year, and on 8th August 1861, a service of two trains for passengers began running each way between Saltburn, Darlington and Tebay. The final development of the line came on 12th April 1862, followed by passenger traffic on 7th June the same year. These services for a short while ran to Clifton & Lowther station on the Lancaster & Carlisle main line, but after a very short period, running powers were obtained to allow the station at Penrith to be used, and a short piece of isolated S&D line, from Eamont Bridge Junction, on the West Coast Main Line, to Redhills Junction on the Cockermouth, Keswick & Penrith line, enabled through running to be made with traffic for the Cumberland area. This piece of line was maintained by the NER and the LNER, till it was lifted in the late 1930s. The signals were NE Southern Division type, and it is interesting to note that NE traffic using the line in the last 15 years of its existence was practically nil, but the line was intact. About 1935, the LMS sent some of their Class 2 4-4-0s to work over the Keswick line, and as the 'table at Penrith was too short to turn a 2, why not use the semi-derelict Redhills loop to turn on? This was duly done, but for some reason or other, probably because of running powers, the LNE whipped a rail out at each end, and the curve lay unused.

Mention can now be made of the final rail development in the Barnard Castle area with the opening in 1865 of the Tees

Valley line, which left our main line at Tees Valley Junction, just west of the Tees Viaduct, and ran to what was then expected to be a temporary terminus at Middleton-in-Teesdale, where the station is in Yorkshire, and the town in Co. Durham. The Directors of this small line, again to be worked by the S&DR, had visions of reaching Alston, but to anyone who knows this area, the intervening distance is amongst the most lonely areas one could name in this country, and they must have expected a mighty amount of lead traffic to cover the cost of a line such as they envisaged.

By the time this little line was opened, the Stockton & Darlington line itself had been taken over by the mighty North Eastern, for the first ten years as a working arrangement only, a factor which kept alive a lot of tradition belonging to the pioneer line. In fact this was carried on as the Central Division of the NE for some 40 years after the initial take-over, and even then it did not die out: an old signalman I knew at Eaglescliffe in the 1930s always referred to "Leeds Northern" and "S&D" platforms at the station, and a long siding at Cockermouth was always called the Stockton siding.

I will now try to make a journey by memory over the route and as good a place as any to start would be at the old West Auckland laden sidings, just west of the shed. Readers will have to imagine we have left Bishop Auckland on the first train, as actually these notes are built around a trip made some 30 odd years ago. In those days rail tours were unknown, and traversing a certain line had to be done the hard way, often by the humble pushbike! By this means, using walking tour and other forms of cheap travel, careful planning could yield a very pleasant outing.

Our steed would be a Durham Class O, working through to Middleton and loaded to some 4-5 bogies. Just before reaching the sheds at Fieldon Bridge, the Shildon Tunnel branch would be noticed on the left. Opened in 1856, it dispensed with the famous Brusselton incline of the old Stockton & Darlington Railway, although the track must have been in fair shape for years after, as Joseph Armstrong, my grandfather, worked a Tebay-Shildon mineral over the route some time in the early '80s, which was reputed to have been the last train over. There was quite a lot of track with the old stone sleepers still in situ as late as 1923, and the pilot used to run from Shildon to the cottages at Brusselton with coal later than that; this side of the incline was laid with normal track in later years.

The next point of interest was West Auckland shed, where one would see a few of those grand little superheater P1s, such as Nos. 1980, 2079, etc., and maybe A No. 41, driven for many years between Middleton, Bishop Auckland, Stockton, and Wellfield by Geordie Armstrong, another uncle. She was a grand engine, and the way Geordie used to bowl her along over Langley Dale was an eye opener; talk about rock and roll! Only a few weeks ago I was talking to a driver on an A4 at Leeds who had fired to him; he said "I can see him yet, coming across the viaduct, one hand holding the reversing lever, the other round the edge of the cab roof, and as soon as we cleared the viaduct, he would open the old girl out for the climb up to Gibbs Neese box. As long as you could give him a good head of steam so he could make her crack going up the bank, he was happy." My driver friend continued, "I once said to him something about the way the Class A seemed to roll a bit, putting it very tactfully: he just laughed and said in reply, "you should have fired to Big Joss (his father) on 1278, he used to really run the old Quaker on a bit of good road".

Back once more, if luck was with us, we would probably see two of the P1s getting ready to follow us out of the laden sidings with a Tebay coke turn, on the left as we proceed, while at the other side there would probably be a Class N

0-6-2T shunting in the long defunct St Helen's Colliery sidings. We are soon at the peculiar West Auckland station with an ordinary platform for the 'up' road, and an island serving the 'down', fenced off from the 'up' line. We are on historic ground here as the original route of the Stockton & Darlington line from Etherley to Shildon was actually on the station site, and the line from Brusselton comes in on the left: the site of the original iron viaduct, the first in the world, was over the River Gaunless just near here. Out of the station we curve sharply left, noting on the right the old line up to Etherley incline, where at the time mentioned, one could see the winding house chimney. At Spring Gardens Junction, about 1¼ miles on, we leave the old Haggerleases line, which carries on along the Gaunless valley to Butterknowle, while we start the first of our heavy climbs, away through Evenwood, with another colliery, now defunct, on the right, with some really good digging at 1 in 60 and harder, passing Woodlands Junction, with lines to a colliery which housed a real museum piece, one of the Stockton & Darlington bank engines that worked on the Skinningrove zigzag. Little trace is left of these sidings today. We next cross the Haggerleases line by a high brick and girder viaduct at Lands, the scenery at this point reminds one very much of the Welsh Valleys, with their crossing and interlacing of tracks. our little tankie is really 'talking to 'em' as we cross Cockfield Fell and halt briefly at the station of that name, just over 7½ miles from Bishop. Very little is to be seen today of the huge battery of bee-hive type coke ovens that once provided much traffic for the line, the next point of note being Gibbs Neese box where sidings serve an opencast working, and where I must digress once more, to refer to Joseph Armstrong, for at this point he had an accident which could have been serious. According to a press cutting in my possession, some 60 years ago, one of the Tebay minerals broke an axle on a private owner's wagon, derailing many wagons, and Joseph must have been pushing up that shift, as the brake gear was knocked off the engine, but, as the paper says, "The driver, named Armstrong, stuck to his engine, and succeeded in stopping the train". His fireman that day was Tom Craig, a grand chap who retired at Middleton. He made me laugh once by his account of the affair. Joseph saw what was likely to happen, shut off, screwed back the reverse, and gave her steam, and with one h*** of a bang, they pulled up, still intact, but off the road. The best part was Joseph, who had quite a good vocabulary when needed, delivering a homily on wagons like that knocking his engine about, and he wasn't exactly whispering either. I might say at this point that the old man was some 6 ft 3 in tall, and weighed about 15-16 stone in his heyday, and I don't think he knew his own strength. An old Kirkby man once told me that Joseph suspected someone had moved his compound 523 in Tebay shed; next time he left her, he screwed his handbrake on so hard it took two men to get it off!

We are now dropping down onto Langley Dale, and swinging over the fine stone viaduct, to make the sharp climb up to Forthburn box, where we take the tablet for the first single line section, just under 1¼ miles to Coal Road Crossing, traversing a deep rock cutting en route. The line here had a peculiar unfinished look, as the crossing embraced two roads, but the crossover was at the far side of the highway, and the down line petered out in a mound of earth. From this point, there is a magnificent view to the west, and one could see a train running into Barnard Castle station quite easily on a good day. We now drop smartly down into Barnard Castle, 14 miles 73 chains from Bishop, and as our train is going up to Middleton, we indulge in a typical bit of North Eastern practice, and run through the station and back into the down bay. I never much cared for this working, and often wonder if anyone ever thought they had overrun their station, before they realised what was happening. Just before we entered the station, the line from Darlington comes in from the left, with the original line going away behind the East box to the goods depot. The connections used to be controlled by a fine bridge of Northern Division signals, with latter girder posts, now alas like the shed, which was on our right, only a memory. The little shed here housed some grand old timers, including 367, the last 901 to remain in service, and 366 of the same class, which broke a side rod going up Sandy Bank a year or two earlier. No. 933, a much rebuilt Fletcher, seemed to live in the shed after she was converted to a 4-4-0. I have been told she would hardly run down bank with steam on! We can expect to see one or two Ns working about; they were employed "shoving up", and on Middleton goods turns, till one got away approaching Tees Valley box off the Middleton branch, and it was decided they had insufficient brake power for those jobs. They were not allowed westwards beyond the Summit, but someone slipped up one day, and one arrived at Kirkby on an inspection special; the loco staff at Kirkby spotted this, and there was some paper flying. She was not allowed back under steam, and lounged around Kirkby for a week or so, before having tanks and bunker emptied, and I believe some motion removed, before being towed back home. I often thought of this when I watched double-headed BR stuff clattering over Belah many years later!

Well, we have now left our train from Bishop, and with a tingle of excitement watch for the 6.50 am from Darlington to round the bend, and here she comes, double-headed, with two 'Tennants'. The pilot would be coming to work at Barney, after shoving us up to the Summit, the load being 5 and the S. Appleby milk vans. As near as memory serves me, the two engines were 1463 and 1465, the latter being that smart one with the capuchon chimney; however 1463 was our train engine. During station work, our assistant engine has run round, and coupled up at the rear with another well known NE feature, the slip coupling, a mixed blessing with the loose cable and always the doubt if it would slip correctly. Sometimes they would refuse to open out and drop off, resulting in much whistling and waving to stop the train at the top, and they have been known to come off the draw hook at times. I once saw one at the Summit dragging in the ballast, luckily with little damage.

What a picture our 2-4-0 made in the morning sun, beautifully turned out, with the brasswork and buffers, etc., gleaming. The valves are just beginning to lift as the Station Foreman gives the ready, the guard waves, followed by that ever thrilling "Cock-a-doodle-do", and we're away on time at 7.35 am. Just before we left, the early train to Darlington left the East bay, with one of Barney's Class G 4-4-0s at the head, No. 222, which would work through to Saltburn. We ourselves soon leave the neat station, with the single main line platform conforming to Central Division standards, and gather speed rapidly up to the Tees Viaduct, the first of the three great viaducts on this route. Once over this, we clear Tees Valley Junction, with the Middleton line alongside at a lower level for a short distance, and our two fliers begin to dig their toes in for the initial climb to Hulands. We swing towards the south on a high embankment, with grades round the 1 in 60 mark, and this is the ruling gradient right to the top. Lartington station is near, and looking back, one sees a wonderful view extending down towards Teesside and the Cleveland Hills and a sudden jerk announces we have shut off steam for Lartington, as the banker buffers up to the train. This station stands in a pleasant wooded cutting, but was a vicious place to start from, up a bank and on a curve. I have vivid memories of seeing 1477, a Kirkby 'Tennant', on the 3

pm ex-Darlington, having a real tussle to get going, the crew were struggling with regulator, reverse, brakes and sanders, and one could well guess they wished that particular 1463 was in a warmer place than York Museum! These 2-4-0s had a tendency to dead centre at times, and seemed to run with a surging action till they got away; I often used to wonder if the fault was at the other end.

That slip coupling caused a block here one snowy Christmas Eve about this time, when the banker to the 5.03 pm 'down' ex-Darlington somehow slipped the hook, and dropped behind the train a few feet, and in the falling snow, the driver had not noticed this, with the result that when they stopped at Lartington, he came up smartly onto the rear vehicle causing a slight derailment and blocking both roads. However, all is well with our two steeds, and they are really rousing the echoes up the rock cutting, past Lartington West box, formerly Lartington Quarry Junction; the site of the old lines can be seen on the right. We are now on to Deepdale Viaduct, a breath-taking structure, not quite as high and long as Belah, but being built on a curve, it was just as thrilling to cross, especially from the footplate of a 'Tennant' on an 'up' train. Older railwaymen used to call this "Cat Castle Viaduct", as there had been a colony of wild cats in the area at one time. Our train is now climbing and rounding the reverse curve known as Boldron Kip, and many of the old timers who ran the Tebay minerals used to reckon this was the toughest bit on the whole run, and in the old days of coal bonus, the driver on the "Shover up", if of a saving disposition, would try the same stunt as mentioned in the "Express" re the working up Nunthorpe bank, by easing off and throwing some soft coal on the fire, to make a good display of sparks, kidding the front end lads that they were "Into 'em". Old Joss spotted this game one night, and when they got through Bowes, did the same at the front; of course, to save face, the chap at the back had to "Lay her over" to keep time, and Joseph never had much more trouble in that direction. Having by now got round the curve, we approach the stone ballast quarries at Hulands, and we halt for a moment to drop off a number of railwaymen who work on the site. There is a modern wooden signal box, and short platforms for each road. The run from here to Bowes is much easier, and known as the "Bowes level", was a very welcome breather before tackling the climb over Stainmore proper. Bowes is just under $6\frac{1}{4}$ miles from Barney, a solid station of local stone.

Although most of the line was doubled many years previously, one can still trace which part of many of the stone bridges was original. Another little point which has some bearing on the quality of enginemanship on the old line was the reference by a writer in one of the journals re the last train over the line, when on the return trip we stopped for a blow up just short of Belah. Treating the matter lightly, he stated that we stuck for steam just as thousands of other engines had done over the years, or words to that effect. A little more knowledge of the old NE would have shown the fact that to stick for steam in the good old days was something of a major crime to a driver and his mate, and they had to have a damned good reason for the delay. There was no question of dirty coal or bad maintenance to clear the matter, and they used to regard the daily run as a challenge to their abilities with an engine. I believe I quoted in my Stainmore notes for the last trip that when Penrith men began running the Lakes expresses from Darlington to Penrith, they had one of the rebuilt "Ginx's babies" for the job, and on the first run, my father, firing to John Stephenson just couldn't make the old girl boil on the non-stop run from Bank Top and North Road to Barney, and they had to take a banker to the Summit. An inspector was soon on the job, to see what the trouble was, as Saltburn men had been running right through from there to

Penrith, stopping at all stations. There was the fault; they were very awkward engines to fire, and very shy steamers, but on a stopping train could just manage to plug along, but to put them on a fast run over a road like this, they just were no good, and were soon replaced by Fletcher's 901 class. I believe they were allowed about 22 mins Barney to Summit pass, and John Stephenson was no slouch when he was running a train. Rumour has it that his reply to a young fireman who was finding it a bit tough to keep the needle round about blowing off point was "Don't worry thisen, lad, ye bray 'em in and I'll bray 'em out". They used to say it was a curtain raiser to have a trip with him over the LNW from Oxenholme to Tebay, with the Penrith turn to Kendal in summer; of course they had to show the "Wessy" men what a real engine could do. "Stuck for steam over Stainmore?" Not likely; those old lads would have asked for another fireman as soon as they got back home!

On our left as we leave Bowes can be seen the main road over the moor, dating back to Roman times, with a fleeting glimpse of the Castle and Dotheboy's Hall of Dickens fame. We soon cross the road by a metal bridge, and it is interesting to recall the paucity of road traffic in those days over here. Ahead of us is the unbroken climb to the Summit cabin, our two old stagers are sending up a fine column of steam and smoke and one can hear the cinders rattling on the roof tops like hail stones; no good wet nursing the old girls up here, if they are steaming well, get at 'em! A pity tape recorders were not thought of then, but memory serves me well, and it is possible to recall a trip like that with ease. The terrain grows wilder as we climb at a steady 26-30 mph, looking out for such landmarks as God's Bridge, and the lonely Spittal cottages, with the signals at Spittal box all off both ways: the W.T.T. says "Closed temporarily" and little did one think that the next shift there would be to pass evacuation specials from Tyneside to the West Coast at the start of World War II, and that would be the end of Spittal box! One feature of the lineside are the posts marking catch points which are tall granite posts, with a square top, vastly different from the ordinary NE wooden type; this idea would be to show the position of the points in deep winter snow, if single line working had to be used.

The line over the moor at this side of the Summit was mostly across wild open terrain, with not too deep cuttings, vastly different from the western climb, climbing as it did through deep cuttings and embankments along the hillside.

As we toil towards the top, Bowes Moor Hotel can be seen high on the roadside above us on the right, with the River Greta tumbling eastwards on the left, in a rough rocky channel. The water supply for the Summit columns was from a large reservoir near the source, which must have been the loneliest piece of North Eastern property.

A long blast on the deep toned Gateshead whistle warns us that the Summit distant is on, the home board just clears as we run up to it, but we halt opposite the cabin, where one or two youngsters are helped into the train by the guard. They live in the nearby railway cottages and will drop off at Barras to attend the school there, returning by the 'up' afternoon train. The halt gives us a fine chance to survey this bleak outpost: the 5.30 am goods ex-West Yard, Darlington, is stood inside waiting for us to clear, with one of Darlington's non-superheater P1s in charge: she should have been at Kirkby by now but traffic delays had held her up. The Summit board is a huge wooden affair, showing height and also mileages to such places as Darlington, Redcar, Tebay, etc., and there is the usual generous array of signals. The old NE never used one signal if two would do! A wave from our guard, with a few sharp puffs, and we start to drop down the bank, leaving our banker looking somewhat forlorn near the

cabin. She will take water, and return to Barney, make another trip up the bank, take a fresh set of men, and work the dinner-time train from Darlington to Tebay, changing over with the set that worked the 'up' 7.32 am mentioned earlier.

We have cleared the Summit cottages, and the main road now leaves us, turning away to Brough, while we hug the hillside by Bleathgill, with the notorious cutting so well known for snow blocks. There is evidence here of more prosperous days on the line, when traffic warranted shorter sections, in the shape of Bleathgill cabin, perched right on the edge of a curved embankment backed by a vista that can extend to Scotland on a clear day. On the historical side there is a reminder of another railway scheme, as between the Summit and Bleathgill can be seen the remains of test bore holes for a line that was to have cleared the summit by means of a tunnel, with the western end at Calva House, just below Barras station. Our route crosses a deep gorge by a stone viaduct, and through a deep cutting into Barras station. The run from Bowes to Barras at one time was the longest in the country without an intermediate station, but friend Beeching has long since broken that record. The view from the station at Barras can hardly be described by writing, the beautiful Eden Valley can be seen for miles, with the Lake District peaks as a backcloth, and away to the north west the hills beyond the Solway Firth. On a clear day it is possible to follow a train on the Midland line away beyond Appleby, right up to Smardale Glen.

I would like to return to the Summit for a brief moment here, as mentioning the view over the valley has recalled a stirring scene one lovely May morning at the Summit, near a favourite spot of mine, where I could see Milepost 29 from Darlington (which now stands in my garden), I was on a cycle tour, and having made an early start, was enjoying a spell at the 'Top'; the time would be about 7.50 am. It was a morning one dreams about, clear, sun just beginning to climb high, and I had got into conversation with the ganger on the line. He was very interested to learn of my keenness over his line, and said, "Wait a few minutes, you'll see t' first passenger come over t' 'Top'." Of course, I hung on, with the result that I had the pleasure of memorising a railway scene I'll never forget; right on 8 am, a dull drumming sound could be heard, and a drift of smoke could be seen in the sky (this phenomenon of drifting smoke was always present on this line - air currents, no doubt). My friend said "By gum, Geordie's warming her backside this morning", and a couple of minutes later she hove in sight, No. 372, one of those grand little 4-4-0s, of which 372 was one of the best. She had four bogies and three sixes for Appleby milk, and no banker, and sure enough it was my friend George Towlard driving. The scene is still vivid in my mind, of his friendly wave as he spotted us, then back into the cab to shut off, no school stop that day, and he slid away down the bank; he must have cleared the Summit at about 30 mph, and the engine was in grand nick. He was only clear of the cottages, when she showed the old "white feather" at the gleaming safety valve trumpet; Geordie gave many such performances while in the 'G' link at Darlington, and he could really handle an engine. His last job before retirement was Test Driver for ex-shops engines, a job he liked immensely; he used to gallop the Zs to Thirsk and back in grand style.

Having known men like Geordie, one realises that one has witnessed the passing of an era, and a type of railwayman gone with the end of steam. From this vantage point at the Summit, I saw with nostalgia, the last whisp of steam and smoke from a steamer, watching the last demolition train away in the distance near Bleathgill, and it was a real North Eastern, a good old T2.

While at Barras, one noticed the large station house, at a

lower level than the platform, and although it is now made into two separate dwellings, a photo in my collection taken just before the line was opened shows it was one house, and I understand it was to have been an hotel. It is up for sale now. The photograph mentioned shows some early Stockton & Darlington signals, but for many years Barras has been a ground frame only.

With a simmer of steam from the safety valves, and the thump-thump of the Westinghouse pump, the driver knocks the brake off and we roll away down the bank towards Belah, the crossing of which we await with great anticipation. Nothing can be seen of the great viaduct from this direction, but from the Kirkby side it stood out on the hillside and visible for miles, as was the deep cleft in the Pennines through which the railway and road ran at the Summit. As we run into the deep rock cutting just over a mile from Barras, a sharp brake application gives us a warning of the viaduct; suddenly we seem suspended in space as we cross at about 20 mph, with that rattling of handrails that always seemed to accompany the crossing. Many times have I crossed it, both walking and riding, and have been all round it underneath, viewing it from all angles, and it never failed to impress me by the apparent lightness of construction and height, yet strong it must have been, to stand 100 years of wind and weather on those lonely fells. The isolated cabin at the west end of the bridge used to show a welcome flash of light when travelling the line in winter, but it was one of the loneliest cabins I knew, and I enjoyed more than one "brew up" in there, whilst listening to a bit of crack from the old timers who worked there. It was far better than book reading to hear the tales of the days when the line was open night and day, with trains at roughly half hourly intervals.

As we gather speed near the two railway cottages near the viaduct we spot the 'up' Belah distant is 'off', for the first 'up' train of the day has cleared Kirkby East, and we cannot afford to miss the chance of seeing another 'Tennant' or a Kirkby G in action. As we swing along over stone viaducts and through deep cuttings, we can see a drift of smoke away over by Rookby Scarth; the old timer is belting up through Big Hill cut, on her Darlington run, where she will be station pilot till 2 pm when she retires to the shed for loco duties before returning home on the 3 pm. This was a Penrith turn at one period, later Kirkby men had the job. As she comes nearer we see it is 'Tennant' No. 1477, about ready for shops by the colour of her paint and the blow at the front end, but although in need of a repaint, she is clean, and making good headway with her three clerestory bogies, a real NE scene as the two drivers give a friendly salute as they pass.

The sight of snow fences on the more exposed sections are grim reminders of what the line can be like in winter, and also one recalls the story of a namesake of mine, driver John Armstrong of Kirkby, a cousin of the redoubtable Joseph. John was the proud possessor of a long and flowing beard which, when he was looking over the cab side at speed used to fly in the wind. Well, one bitter winter day, snowing like mad, he and his mate were approaching the long defunct cabin at Rookby Scarth (I believe their engine was 840, a 901) and John, as usual, was hanging over the side. He sees the boards are all clear, and tries to turn back into the cab for a spell, but no, his beard was well and truly frozen to the cab side, and his mate had to bring the train into Kirkby where hot water and some scissors had to be used before John could be released. That little episode took some living down, and a shorter beard was the result!

We are now running on the last fast stretch before Kirkby, which can be seen nestling in the valley on our right, and from speeds up to the 70 mark, we slip past Merrygill box controlling the lines into Hartley quarries on the left. We are soon running past Stenkrith sidings, with the mighty snow-ploughs stored there, and the power house worked by water from the River Eden, which gave the NE Railway electricity to light their station premises, signals, and power for the shed at Kirkby. The ancient 'up' advance starter was worth noting, a relic of olden days where the minerals used to "Grow up" as they were right away for the long grind up the bank. There was no help from this side, the climb started as soon as they passed the East box. Plenty of activity in the goods yard today, 800 is making mighty efforts at shunting, between trips up the bank, and we run into the clean island platform, making a real Westinghouse stop. Here the 'Tennant' comes off, and a Kirkby engine goes forward to Penrith, after dropping one bogie; as far as I can recollect it was G No. 1107 that day. Meanwhile, our Darlington 2-4-0 has taken water and collected a couple of clerestories from the carriage slip, backed into the 'down' platform, ready for Tebay away at 8.34 am; there are not many passengers for the trip, most of them are evidently railway people by the cheerful banter with our enginemen.

The brief pause while we wait gives one time to have a look at this North Eastern outpost, the substantial stone buildings, reception sidings on the left, and the four-road fan-shaped shed on the opposite side, which, like Barnard Castle, housed some rare types in its day, as well as creating a breed of enginemen of the real old school, many of whom as promotion came due moved away to places like York and Gateshead, Leeds and Hull, continuing their tradition by good running and sound enginemanship. It used to be grand to hear the rich Westmorland dialect, "Noo, Tom, what thi turn today? I'se away ower 'top with a double layad". A recent visit to the scene made one realise what a tragedy the closing of this line was. We were not looking at some remote branch line killed by road transport, but an ex-main line entirely wiped out. Weeds and rubbish all over the place, shed roof falling down, and marvellous to relate, the old slip coupling was still hanging in position on the station wall! Whilst I stood and thought of happier days when one watched a 'down' mineral grinding to a stop with a load of those huge NE 20-tonners, brake blocks red hot after their long grind down the bank, or when one could hear that "Cock-a-doodle-do" swept back by the wind that blew down from the Line Standards as the 2.30 pm goods got away for Darlington, a voice behind me said, "It's a good job thi' old Grandad can't see this lot, it would have broken his heart". I was delighted to see a real old timer who used to be carriage and wagon examiner there way back in the 1920s, and although nearing his 90th birthday, still had vivid recollections of compound 523 and 'Big Joss' hammering away up the bank. He told me he once saw him 'running amain', as it was termed when the load got away down the bank: he had tied down both whistles and went crashing and screaming through the 'down' goods line with a smell of burning fat from the wagon axle boxes, and flaming brake blocks. He had the engine in reverse and pulled up well beyond the West box; in cases like this the runaway was always turned up the sharp gradient on the Tebay line. When Joseph set back into the yard somebody said, "everything alright, Joss? We thought you were coming off the road", to which he replied, "There's nowt to worry thisen about, the old B****** had to stop somewhere".

On our trip we notice a couple of Cs at the shed, 668 and 960; 'Tennant' 1471 is under the sheer legs, and a similar engine is in steam inside the shed. Over in the 'down' reception sidings P1 No. 1866 is making ready to leave for Cockermouth with a mineral: this was the last haunt of the old "Quakers" in the area, and by now the Redhills curve has only the occasional Q turn to deal with.

We are now 'right away' and 1463 chatters away in good style past the West box, where we pick up the tablet for the single line stretch to Sandy Bank box. On the left of the West cabin (which is in the fork of the Tebay and Penrith lines) can be seen the original cabin that served the junction. Whilst the Eden Valley line bears away to the right on an easy gradient we are faced by a stiff climb right up to Smardale station, a small single platform; in fact the smallest station on the line. It served a few farms but no village of any size. From here till Smardale Viaduct the grade is rather easier and the old 'Tennant' ambles along in great style, under the Midland's massive stone viaduct across Smardale Glen, whilst our route takes us through the beautiful glen itself, with the stream deep down on the right, and Ash Fell towering up on the left, straight off the lineside: it is indeed a picturesque place. We then sweep over the Smardale Viaduct of the NE, a stone structure, built for double road but the single track across was placed on a slant to ease the reverse curve a little. We are now in the wild and remote spot, with a couple of railway houses as the only sign of human life. The line curves and climbs in a deep cutting, and I often wonder how old John Stephenson coaxed his little Fletcher 'single' up there on a rough day, when my father was firing to him from Penrith. That was before they got the 901s, which were big engines to them in those days. At the time of our trip the single line section ended at the bank top, where on the right was a ground-level box, Sandy Bank, but in the early thirties the single line was extended to Ravenstonedale and Sandy Bank was no more.

There have been a few human tragedies about Sandy Bank: they all form part of the history of the line. The first one I recall concerns my grandfather and Uncle jack, who was firing to him at the time. In those days, about 1895, the box at Sandy Bank was a tall affair, reached by a long flight of steps. They had left Tebay at 2.20 am on a Monday in January with the first turn to West Auckland: my uncle recalled that it was a wild morning but dry, and they had settled down to work nicely. Old 523 had just got warmed up as they approached Ravenstonedale where surprisingly the distant was on: they knew nothing had been over since the last home trip to Tebay about 4 am on the Sunday, so shutting off, they approached the home board, which cleared as they crept up, but the signalman stopped them at the box with a red light. Big Joss leaned out of the cab and wanted to know what the blue pencil was up, to which the signalman said he thought something had gone wrong at Sandy Bank, as the chap there had given correct 'opening cabin' signals, but he had made no response to repeated 'be ready to receive' signals, so he told the chaps on 523 to go forward at caution and see what the trouble was. It was too dark to see if there were any wires down, but approaching Sandy Bank they could see the flickering oil light was burning, and the cabin door was open, but no sign of life. They pulled up at the box, and young John was sent to investigate, and had an awful shock when he entered the cabin; there was an overturned bucket of coal on the floor, and the old signalman was laid dead over the lever frame. He was nearly 70, and in those days it was a 12-hour shift. The inquest said that no doubt the old chap had been knocked about by the wind getting to work, and climbing the stairs with a bucketful of coal had finished him completely. That incident was firmly impressed on the mind of a young fireman to the end of his days.

The next affair was not quite so tragic, but bad enough; this concerned my father when he was firing to John Stephenson on a 901; I think it was 911. They were working the Penrith morning turn to Tebay and Kendal via Kirkby; it was a glorious day, and John was no doubt enjoying the run along Smardale Glen and up the bank. They had just crossed the viaduct, young Robert was just dropping a few towards the front end of the box, and John had just dropped the reverse down a couple of notches, climbed back onto his seat, and suddenly shouted to my father that he felt cold, and collapsed on the cab floor. Dad lifted him up as best he could, and at Sandy Bank stopped to see what could be done. The signalman rang Ravenstonedale, who arranged to have a doctor ready, also a porter who could fire to Tebay. On arrival at Ravenstonedale, a stroke was diagnosed, and poor John never drove again. He was conveyed back to Kirkby on the next train, and actually outlived my Dad! Meanwhile, young Robert was getting on towards Tebay, where he picked up a spare fireman, and they worked the job till arriving back at Kirkby, where a relief driver was obtained.

The third incident concerns a Barney 901, No. 366, which was working the dinner-time train from Darlington. This train went through to Tebay, and was an engine change job for Barney (due 1.14/8 pm). The train was right on time, and had left Smardale as booked at 2.12 pm; the load would only be a couple of bogies, it was the first few months of the 1923 Grouping, and winter loading was still in force. All seemed well as they swung over the viaduct and into the bank when, without any warning, the cab was a mass of scalding steam from a boiler gashed open by a flailing side rod that had come adrift at one end. The fireman was blown back into the tender, and was scalded badly enough, but his mate was injured much more seriously, as he made a gallant and successful attempt to get the brake on and hold the train on the bank. At the subsequent inquiry, the Inspector made some drastic remarks about the way the coupling-rod key had been over-driven and had gradually worked loose. The engine was never in service again.

The final incident was, in my opinion, the most tragic of all, as the enginemen and the victim's wife saw what was going to happen and could do nothing to avert the tragedy. An old retired railwayman had taken one of the lonely cottages on Sandy Bank, and with his wife, looked after a few poultry just down the line. To reach these, they used the path at the lineside, well clear of traffic. The line was normally closed on Sundays, but this particular Sunday there was an excursion from the West Hartlepool area to Barrow, and although the old couple may have seen it in the morning, they must have forgotten all about it by the time it came to feed the hens at night (I forgot to mention the old man was stone deaf). They set off on their usual little walk down the line, the old man had gone on ahead, with his wife following some distance behind; she saw him, for some unknown reason, step off the path and start to walk in the four-foot, but thinking there was nothing about, this did not concern her unduly, till suddenly she heard the noise of the return trip coming at a good lick round the curve half way down the bank. She then realised the danger and tried to catch up to her husband, shouting was no good, but her efforts were of no avail, and she saw the train, hauled by a West Hartlepool C, sweep her husband down. The driver had spotted him, given a full brake application, and blew like mad, but the poor old chap never even looked round. It was an awful shock to the old lady, and to the driver and fireman, helpless to do a thing.

It is about time we left the scene of such tragedies, and continue on towards Ravenstonedale, which is actually at Newbiggin on Lune, but was renamed many years ago. This is a station with staggered platforms and one of the best gardens I have seen on a railway station. One of the old signalmen here was a most interesting chap, and most surprising, he had a brother who had fired on the old Manchester, Sheffield & Lincolnshire line, and who had retired as a top link man on the Manchester-Marylebone link. We now travel gently along the pleasant Lune Valley, with double road and easier grades, with wonderful views of Wild Boar Fell, and other grim peaks, and at Gaisgill, the last North Eastern station, we can see our first glimpse of the mighty Shap on the right. The line swings southwards and we pass the box at Tebay Yard No. 3, a real Central Division box, noting the old NE shed on the left, and come to a halt in that grim cavern at Tebay known as the "Geordie" platform.

The engine looses off and away to the shed for loco duties, but the shed itself has only memories now. There is a quaint disc signal near the end of the shed, but enquiries do not give it any great historical value. Uncle Jack just says, "It wasn't there when I was firing", and you can take it that he is right. Shutting one's eyes, one can in memory see Big Joss getting his beloved compound out of the shed, 523, with the grained and varnished cab interior, and the two sliding panels he had got fitted personally at North Road, and which enclosed the cab entirely on a rough night. I am told he had a unique method when he brought her out for the day's work; he used to screw the hand brake fairly hard on, open the cylinder taps, and give her the works up the shed yard. The whole of Tebay knew when he was on the job, by the hefty bark the old hoss . gave at this treatment, but his idea was to clear water and condensation out before pulling away. He also had a natty little ball of wagon fat on each big end, which gave early indication of any tendency to run warm, not that such a thing would happen; it was in the same class as sticking for steam on the bank. He had this engine from bringing her new from Darlington in 1889 till 1903, and his only two failures were both unforeseeable, both were broken crank pins. An old chap I met at Tebay told me he was the best chap they had for driving one of those Worsdell compounds; they were good engines on the road, but a bit skittish at starting. One notorious place was out of Woodlands sidings up to Cockfield, but Joseph used to handle the old girl like a baby. He told me the LNW people had an engine off the road on time, and were

about whacked by the failure to get her rerailed, when some bright bod thought about getting the Geordie lads to have a try. So they sent over for help, and over lands Joseph with his compound; after surveying the scene, they got fitted up with some NE ramps, Joss hangs on and with a tremendous heave, gets the old "Wessie" back on the straight and level again. There was much less formality in those days, and the job was squared up by a drink at the Cross Keys.

I might further add that the day was continued over Shap behind a 'Precursor' tank to Penrith, and a pleasant run along the Eden Valley through Appleby by yet another 'Tennant', this time No. 1464, and after halting at Kirkby and exploring the shed, etc., the trip home was on the last train of the day to Darlington, behind 372. It is, however, another story to be told later, but it is worth noting that 372 often made the double trip Darlington to Tebay daily. These little engines were so good over that road than when it was time for their demise, rumour had it that some more were to be built at North Road, but as to what we did get, least said the better.

Class G5 0-4-4 tank No. 238 poses with staff outside the shed at Tebay. No. 238 replaced S&DR 0-6-0 No. 1177 at Tebay in about 1889.

J. W. Armstrong

Appendix I

Station Masters

1894

Kirkby Stephen	: William Hoggs		Appleby	: Lancelot Askew
Ravenstonedale	: William Moss		Kirkby Thore	: John Best
Gaisgill	: Hugh Baker		Temple Sowerby	: William Appleby
Tebay Junction	: Thomas Brinnard		Cliburn	: Joseph W. Burton
Musgrave	: John Atkinson Kirk		Clifton Moor	: Stephen George Eltringham
Warcop	: George Capstick Braithwaite			

1925

Barras	: Albert Hope		Warcop	: W.H. Simpson
Kirkby Stephen	: Frederick Smith		Appleby	: Henry Blake
Smardale	: Isaac Potts Ruddick		Kirkby Thore	: Joseph Marshall
Gaisgill	: J.W. Jackson		Temple Sowerby	: Joseph Marshall

By 1938 the names of local station masters were omitted from Westmorland Directories, although station masters continued to work at many locations until the line closed in 1962. The post Second World War period to the end included the following:

Kirkby Stephen (East): Mr Sinclair, Mr W. Sanderson, Mr W. Hill and finally Mr P. Sarginson

Warcop: Mr E. Lee, Mr W.J. Millard, Mr J.L. Sutton and finally Gordon Walton who had started work as clerk in 1951, being made redundant after closure. (Mr W.H. Simpson who appeared on the 1925 list was Gordon's grandfather).

Musgrave: The last station master was a Mr Smith before Musgrave was merged with Kirkby Stephen.

Appleby (East): Mr R. Murray promoted from Musgrave. Then Appleby East and West station master duties were merged, as were those at Kirkby Stephen East and West. Mr McKenzie.

KirkbyThore/ Temple Sowerby: Mr N. Greenhow
Clifton Moor: Mr W. Hamilton

Appendix II

Surviving Structures, June 1992

The main line from Bernard Castle to Tebay

Location	Notes
Percy Beck Viaduct	Intact.
Tees Valley Viaduct	Stone buttresses of the viaduct.
Lartington station	Main building as a private dwelling.
Lartington West Box	Derelict.
Deepdale	Stone buttresses of the viaduct.
Bowes Gate cottages	Splendidly renovated as a private dwelling.
Bowes station	Derelict main buildings and signal box.
God's Bridge cottages	Intact as holiday cottages.
Spital cottages	Intact as holiday cottages.
Reservoir to the south of Stainmore Summit	Intact.
Barras station	Remarkably intact as a private dwelling.
Barras cottages (Crag Green)	Intact as a private dwelling.
Belah	Stone buttresses of viaduct remain, as do certain pier foundations, signal box in derelict condition. Signalmen's cottages as a private dwelling.
Belah cottages	Undergoing renovation.
Aitygill	Viaduct intact, excellent timber over bridge still in use.
Merrygill	Viaduct intact.
Podgill	Viaduct intact.
Hartley Castle	Metal overbridge.
Kirkby Stephen	Goods shed in private industrial use. Main station building in use, albeit extensively modified for industrial purposes. Lattice overbridge and five-arch road overbridge intact.
Smardale	Main house building well preserved as a private dwelling.

Location	Notes
Smardale – Smardale Gill	National Trust Nature Reserve – private. Some excellent features remain on this stretch including Smardale Gill Viaduct and NER lime kilns and derelict cottages.
Sandy Bank	Stone lined cutting.
Ravenstonedale	Well preserved station building as private dwelling.
Kelleth	Crossing cottage.
Gaisgill	Station buildings as private dwelling.

The Eden Valley branch from Kirkby Stephen East to Eden Valley Junction.

Location	Notes
Waitby	Crossing cottage.
Musgrave	Station buildings as a private dwelling.
Warcop	Main buildings as a private dwelling. Platform, signal box derelict. Present limit of branch from Appleby. Run-round facility and sidings. A derelict lattice post signal.
Coupland Beck	Viaduct intact.
Appleby East	Main station buildings as a private dwelling. Goods shed intact. Crossing cottages.
Temple Sowerby	Main station buildings as a private dwelling.
Cliburn	Main station buildings as a private dwelling. Semi-derelict signal box.
Clifton Moor	Main station buildings as private dwellings. The timber lean-to signal box has been moved and is now used as a garden shed.

The stations at Barnard Castle, Tebay and Kirkby Thore have disappeared, almost without trace. Signal boxes at Barnard Castle, Tees Valley Junction, Hulands, Spital, Stainmore, Bleathgill, Kirkby Stephen East and Junction, Sandy Bank, Ravenstonedale, Gaisgill and Tebay No. 3 have all disappeared. Also gone are those at Waitby Crossing, Appleby East and Junction, Kirkby Thore, Clifton Moor and Eden Valley Junction. Many incidental and interesting bridges, bits of bridges, etc., still remain at a variety of locations.

A last look at the signal box at Stainmore in 1965, three years after closure.

Author

The almost intact shell of Bleathgill box remained for many years after the line's closure. This picture of the eastern elevation was taken in 1975. It is ironic that this box was one of the last to collapse, despite being out of normal use for a long period prior to the closure of the line in 1962. A crossover here allowed single line working in emergencies. The windows were boarded over to protect the box internals which were used in exceptional circumstances as indicated by the entry in the Stainmore box occurrence book on 30th March 1953.

"Received a telephone message from the guard of the 5.15 St Helens to Tebay return mineral, that the train engine (5092) had blown a lump out of the front cylinder cover and was disabled at Bleathgill. (46473) engine and van entered section at Belah under regulation 14 at 9.48 pm. Guard stated that he had been forced to break down the door of Bleathgill Cabin to enable the driver to enter".

Author

The stone overbridge immediately to the west of the Summit. Beyond the bridge there were railway cottages on the north side of the line. Both cottages and bridge have disappeared without trace, the site now being partially covered by the A66 trunk road "improvement".

Author

The fine river underbridge (now demolished) at Stenkrith.
Author

The metal overbridge to the east of Sandy Bank Summit in 1986.

Author

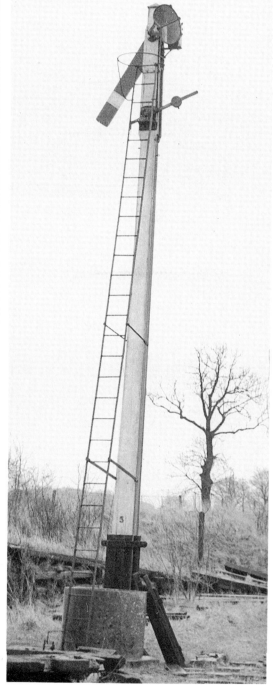

Still standing intact after track removal, Clifton Moor's No. 17 'down' home signal high upon the embankment, on the northside of the overbridge, immediately to the south of the station.

Author

The 'up' starter on the same day. The signalling equipment was still operational; (I couldn't resist pulling the wire for the photograph, and presumably the last time).

Author

207

The tree-shrouded Percy Beck Viaduct, still standing in 1986. *Author*

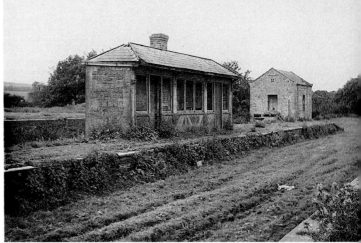

The derelict remains of the island platform waiting room and the goods shed at Bowes in 1974. The waiting room has since been demolished. Note the unusual, agricultural-looking goods shed beyond.

Author

Miraculously, in January 1986 the shell of Bowes station remained.

Author

The main buildings at Bowes, still standing in 1974, but ravaged by the Pennine weather.

Author

The abandoned trackbed near Spital, looking west. It is hard to imagine successions of coke trains fighting up the last few miles from here to Stainmore Summit. Spital once possessed a signal cabin and crossover facility. This box was allegedly last used in 1942 to cater for a number of 'evacuation specials' which crossed Stainmore.

Author

The isolated double and single storey cottages stand to the north side of the abandoned trackbed at Spital in 1986.

Author

1984 and Belah box still stands.

Author

The east elevation of the station house at Barras in use in 1986 as a private dwelling. The original plans detail a structure vastly different from the one shown in this picture. Rumour suggests that at one time this building may have been considered to incorporate a hotel.

Author

There were a number of different styles of accommodation built for railwaymen along the routes. Some cottages were single storeyed like those at Bowes Gate, God's Bridge, Belah, etc., and others were houses such as this example at Barras, photographed in 1986.

Author

Bridge No. 120 between Belah cottages and Aitygill Viaduct, still standing in 1985.

Author

One of the remaining stones at Belah showing the pillar stud key arrangement. See also the relevant detailed plan.

Author

Aitygill Viaduct surrounded by trees, is difficult to photograph in its entirety today.

Author

The 'Railwaymens' Pub' – The Croglin Castle Hotel in 1983. Note the railway bridge in the left background. Even now, twenty years after closure, one or two former NE men still frequent "The Crog".

Author

Sunset over the remains of Podgill Viaduct.

Author

In 1985 the trackbed between Smardale Halt and Smardale Gill Viaduct had become a part of a private nature reserve.

Author

Top left: No photograph can do justice to the gentle grace with which Smardale Gill Viaduct crosses the Scandal Beck. This view looks towards the West. The NER-served kilns can be seen in the middle distance, as can Sandy Bank cottages and an occupation bridge illustrated in close up.

Author

Left centre and bottom: Two further views of the viaduct, this time from the north western side. The stone used to build the viaduct was quarried further down the valley and transported to the site via the lane in the background.

Author

211

All that remains. The station at Ravenstonedale building as a private dwelling in 1966.

Author

In 1985 the occupation bridge at Smardale is still stained with soot, over twenty years since a train blasted through it for the last time.

Author

Milepost 8 still in position in May 1986. The NER mileposts were effectively square as illustrated, with the distance to/from Kirkby Stephen West (Junction) in the case of the valley branch. The half mile posts were circular, with two horizontally opposed triangular protrusions. The quarter mileposts had one protrusion on top and three quarter mile posts had protrusions on top and both sides.

Author

The only viaduct left available for use – Coupland Beck.

Author

Temple Sowerby finial, still in position in 1986.

Author

The last signal on the line, Warcop's 'up' distant as still standing in 1986.

Author

The main buildings at Temple Sowerby relatively intact, following track lifting and conversion into a private dwelling. The waiting room screen having been removed exposes the original support columns. The main house chimney has since been removed.

Author

The stone underbridge to the north of Wetheriggs Pottery, at the site of the former junction with the line which once provided a southward facing junction with the LNWR main line at Clifton Old Junction. This line closed officially in 1875 but very little traffic must have used the facility after the construction of Eden Valley Junction and the Redhills curve in 1866.

Author

Approximately one hundred years after the line was last used, a bridge girder still remains in place between the junction at Wetheriggs Clifton Old Junction, in 1986.

This girder was left in place to carry a spring crossing the gap, as can be seen from the picture taken from the tree-grown track-bed. It seems hard to imagine an early S&DR locomotive here guiding its haul of coke from the North East towards West Cumberland.

Ron Herbert

Appendix III

Belah Viaduct

The actual construction of Belah Viaduct began on 25th November 1857 when the foundation stone was laid by Henry Pease of Darlington, who was vice chairman of the SD&LUR. He was also MP for the Southern Division of the County of Durham.

A contemporary account from the *Durham Chronicle* of 4th December 1857 of the laying of the foundation stone reads:

"The morning was clear and frosty, the hills of Stainmore were covered with snow and the scenery around the steep valley of the River Belah was exceedingly wild and imposing.

Where it all began. The specially constructed track to the rear of Belah box where the stone used to build the massive buttresses of the viaduct was dragged to site from a quarry, between Belah and Tan Hill. Ironically, well over 100 years since it was used for this purpose, it is one of the best defined remnants of the route.

Author

Mr J. Whitwell of Kendal addressed the audience. He said they had met amidst the sublime scenery which surrounded them to see the immense gap over which Mr Bouch, the engineer of the South Durham & Lancashire Union Railway proposed to leap, an effort, the magnitude of which had astonished everyone in the district.

These engineers must be bold fellows to undertake this monster leap; but bold and vast as the project was, he believed that with the assistance of neighbouring contractors who had undertaken the work, it would be accomplished.

The mere spanning of this stream wonderful as it was, attained its importance from the circumstance that it was part of a system of railways which was to connect the County of Westmorland and the western coast of England immediately beyond it, with the important districts of Durham and Cleveland, affording opportunities for the frequent interchange of all social and commercial relations and giving the means for advancing more completely than heretofore, the happiness of a large portion of the community.

Mr Pease, in laying the foundation stone, also buried a bottle containing a paper giving details of the ceremony and a florin - one of the coins of the realm at that time, says the report.

He placed the bottle in the stone. The foundation stone was then lowered and with a silver trowel and a mahogany mallet Mr Pease performed the ceremony. In doing so, he called to his assistance as representatives of the rising generation, three interesting children who were near him – Master Thomas Mason King and Miss Jane King, children of the Incumbent of Kirkby Stephen and Miss Elizabeth Mason daughter of Thomas Mason Junior of the same place.

Mr Pease said the grand gorge upon which they were standing was to be spanned by a viaduct, the first stone of which had just been laid, and would be about 200 feet high, 1,000 feet in length and would have 15 iron piers.

'A few years ago the erection of such a work must necessarily be of stone, occupying four years or more in its construction. Now it would be of iron, 18 months would suffice for its erection and it would be put up probably without scaffolding except what itself furnished'."

Twenty months after the ceremony of 25th November 1857 work began upon the viaduct. The contractors, Gilkes, Wilson & Company erected the viaduct extremely quickly. It took 43 days to reach the central (8th) pier from the Barras end of the viaduct.

The method of construction was to set up a crane on the stone abutment and assemble the components onto the stone foundations to form the first pier. The resultant gap was then bridged and the crane moved onto the first pier to build the second and so on. No modern equipment, communication or method was used: neither was any scaffolding needed nor provided. Not a single accident occurred during the construction.

A unique feature of Belah Viaduct (and that at

Deepdale) was the tapering of the main ironwork from a 50 ft dimension at the base to less than half that at the top. Belah, 1,040 ft long and 196 feet high spanned the deep valley by means of 15 vertical piers (sixteen spans) each composed of cast iron, 12 in dia columns arranged in two parallel lines of three each and braced to each other by cross girders at 5 ft intervals. This main framework was tied together with wrought iron bars. The 15 piers were pitched at a nominal 60 ft apart and were topped with a lattice girder arrangement which included an integral, internal walkway. Large, special timbers were provided for the decking, ornamental cast parapets on both sides of the decking, 24 ft apart and topped with timber handrailing completed this marvellous structure - referred to by one Stainmore enthusiast as a "Meccano Fantasy".

When Belah Viaduct was demolished, starting on 4th July 1963, a document was recovered from the central (8th) pier which read:

Two pictures showing details of the Viaduct, taken on 7th June 1956.

Turners (Photography) Ltd

Beelah Viaduct
on Tuesday the 6th September, 1859
A document
was deposited in the inside (from the top) of one of the centre columns of the Eighth Pier, to commemorate the hitherto successful efforts of the Workmen engaged in the erection.

The erection of this gigantic and beautiful Iron Structure - the Beelah Viaduct - measuring One Thousand Feet in length and Two Hundred Feet in height, was commenced on the 19th day of July in the year of our Lord, 1859, from the Eastern end, and to this, one of its highest piers, of 200 feet, which we raise as our Ebenezer - was the work completed in the extraordinary short space of 43 days, without an accident occurring to anyone concerned.

To future ages these lines tell
Who built this structure O'er the dell
Gilkes, Wilson with their eighty men
Rais'd Beelah's Viaduct O'er the glen.

Contractors: Gilkes, Wilson & Co. Middlesbrough
Manager: John Hewitson
Cashier: F.W. Hull
Time-Keeper: Robert Tindle
Fitting department: (then follow 15 names)
Smith and Boiler Smith Department: (27 names)
Joinering Department: (5 names)
Ailors: (4 names)
General Workmen: (25 names)
Company Surgeon: Thomas Dalston

See! now Beelah's beauteous sights begin!
Whose curling stream shall ever flow within,
And underneath this splendid monster bridge,
Shall floods henceforth descend from every ridge;
Westmorland's honour form'd by the skill of man
Shall ever o'er thy spacious landscape span,
And thousands wonder at the glorious sight,
When trains will run aloft both day and night,
For ages past, no human tongue could tell
Of such a structure o'er thy monster gill
Time will roll on, and mortals may increase
When those who see it now, we hope will rest in Peace.

Charles Davis Brough.

The awe with which the new structure was regarded is evident in this description of it in a Westmorland directory published a few years later:

"The Belah Viaduct, over which the N.E. Railway is conveyed, is one of the most imposing triumphs of engineering skill in the British Isles. It rests upon what appears to be very light, and yet are very strong, though graceful, groups of open columnar iron work, planted on solid stone foundations of an almost cyclopean character. No adequate idea of the wonderful height of the viaduct can be formed unless a person walks underneath it, and then views it at a short distance. Seen in a clear moonlight, when the snow is on the ground or a fleecy cloud of mist partly envelops it, and one of the long trains happens to be passing, the whole appears to be more like the work of enchantment than a very solid reality".

The total cost of construction for Belah Viaduct was £31,630.

With indecent haste and in the wake of considerable protest, this unique viaduct at Belah was demolished during 1963 just over one year since the last train, the "Stainmore Limited" had blasted eastward over the high girders for the final time. The detail of the decking, catwalk and bracing can be seen in this view taken on 15th June 1963.

J. L. Birkbeck

Belah Viaduct on 7th June 1956.

Turners (Photography) Ltd

The first span at the Kirkby Stephen end is destroyed on 13th August 1963.

J. L. Birkbeck

The last span is destroyed. Notice the freshly applied paintwork of 1956, only seven years old – your money and mine!

J. L. Birkbeck

Belah Viaduct

Extract from an early Brough Guide.

The epitome of Belah. A three-car diesel multiple unit descends towards Kirkby Stephen as the sun catches the beautifully light cast and wrought iron structure.

J. T. Hall

Appendix IV

Signalling Diagrams

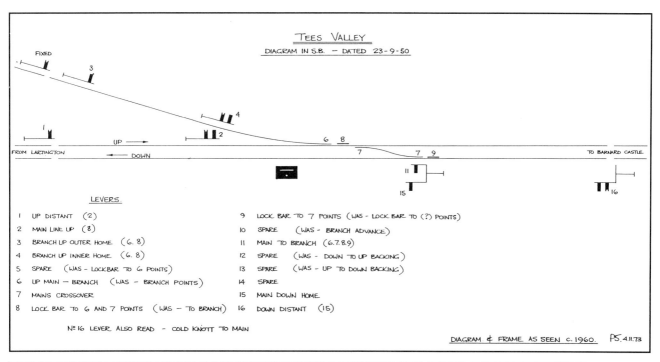

TEES VALLEY
DIAGRAM IN S.B. — DATED 23-9-50

FIXED

3

4

1

2

UP →

6   8

FROM LARTINGTON   ← DOWN   7   7   9   TO BARNARD CASTLE

11

15   16

LEVERS

1	UP DISTANT (2)	9	LOCK BAR TO 7 POINTS (WAS - LOCK BAR TO (?) POINTS)
2	MAIN LINE UP (8)	10	SPARE (WAS - BRANCH ADVANCE)
3	BRANCH UP OUTER HOME (6. 8)	11	MAIN TO BRANCH (6.7.8.9)
4	BRANCH UP INNER HOME (6. 8)	12	SPARE (WAS - DOWN TO UP BACKING)
5	SPARE (WAS - LOCKBAR TO 6 POINTS)	13	SPARE (WAS - UP TO DOWN BACKING)
6	UP MAIN - BRANCH (WAS - BRANCH POINTS)	14	SPARE
7	MAINS CROSSOVER	15	MAIN DOWN HOME
8	LOCK BAR TO 6 AND 7 POINTS (WAS — TO BRANCH)	16	DOWN DISTANT (15)

Nº 16 LEVER ALSO READ - COLD KNOTT TO MAIN

DIAGRAM & FRAME AS SEEN c.1960.   PS. 4.11.73

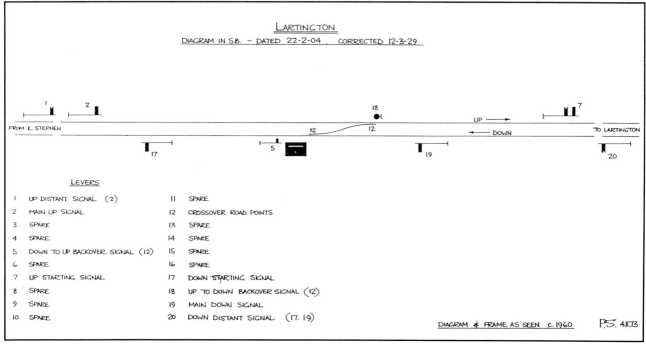

LARTINGTON
DIAGRAM IN S.B. — DATED 22-2-04 , CORRECTED 12-3-29

1   2

18

7

UP →

FROM K. STEPHEN   12   12   ← DOWN   TO LARTINGTON

17   5   19   20

LEVERS

1	UP DISTANT SIGNAL (2)	11	SPARE
2	MAIN UP SIGNAL	12	CROSSOVER ROAD POINTS
3	SPARE	13	SPARE
4	SPARE	14	SPARE
5	DOWN TO UP BACKOVER SIGNAL (12)	15	SPARE
6	SPARE	16	SPARE
7	UP STARTING SIGNAL	17	DOWN STARTING SIGNAL
8	SPARE	18	UP TO DOWN BACKOVER SIGNAL (12)
9	SPARE	19	MAIN DOWN SIGNAL
10	SPARE	20	DOWN DISTANT SIGNAL (17. 19)

DIAGRAM & FRAME AS SEEN c.1960   PS. 4.11.73

219

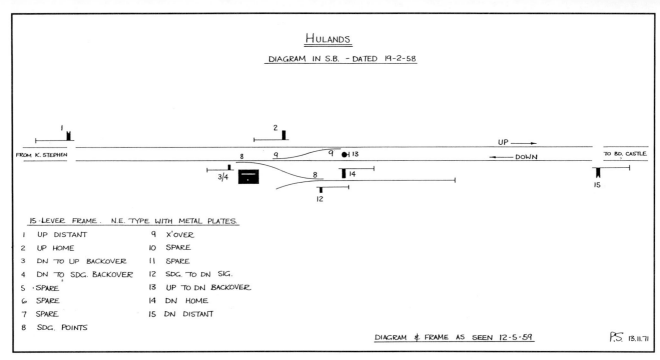

HULANDS

DIAGRAM IN S.B. - DATED 19-2-58

FROM K. STEPHEN
UP →
← DOWN
TO BD. CASTLE

15-LEVER FRAME. N.E. TYPE WITH METAL PLATES.

1 UP DISTANT
2 UP HOME
3 DN TO UP BACKOVER
4 DN TO SDG. BACKOVER
5 ·SPARE
6 SPARE
7 SPARE
8 SDG. POINTS
9 X'OVER
10 SPARE
11 SPARE
12 SDG. TO DN SIG.
13 UP TO DN BACKOVER
14 DN HOME
15 DN DISTANT

DIAGRAM & FRAME AS SEEN 12·5·59   PS. 13.11.71

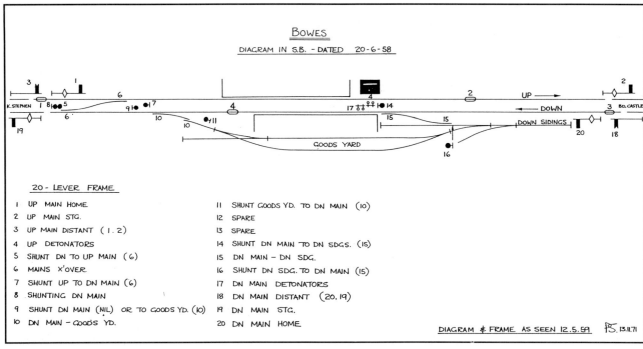

BOWES

DIAGRAM IN S.B. - DATED 20-6-58

K. STEPHEN
UP →
← DOWN
BD. CASTLE
DOWN SIDINGS
GOODS YARD

20 - LEVER FRAME

1 UP MAIN HOME
2 UP MAIN STG.
3 UP MAIN DISTANT (1.2)
4 UP DETONATORS
5 SHUNT DN TO UP MAIN (6)
6 MAINS X'OVER
7 SHUNT UP TO DN MAIN (6)
8 SHUNTING DN MAIN
9 SHUNT DN MAIN (NIL) OR TO GOODS YD. (10)
10 DN MAIN - GOODS YD.
11 SHUNT GOODS YD. TO DN MAIN (10)
12 SPARE
13 SPARE
14 SHUNT DN MAIN TO DN SDGS. (15)
15 DN MAIN - DN SDG.
16 SHUNT DN SDG. TO DN MAIN (15)
17 DN MAIN DETONATORS
18 DN MAIN DISTANT (20,19)
19 DN MAIN STG.
20 DN MAIN HOME

DIAGRAM & FRAME AS SEEN 12.5.59   PS. 13.11.71

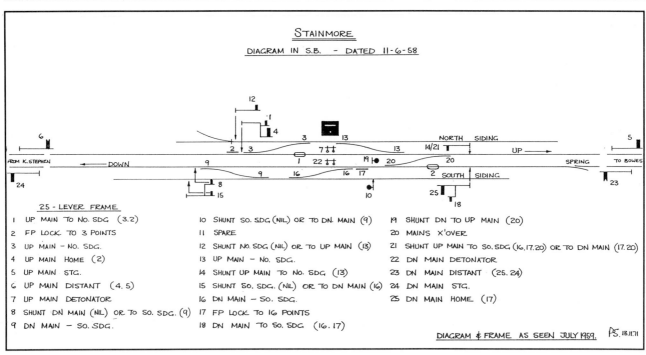

STAINMORE

DIAGRAM IN S.B. - DATED 11-6-58

FROM K. STEPHEN
← DOWN
UP
NORTH SIDING
SOUTH SIDING
SPRING
TO BOWES

25 - LEVER FRAME

1 UP MAIN TO No. SDG (3.2)
2 FP LOCK TO 3 POINTS
3 UP MAIN - No. SDG.
4 UP MAIN HOME (2)
5 UP MAIN STG.
6 UP MAIN DISTANT (4.5)
7 UP MAIN DETONATOR
8 SHUNT DN MAIN (NIL) OR TO So. SDG. (9)
9 DN MAIN - So. SDG.
10 SHUNT So. SDG. (NIL) OR TO DN. MAIN (9)
11 SPARE
12 SHUNT No. SDG. (NIL) OR TO UP MAIN (13)
13 UP MAIN - No. SDG.
14 SHUNT UP MAIN TO No. SDG. (13)
15 SHUNT So. SDG. (NIL) OR TO DN MAIN (16)
16 DN MAIN - So. SDG.
17 FP LOCK TO 16 POINTS
18 DN MAIN TO So. SDG. (16.17)
19 SHUNT DN TO UP MAIN (20)
20 MAINS X'OVER
21 SHUNT UP MAIN TO So. SDG (16.17.20) OR TO DN MAIN (17.20)
22 DN MAIN DETONATOR
23 DN MAIN DISTANT (25.24)
24 DN MAIN STG.
25 DN MAIN HOME (17)

DIAGRAM & FRAME AS SEEN JULY 1959.   PS. 13.11.71

220

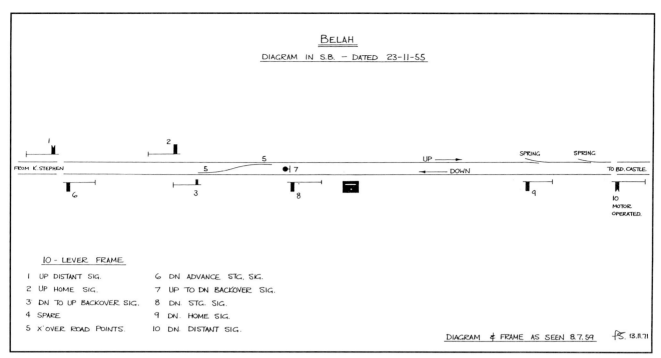

BELAH

DIAGRAM IN S.B. – DATED 23-11-55

FROM K.STEPHEN

UP →

← DOWN

SPRING   SPRING

TO BD. CASTLE

10 MOTOR OPERATED.

10 - LEVER FRAME

1 UP DISTANT SIG.	6 DN ADVANCE STG. SIG.
2 UP HOME SIG.	7 UP TO DN BACKOVER SIG.
3 DN TO UP BACKOVER SIG.	8 DN. STG. SIG.
4 SPARE	9 DN. HOME SIG.
5 X'OVER ROAD POINTS.	10 DN. DISTANT SIG.

DIAGRAM & FRAME AS SEEN 8.7.59   P.S. 13.11.71

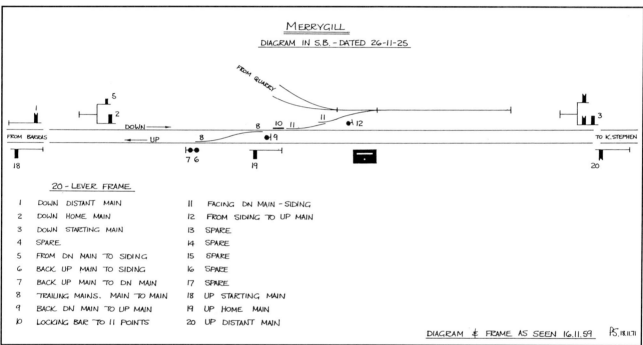

MERRYGILL

DIAGRAM IN S.B. – DATED 26-11-25

FROM QUARRY

DOWN →

← UP

FROM BARRAS

TO K.STEPHEN

20 - LEVER FRAME

1 DOWN DISTANT MAIN	11 FACING DN MAIN - SIDING
2 DOWN HOME MAIN	12 FROM SIDING TO UP MAIN
3 DOWN STARTING MAIN	13 SPARE
4 SPARE	14 SPARE
5 FROM DN MAIN TO SIDING	15 SPARE
6 BACK UP MAIN TO SIDING	16 SPARE
7 BACK UP MAIN TO DN MAIN	17 SPARE
8 TRAILING MAINS. MAIN TO MAIN	18 UP STARTING MAIN
9 BACK DN MAIN TO UP MAIN	19 UP HOME MAIN
10 LOCKING BAR TO 11 POINTS	20 UP DISTANT MAIN

DIAGRAM & FRAME AS SEEN 16.11.59   P.S. 18.11.71

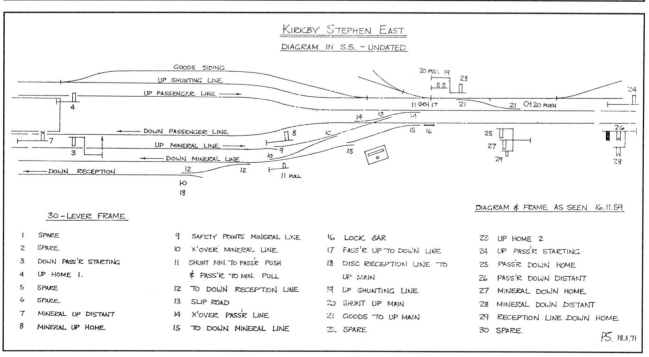

KIRKBY STEPHEN EAST

DIAGRAM IN S.B. – UNDATED

GOODS SIDING

UP SHUNTING LINE

UP PASSENGER LINE →

DOWN PASSENGER LINE

UP MINERAL LINE →

← DOWN MINERAL LINE

← DOWN RECEPTION

DIAGRAM & FRAME AS SEEN 16.11.59

30 - LEVER FRAME

1 SPARE	9 SAFETY POINTS MINERAL LINE	16 LOCK BAR	23 UP HOME 2
2 SPARE	10 X'OVER MINERAL LINE	17 PASS'R UP TO DOWN LINE	24 UP PASS'R STARTING
3 DOWN PASS'R STARTING	11 SHUNT MIN. TO PASS'R PUSH & PASS'R TO MIN. PULL	18 DISC RECEPTION LINE TO UP MAIN	25 PASS'R DOWN HOME
4 UP HOME 1.	12 TO DOWN RECEPTION LINE	19 UP SHUNTING LINE	26 PASS'R DOWN DISTANT
5 SPARE	13 SLIP ROAD	20 SHUNT UP MAIN	27 MINERAL DOWN HOME
6 SPARE	14 X'OVER PASS'R LINE	21 GOODS TO UP MAIN	28 MINERAL DOWN DISTANT
7 MINERAL UP DISTANT	15 TO DOWN MINERAL LINE	22 SPARE	29 RECEPTION LINE DOWN HOME
8 MINERAL UP HOME			30 SPARE.

P.S. 18.11.71

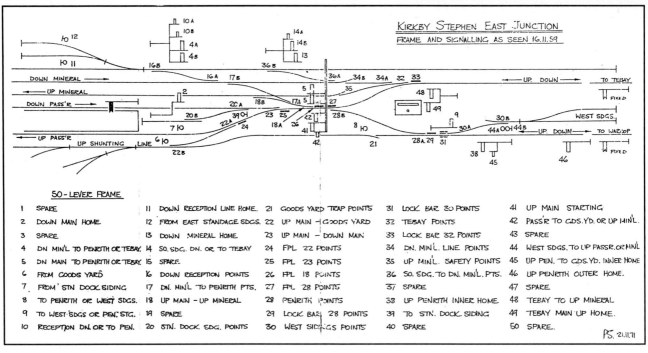

50-LEVER FRAME

1 SPARE	11 DOWN RECEPTION LINE HOME.	21 GOODS YARD TRAP POINTS	31 LOCK BAR 30 POINTS	41 UP MAIN STARTING
2 DOWN MAIN HOME	12 FROM EAST STANDAGE SDGS.	22 UP MAIN - GOODS YARD	32 TEBAY POINTS	42 PASS'R TO GDS.YD. OR UP MIN'L.
3 SPARE	13 DOWN MINERAL HOME.	23 UP MAIN - DOWN MAIN	33 LOCK BAR 32 POINTS	43 SPARE
4 DN MIN'L TO PENRITH OR TEBAY	14 SO. SDG. DN. OR TO TEBAY	24 FPL 22 POINTS	34 DN. MIN'L. LINE POINTS	44 WEST SDGS. TO UP PASS'R. OR MIN'L
5 DN MAIN TO PENRITH OR TEBAY	15 SPARE	25 FPL 23 POINTS	35 UP MIN'L. SAFETY POINTS	45 UP PEN. TO GDS.YD. INNER HOME
6 FROM GOODS YARD	16 DOWN RECEPTION POINTS	26 FPL 18 POINTS	36 SO. SDG. TO DN. MIN'L. PTS.	46 UP PENRITH OUTER HOME.
7 FROM STN DOCK SIDING	17 DN. MIN'L TO PENRITH PTS.	27 FPL 28 POINTS	37 SPARE	47 SPARE
8 TO PENRITH OR WEST SDGS.	18 UP MAIN - UP MINERAL	28 PENRITH POINTS	38 UP PENRITH INNER HOME	48 TEBAY TO UP MINERAL
9 TO WEST SDGS OR PEN. STG.	19 SPARE	29 LOCK BAR 28 POINTS	39 TO STN. DOCK SIDING	49 TEBAY MAIN UP HOME.
10 RECEPTION DN. OR TO PEN.	20 STN. DOCK SDG. POINTS	30 WEST SIDINGS POINTS	40 SPARE	50 SPARE.

P.S. 21.11.71

SMARDALE
I'ANSONS FRAME, STEVENS LOCKING - 1879
4½" SQ. LEVER PLATES, 1-E.R.
WOODEN S.B. SIG. LAMPS :- OIL.

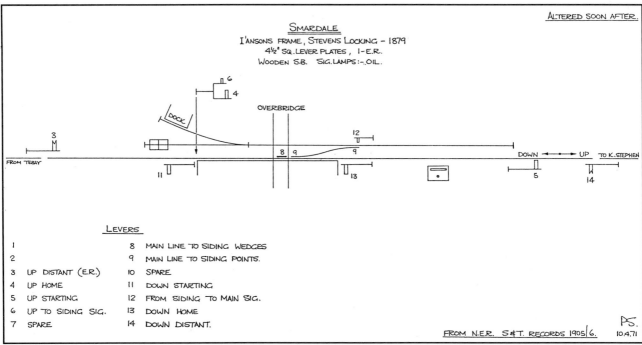

LEVERS

1	8 MAIN LINE TO SIDING WEDGES
2	9 MAIN LINE TO SIDING POINTS.
3 UP DISTANT (E.R.)	10 SPARE
4 UP HOME	11 DOWN STARTING
5 UP STARTING	12 FROM SIDING TO MAIN SIG.
6 UP TO SIDING SIG.	13 DOWN HOME
7 SPARE	14 DOWN DISTANT.

FROM N.E.R. S&T. RECORDS 1905/6.

P.S. 10.4.71

SMARDALE
STEVENS FRAME & LOCKING 12/1907
WOODEN S.B. SIG. LAMPS :- OIL.

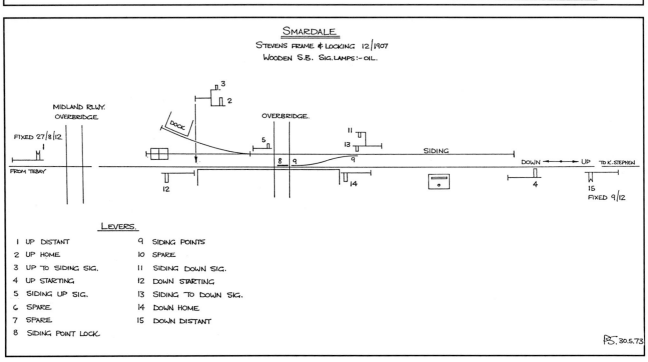

LEVERS.

1 UP DISTANT	9 SIDING POINTS
2 UP HOME	10 SPARE
3 UP TO SIDING SIG.	11 SIDING DOWN SIG.
4 UP STARTING	12 DOWN STARTING
5 SIDING UP SIG.	13 SIDING TO DOWN SIG.
6 SPARE	14 DOWN HOME
7 SPARE	15 DOWN DISTANT
8 SIDING POINT LOCK	

P.S. 30.5.73

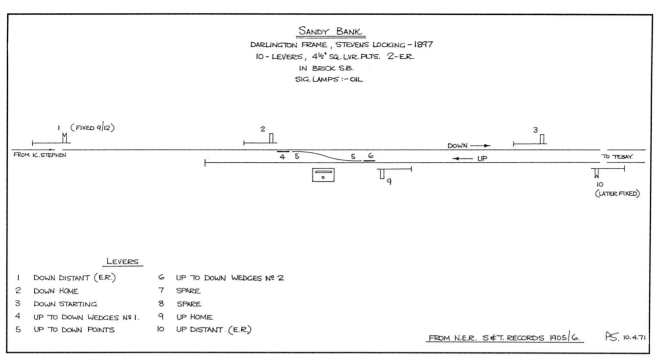

SANDY BANK

DARLINGTON FRAME, STEVENS LOCKING – 1897
10 - LEVERS, 4½" SQ. LVR. PLTS. 2-E.R.
IN BRICK S.B.
SIG. LAMPS :– OIL

I (FIXED 9/12)

FROM K. STEPHEN

DOWN →

← UP

TO TEBAY.

10 (LATER FIXED)

LEVERS

1	DOWN DISTANT (E.R.)	6	UP TO DOWN WEDGES Nº 2
2	DOWN HOME	7	SPARE
3	DOWN STARTING	8	SPARE
4	UP TO DOWN WEDGES Nº 1.	9	UP HOME
5	UP TO DOWN POINTS	10	UP DISTANT. (E.R.)

FROM N.E.R. S&T. RECORDS 1905/6.   PS. 10.4.71

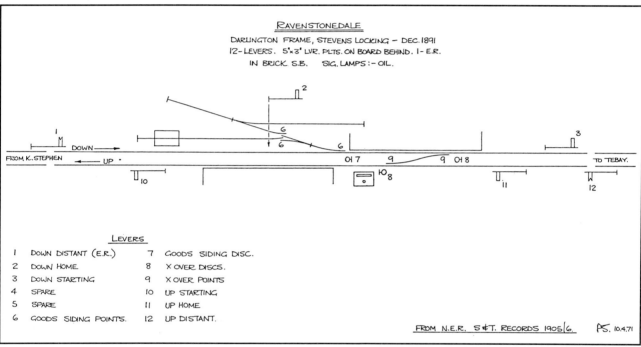

RAVENSTONEDALE

DARLINGTON FRAME, STEVENS LOCKING – DEC. 1891
12 - LEVERS. 5"×3" LVR. PLTS. ON BOARD BEHIND. 1 - E.R.
IN BRICK S.B.   SIG. LAMPS :– OIL.

FROM K. STEPHEN

DOWN →

← UP

TO TEBAY.

LEVERS

1	DOWN DISTANT (E.R.)	7	GOODS SIDING DISC.
2	DOWN HOME	8	X OVER DISCS.
3	DOWN STARTING	9	X OVER POINTS
4	SPARE	10	UP STARTING
5	SPARE	11	UP HOME
6	GOODS SIDING POINTS.	12	UP DISTANT.

FROM N.E.R. S&T. RECORDS 1905/6.   PS. 10.4.71

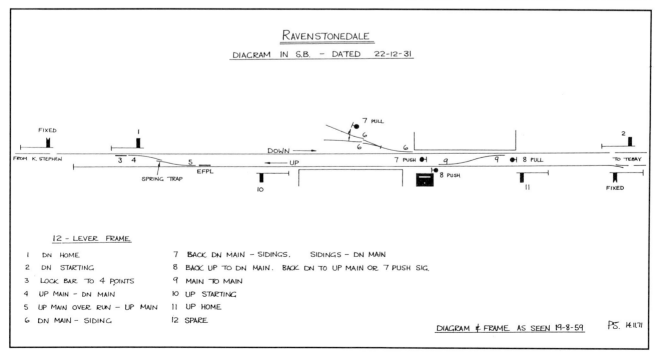

RAVENSTONEDALE

DIAGRAM IN S.B. – DATED 22-12-31

FIXED

FROM K. STEPHEN

DOWN →

← UP

SPRING TRAP

EFPL

TO TEBAY

FIXED

12 - LEVER FRAME

1	DN HOME	7	BACK DN MAIN – SIDINGS. SIDINGS – DN MAIN
2	DN STARTING	8	BACK UP TO DN MAIN. BACK DN TO UP MAIN OR 7 PUSH SIG.
3	LOCK BAR TO 4 POINTS	9	MAIN TO MAIN
4	UP MAIN – DN MAIN	10	UP STARTING
5	UP MAIN OVER RUN – UP MAIN	11	UP HOME
6	DN MAIN – SIDING	12	SPARE

DIAGRAM & FRAME AS SEEN 19-8-59   PS. 14.11.71

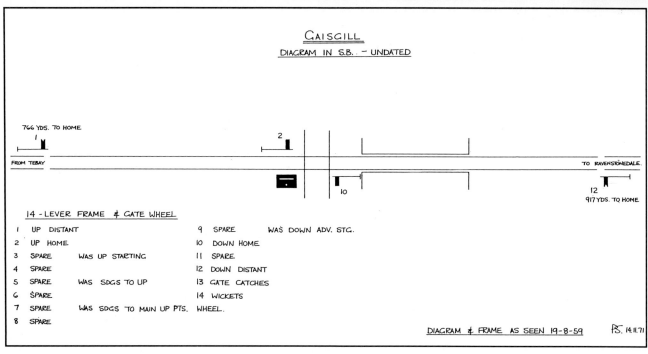

GAISGILL

DIAGRAM IN S.B. – UNDATED

766 YDS. TO HOME

FROM TEBAY

TO RAVENSTONEDALE.

917 YDS. TO HOME.

14 - LEVER FRAME & GATE WHEEL

1	UP DISTANT	9	SPARE WAS DOWN ADV. STG.
2	UP HOME	10	DOWN HOME
3	SPARE WAS UP STARTING	11	SPARE
4	SPARE	12	DOWN DISTANT
5	SPARE WAS SDGS TO UP	13	GATE CATCHES
6	SPARE	14	WICKETS
7	SPARE WAS SDGS TO MAIN UP PTS. WHEEL.		
8	SPARE		

DIAGRAM & FRAME AS SEEN 19-8-59   PS. 14.11.71

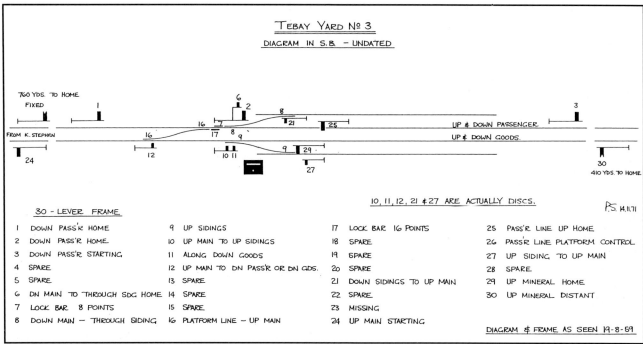

TEBAY YARD № 3

DIAGRAM IN S.B. – UNDATED

760 YDS. TO HOME
FIXED

FROM K. STEPHEN

UP & DOWN PASSENGER
UP & DOWN GOODS.

410 YDS. TO HOME.

10, 11, 12, 21 & 27 ARE ACTUALLY DISCS.

PS. 14.11.71

30 - LEVER FRAME

1	DOWN PASS'R HOME	9	UP SIDINGS	17	LOCK BAR 16 POINTS	25	PASS'R LINE UP HOME
2	DOWN PASS'R HOME	10	UP MAIN TO UP SIDINGS	18	SPARE	26	PASS'R LINE PLATFORM CONTROL
3	DOWN PASS'R STARTING	11	ALONG DOWN GOODS	19	SPARE	27	UP SIDING TO UP MAIN
4	SPARE	12	UP MAIN TO DN PASS'R OR DN GDS.	20	SPARE	28	SPARE
5	SPARE	13	SPARE	21	DOWN SIDINGS TO UP MAIN	29	UP MINERAL HOME
6	DN MAIN TO THROUGH SDG HOME	14	SPARE	22	SPARE	30	UP MINERAL DISTANT
7	LOCK BAR 8 POINTS	15	SPARE	23	MISSING		
8	DOWN MAIN — THROUGH SIDING	16	PLATFORM LINE – UP MAIN	24	UP MAIN STARTING		

DIAGRAM & FRAME AS SEEN 19-8-59

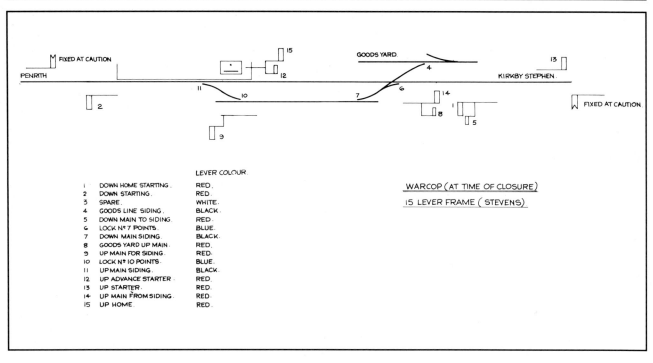

FIXED AT CAUTION

PENRITH

GOODS YARD

KIRKBY STEPHEN.

FIXED AT CAUTION

LEVER COLOUR.

1	DOWN HOME STARTING.	RED.
2	DOWN STARTING.	RED.
3	SPARE.	WHITE.
4	GOODS LINE SIDING.	BLACK.
5	DOWN MAIN TO SIDING.	RED.
6	LOCK № 7 POINTS.	BLUE.
7	DOWN MAIN SIDING.	BLACK.
8	GOODS YARD UP MAIN.	RED.
9	UP MAIN FOR SIDING.	RED.
10	LOCK № 10 POINTS.	BLUE.
11	UP MAIN SIDING.	BLACK.
12	UP ADVANCE STARTER.	RED.
13	UP STARTER.	RED.
14	UP MAIN FROM SIDING.	RED.
15	UP HOME.	RED.

WARCOP (AT TIME OF CLOSURE)

15 LEVER FRAME (STEVENS)

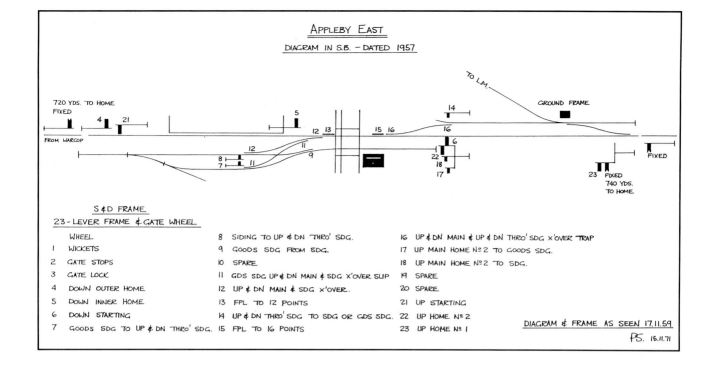

APPLEBY EAST

DIAGRAM IN S.B. — DATED 1957

720 YDS. TO HOME.
FIXED

FROM WARCOP

TO L.M.

GROUND FRAME.

FIXED

23 FIXED
740 YDS.
TO HOME.

S & D FRAME

23 - LEVER FRAME & GATE WHEEL

	WHEEL	8	SIDING TO UP & DN THRO' SDG.	16	UP & DN MAIN & UP & DN THRO' SDG X'OVER TRAP
1	WICKETS	9	GOODS SDG FROM SDG.	17	UP MAIN HOME Nº 2 TO GOODS SDG.
2	GATE STOPS	10	SPARE	18	UP MAIN HOME Nº 2 TO SDG.
3	GATE LOCK	11	GDS SDG UP & DN MAIN & SDG X'OVER SLIP	19	SPARE
4	DOWN OUTER HOME	12	UP & DN MAIN & SDG X'OVER.	20	SPARE
5	DOWN INNER HOME	13	FPL TO 12 POINTS	21	UP STARTING
6	DOWN STARTING	14	UP & DN THRO' SDG TO SDG OR GDS SDG.	22	UP HOME. Nº 2
7	GOODS SDG TO UP & DN THRO' SDG.	15	FPL TO 16 POINTS	23	UP HOME Nº 1

DIAGRAM & FRAME AS SEEN 17.11.59

PS. 16.11.71

Left: Tebay NE Yard and No. 3 box from the west.

J. F. Mallon

Below: The view to the west from the end of the platform at Kirkby Stephen East at the time of closure.

J. T. Hall

225

NORTH EASTERN RAILWAY.

Office of Superintendent of the Line,

YORK, 16th May, 1895.

Circular No. 32/1895

SINGLE LINE WORKING.

Referring to Rule 368 of the General Rules and Regulations, and paragraph 8 of page 127 of the Appendix, in reference to the working of Single Lines. In future a train following board during the day or an extra tail lamp at night must be put on all trains which do not carry the staff, excepting the last train over the Branch before the line is closed for the night and when the staff is left for the first train the next day, except between the following points :—

Carlin How Junction to Loftus.
Crook and Consett:
Dearness Valley Branch.
Eden Valley Branch.
Forcett Junction and Barnard Castle.
Kirkby Stephen and Sandy Bank.
Lanchester and Blaydon Junction.
Prospect Hill and Bog Hall Junction.
Spring Gardens and Barnard Castle.
Tees Valley Branch.
Wear Valley Branch.
West Cliff and Prospect Hill,

but on these lines, when a passenger train is run in duplicate, and the second train has not been previously advised, the first train must carry a train following board or an extra tail lamp.

JOHN WELBURN,

Superintendent of the Line.

Acknowledge receipt to your District Superintendent.

LNER S.892.36 5,000

London & North Eastern Railway
(North Eastern Area).

SUPERINTENDENT'S OFFICE,
YORK.

O. 3024

1st November 193 6

To the Signalman at

Appleby West ....Box.

Block Regulation 5.

Authority is hereby given for trains not conveying passengers, light engines, light engines coupled together, and engines with not more than two **brake vans** attached, to be accepted from the direction of :—

Kirkby Thore ....

in accordance with Regulation 5, IN CLEAR WEATHER ONLY, provided the line between the Home signal and the prescribed clearing point for Regulation 4 is not occupied or about to be occupied by a train conveying passengers.

Notes.

(1) This authority does not apply when the section extends beyond

Kirkby Thore ....Signal Box

and ....Signal Box.

(2) This authority may be applied in the case of Engineer's Rail Motors and Velocipede cars where such are specially authorised to work.

G. M. JENKIN JONES,
Superintendent.

(O. 7361)

Stainmore Miscellany

Many years after the closure of the East station, the signs in and around the town of Appleby still directed would-be passengers to both the stations.

Author

The page of the Train Register book from Merrygill signal box. The signalman was the late Fred Marshall. Notice the date, 22nd January 1962, the first operational day after the closure of the line 'over the top". Fred still tested through to Tees Valley box.

Author

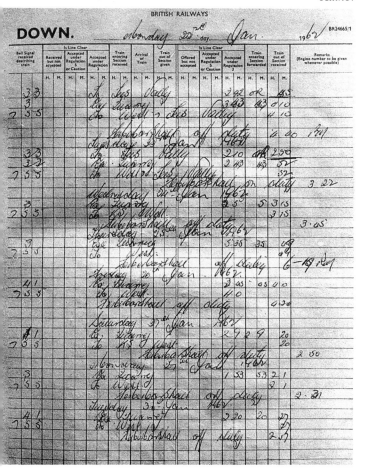

There are very few overbridges on the Valley branch between Appleby and Clifton Moor. One remaining bridge, albeit in poor condition, possessed a decorative iron railing parapet rather than the usual stone type. As we can see from this 1986 picture the trackbed is used for vehicular access. The bridge is located about one mile south of Cliburn, very close to where work on the Eden Valley branch first began.

Author

A single line tablet from the Valley branch.　　*Author*

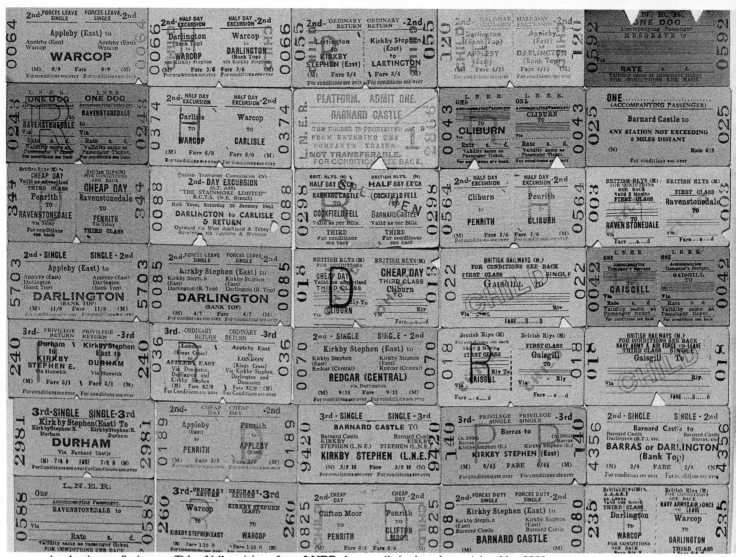

A selection at Stainmore/Eden Valley tickets from LNER days until the last day – ticket No. 0088.

A selection of Stainmore/Eden Valley tickets from British Railways days.

The dual-purpose British Railways sign from Appleby.

Author

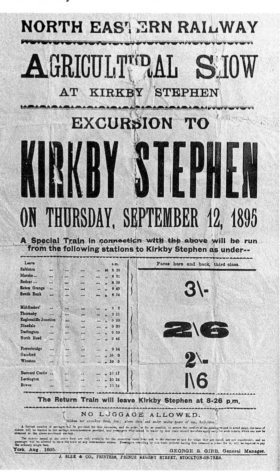

An excursion poster from 1895.

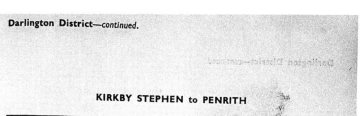

DARLINGTON to TEBAY

Down	Distance M.	C.		B Mins.	C Mins.	D Mins.
Darlington (Down Sidings)	—	—	dep.	—		5
Hope Town	—	41	pass	—	….	
Piercebridge	4	47	,,	—	….	13
Forcett Jct.	⊕ 1	44	,,	—	22(arr.)	6 arr.
Gainford	1	17	,,	—	….	5 ,,
Winston	⊕ 2	7	,,	—	10	10 ,,
Broomielaw	⊕ 3	52	,,	—	15(arr.)	15 ,,
Barnard Castle	1	79	,,	40	6	6 ,,
Stainmore	13	51	,,	—	54	54 ,,
Kirkby Stephen	⊕ 9	21	,,	—	25	25 ,,
				L.Eng.		
Ravenstonedale	⊕ 5	52	,,	12	20	22
Tebay	6	6	arr.	14	15	18

TEBAY to DARLINGTON

Up	Distance M.	C.		B Mins.	C Mins.	D Mins.
Tebay	—	—	dep.	L.Eng.		
Ravenstonedale	⊕ 6	6	pass	14	19	21	—
Kirkby Stephen	⊕ 5	52	,,	12	16	19	—
Stainmore	9	21	,,	—	34	40	—
Barnard Castle	13	51	,,	—	31	35	—
Broomielaw	⊕ 1	79	,,	—	….	7	7
Winston	⊕ 3	52	,,	—	….	13	15
Gainford	2	7	,,	—	….		10
Forcett Junction	1	17	,,	—	….	10	4
Piercebridge	1	44	,,	—	…		6
Hope Town	4	74	,,	—	….		13
Up Sidings	—	73	arr.		42	23	6

KIRKBY STEPHEN to PENRITH

Down	Distance M.	C.		C Mins.	D Mins.
Kirkby Stephen	⊕ —	—	dep.	—	dep. —
Musgrave	⊕ 4	11	pass	….	arr. 13
Warcop	⊕ 1	52	pass	15	,, 6
Appleby	⊕ 5	20	arr.	15	,, 15
Kirkby Thore	⊕ 4	5	pass	12	,, 13
Temple Sowerby	1	63	,,	….	,, 5
Cliburn	1	54	,,	….	,, 5
Clifton Moor	⊕ 2	67	,,	20	,, 8
Penrith	3	58	—	….	,, 10

PENRITH to KIRKBY STEPHEN

Up	Distance M.	C.		C Mins.	D Mins.
Penrith	—	—	—	—	dep. —
Clifton Moor	⊕ 3	58	pass	….	arr. 12
Cliburn	2	67	,,	….	,, 8
Temple Sowerby	1	54	,,	….	,, 5
Kirkby Thore	⊕ 1	63	,,	17	,, 8
Appleby	⊕ 4	5	arr.	15	,, 15
Warcop	⊕ 5	20	pass	15	,, 15
Musgrave	1	52	,,	….	,, 6
Kirkby Stephen	⊕ 4	11	arr.	15	,, 15

Darlington District Control extracts showing distances and schedules.

A splendid lamp, purported to be from Warcop.

Another lamp variant from the same area.

The single-line staff for the remnant of the Eden Valley/Stainmore line. Note the key for Appleby East crossing gates.
Author

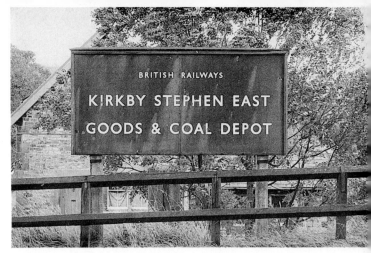

The sign adjacent to the goods yard at Kirkby Stephen East.
Author

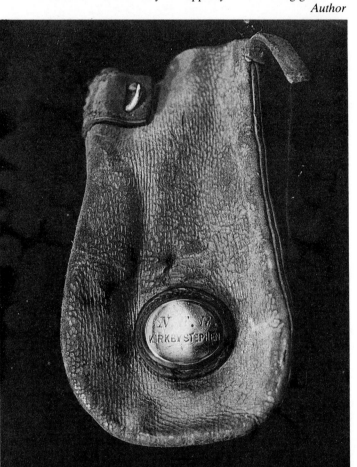

The Kirkby Stephen cash bag.
Author

The usage of the railway in its heyday for all kinds of traffic is illustrated by these two examples of surviving milk churn plates.

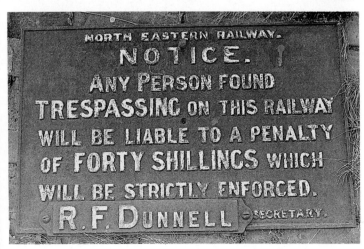

The cast iron warning notice at Wetheriggs Pottery siding.
Author

The train indicators at Darlington North Road station, now a splendid museum operated by Darlington Borough Council.
Author

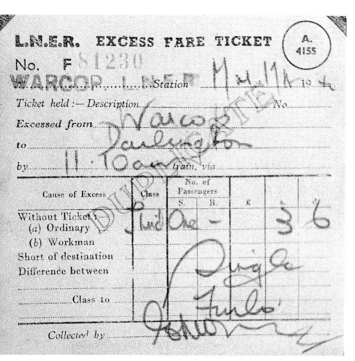

An extract from an excess fare book.

Author

The cast iron signal box lever plates from Eden Valley Junction box referring to the Valley branch.

Author

The station seat nameplates from Kirkby Thore, Barras and Ravenstonedale.

Author

A typical platform lamp at Clifton Moor.

Author

Some of the fine items of furniture carved, about the turn of the century, by the Bleathgill signalman Mr George Bowron apparently manufactured during 'quiet spells' on the box.

Author

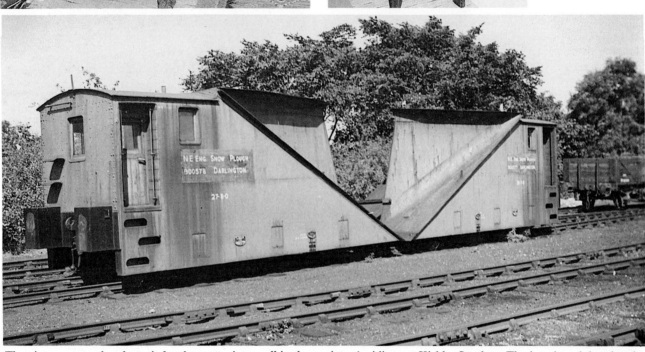

The vintage snowploughs wait for the next winter call in the engineer's sidings at Kirkby Stephen. The interior of the ploughs provided rudimentary comforts for the men who would be involved in the battle against the elements over Stainmore. Ambulance equipment, ramps, detonators, tools, etc. During potentially difficult times the stoves in the ploughs were kept burning continually – just in case!

Neville Bousfield

The last freight from Kirkby Stephen trundles along the Eden Valley branch on a rainy 31st October 1974, between Kirkby Stephen East and Musgrave. Like the first train in 1862 there was no ceremony.

Author